TURNING DATA INTO WISDOM

HOW WE CAN COLLABORATE WITH DATA TO CHANGE OURSELVES, OUR ORGANIZATIONS, AND EVEN THE WORLD

KEVIN HANEGAN

Turning Data into Wisdom

How We Can Collaborate with Data to Change Ourselves, Our Organizations, and Even the World

www.turningdataintowisdom.com

First edition.

ISBN: 978-0-578-63987-1

Editor: Andrea Barilla, www.andreabarilla.com
Cover Design: JD&J Book Cover Design, www.jdandj.com
Book Interior: Robin Krauss, Book Formatters, www.bookformatters.com

DEDICATION

This book is dedicated to my family.

To my parents and my brother. Thank you for teaching me the importance of perspectives and to always drive toward a goal.

To my wife, Shannon, and my children: Parker, Brayden, Jackson, and Colby. Your unique perspectives continue to inspire me to learn more about the world and how we can all work better together.

TABLE OF CONTENTS

Note to the Reader xi

Introduction 1

Chapter 1: The Power and Potential of Data 3

- **Positive Potential of Data on Society** 4
- **Potential Risks with Data** 5
- **Summary and Key Takeaways** 12

Chapter 2: Introduction to Data-Informed Decision-Making 13

- **The 6-Phase Data-Informed Decision-Making Process** 14
- **The 12-Step Data-Informed Decision-Making Methodology** 16
- **Top-10 Data-Informed Decision-Making Skills** 17
  - Top-5 Hard Skills 18
  - Top-5 Soft Skills 20
- **Summary and Key Takeaways** 22

Chapter 3: The Science of Decision-Making 23

- **Going from Data to Wisdom** 23
- **Understanding How the Brain Makes Decisions** 26
  - The Unconscious Mind 26
  - System 1 and System 2 Decisions 28
  - How the Brain Processes Information 29
    - Heuristics 30
    - Mental Models 33
    - Perception and Interpretation 34
- **Understanding Cognitive Bias** 38
  - Common Categories of Cognitive Bias 38

Examples of Cognitive Bias in Action 40
Test Your Bias 41
Understanding Groupthink **42**
The Impact of Organizational Culture on Decisions **43**
Summary and Key Takeaways **44**

Chapter 4: Phase One – The Ask Phase **45**
Turning Business Questions into Analytical Questions **46**
Formulating Good Analytical Questions 46
Example Analytical Question 47
Classifying the Decision **48**
Summary and Key Takeaways **50**

Chapter 5: Phase Two – The Acquire Phase **51**
Finding and Sourcing All Relevant Data **51**
Taking a Systems Perspective 52
The Importance of Using a Variety of Data Sources 58
The Importance of Discussing Data with People 59
Sources of Insight 59
Ensuring That Data Can Be Trusted: Having a Data Strategy **60**
Data Quality 61
Characteristics of Quality Data 61
Data Collection 62
Data Governance and Data Management 63
Summary and Key Takeaways **64**

Chapter 6: Phase Three – The Analyze Phase **65**
Understanding Analytics **66**
Analytics and Statistics 66
Analytics Strategy and Framework 67

Using a Measurement Framework for Descriptive Analytics **69**

Descriptive Analytics **71**

Descriptive Analytics Terminology 72

Describing the Data 73

Organizing the Data 76

Central Tendency 79

Dispersion 82

Frequencies and Percentages 84

Total 85

Visualizing the Data 85

Visualizing Distributions and Comparisons 86

Visualizing Patterns and Relationships 91

Visualizing Summary Measures 94

Limitation of Descriptive Analytics 95

Example: Analyzing Expense Reports 95

Drilling into Data with Diagnostic Analytics **96**

Example: Online Ordering of Car Parts 97

Example: A Soup Company's Loss of Market Share 99

Inferring from Samples of Data Using Inferential Statistics **101**

Inferential Statistics versus Descriptive Analytics 101

Inferential Statistics Terminology 102

Types of Inferential Statistics 103

Reviewing Relationships between Variables 104

Comparing Means 109

Predicting Future Actions by Leveraging Predictive Analytics **111**

Types of Predictive Analytics 111

Linear Programming 111

Break-Even Analysis 112

Crossover Analysis 113

Cluster Analysis 114

Simulations 115

Decision Trees 116

Markov Analysis 117
Sentiment Analysis 118

Automating Decisions Using Prescriptive Analytics 119

Summary and Key Takeaways 119

Chapter 7: Phase Four – The Apply Phase 121

Balancing Data, Experience, and Intuition 122

Challenging the Data and Your Assumptions 123

Challenging the Data 124
Challenging Your Assumptions 124

Becoming Aware of and Mitigating Bias and Groupthink 125

Situations That Trigger Bias 126
Mitigating Bias 127
Strategies for Mitigating Bias at the Individual Level 127
Strategies for Mitigating Bias at the Group Level 130
Strategies for Mitigating Bias at the Organizational Level 136

Making a Decision 137

Summary and Key Takeaways 138

Chapter 8: Phase Five – The Announce Phase 139

Defining Your Audience 140

Cultural Implications for Communication 141
Differences in Interpreting Context 141

Planning the Story 142

Crafting the Story 144

The Visuals 144
The Three Types of Memory 145
Applying Principles of Perception to Visuals 146
The Story 153
The Pyramid Principle 154

The Rule of Three 155
An Example Story 155
Acting on the Decision **158**
How Do We Unlearn? 158
Automating Decisions and Actions Using Prescriptive Analytics 159
Prescriptive Analytics Terminology 159
Machine Learning's Value in Business 160
Examples of Prescriptive Analytics in Action 161
Bias in Prescriptive Analytics 161
Summary and Key Takeaways **163**

Chapter 9: Phase Six – The Assess Phase **165**
Monitoring and Assessing the Outcome **165**
Performing a Metaevaluation of the Decision **166**
Codifying the Decisions **166**
Decision-Making Journals 167
Summary and Key Takeaways **168**

Chapter 10: Tools, Frameworks, and Models **169**
Logic Model **169**
Example of a Logic Model 171
OODA Loop **173**
Behavior Engineering Model (BEM) **176**
Vroom-Yetton-Jago Model **178**
Pugh Matrix **181**
Force Field Analysis **184**
Zig-Zag Process Model for Problem-Solving **186**
Ladder of Inference **190**
Strategic Foresight **192**
Future Search **193**
Theory of Constraints **194**

Assessing Organizational Culture: Competing Values Framework 197
How Do I Assess My Organization's Culture? 199

Chapter 11: Templates and Job Aides 201
6-Phase Data-Informed Decision-Making Process 201
12-Step Data-Informed Decision-Making Methodology 202
Logic Model 203
Behavior Engineering Model (BEM) 204
Pugh Matrix 205
Force Field Analysis 206
Zig-Zag Process Model for Problem-Solving 207
Pyramid Principle and Rule of Three 208

Chapter 12: Example Use Cases and Case Studies 209
Example #1 – A Personal Data-Informed Decision 209
Example #2 – Declining Revenue 213
Example #3 – Missing Sales Quotas 215
Example #4 – Declines in Soup Sales 220
Example #5 – Lower-Than-Planned Profits 224

Glossary of Terms 231
Endnotes 237
Bibliography 247
About The Author 255

NOTE TO THE READER

Terms in boldface throughout this text can be found in the Glossary of Terms at the end of the book. This resource is meant to help you whenever you need a refresher on a term or a concept.

Also, screenshots of data visualizations were made in-house using software by Qlik: www.qlik.com.

INTRODUCTION

Growing up, I often heard sayings like "don't judge a book by its cover" and "there are two sides to every story" that I didn't really believe and just thought were cliché. At that point, I thought I knew everything there was to know, but in reality, I knew very little about anything.

As I grew older, I studied math and statistics in school and was taught there is only one answer to a given problem. Whether it was a calculation, the truth value of a statement for a theorem, or something else, there was always only one right answer. Everything was black and white.

Then, as I got older and had a family, I was presented with a challenge. My oldest son is autistic. Without going into much detail, it can be very frustrating because the way he looks at the world and perceives things is very different than how I perceive things or how other kids perceive things. To him, the world is just like we are taught in math and statistics: black or white, right or wrong, true or false. There is no room for interpretation, and there are not multiple sides to every story.

Eventually, I started diving more into data literacy and had a realization. Each data point, bit of evidence, or observation is a piece of a greater puzzle. There is a story there waiting to be unlocked. Yes, the value of a point of data may be the number two or the color yellow, but what does that really mean, and what can we do with that information? This ties to the concept of data-informed decision-making. A single data point, bit of evidence, or observation *is* one-dimensional. However, when you start to combine data together, you are starting to put the pieces of the puzzle together. Then, when you add in your experiences and beliefs along with the experiences and beliefs of others, the data starts to come to life and tell you a story—a story that can give you great wisdom and insights. This is one reason why decision-making should celebrate diversity and inclusion and be a team sport, as these different perspectives allow you to see multiple sides of the data and what its story is.

With that realization and gained wisdom, I started to apply this thinking to my son. I stopped looking at his attitudes and behaviors as wrong. Just like with data, there is a story there and a puzzle that was waiting to be put together. I just needed to put aside my bias and try to understand his side of the story based on his experiences and beliefs.

My goal now is to continually educate him on different perspectives in the hope he will be well rounded and cultured one day and see that the world is not black and white. While this has not been a total success yet, the tenets in **data literacy** are the same ones I now apply to him. I am always curious why he believes what he believes and why he does what he does. I challenge him often, and I ask him sometimes to think through his thought process so that I can hear his perspective. In many cases, I have left the conversation realizing it was I who had tunnel vision and bias, not him. This practice with my son has opened up an entirely new world of collaboration between us, and I have a ton more wisdom than I did before as a result.

Let's go back to data for a second. In business, we should not think like we did back in school that there is only one right answer when it comes to data and **analytics**. Your experiences combined with others' experiences will allow you to turn that data into insights and wisdom that will continue to help businesses, society, and our planet. Continue to be curious about the data, and challenge it. Try to find ways to disprove your **assumptions** and beliefs rather than looking to justify them. And, just like I now celebrate my son's diversity and unique perspectives, I also preach that businesses should do the same when they are making decisions. Seeking diverse perspectives will help you understand the different sides and stories data can tell, and it can truly change the world by helping you make more-informed decisions.

This book provides a six-phase process and a twelve-step methodology to follow regarding how you can take data and apply the perspectives of yourself and others to make data-informed decisions. Investments in **data strategy** and analytics will be useless—and can even be harmful—unless individuals and organizations can leverage anthropological skills and understand behaviors and psychology to provide the right **context** for the data (in addition to the more technical skills around data and analytics).

Therefore, this book and the process and methodology described within it are a combination of multiple areas, including analytics, psychology, anthropology, and enterprise thinking.

This book can be used by anyone who needs to make decisions at any level of an organization. The **data-informed decision-making** process is iterative and not linear, and different types of decisions may require different parts of the steps or different tools within each step. Therefore, there are a wide range of tools and models discussed in this book. The tools and models are not discussed in any great length, as entire books can be and are devoted to them. Instead, think of them as a tool kit you can pull from when making decisions.

I hope you enjoy this book, and, more importantly, I hope that you receive the same value from the knowledge within it that I have received over the years.

CHAPTER 1

THE POWER AND POTENTIAL OF DATA

> *"We're entering a new world in which data may be more important than software."*[1]
>
> —Tim O'Reilly

We are living in a truly unprecedented time—one that is radically changing the way we work, the way we live, and the way we communicate with each other. This is the dawn of the *fourth industrial revolution.*

The first industrial revolution used coal and water to make steam to mechanize. The second industrial revolution used electricity to mass-mechanize and mass-produce. The third industrial revolution leveraged electricity to bring about the rise of electronics, both to miniaturize (microprocessors) and automate (automatons and robots). The fourth industrial revolution (a term coined by economist Klaus Schwab and the title of his book of the same name) includes technology breakthroughs like machine learning, IoT, 3D printing, nanotechnology, biotechnology, and energy storage. And what powers all of this? Data. Need more proof of the value data will play? The market intelligence firm International Data Corporation (IDC) predicts that by 2027, data will be something that can be valued on a company's balance sheet.[2]

What really makes these technological breakthroughs unprecedented are the speed and the scope of the changes occurring during this revolution. The speed at which these breakthroughs are happening is exponential compared to previous industrial revolutions. The advancements in cognitive learning and the ability of computers to learn things by themselves (**machine learning**) are literally happening at inhuman speeds. The scope is much broader as well. These advancements are impacting and disrupting just about every industry and doing so in just about all parts of the world.

Before we get into data-informed decision-making and a framework to support it, let's start all the way upstream at the raw source. Let's talk about the importance of data itself, which is sometimes referred to as the "new oil" or the "new currency" in today's business world. What can data do for you with regard to making better decisions?

- It can provide a cohesive and objective view of your company's activities.
- It can provide a view into the macro- and external trends happening in your industry or environment.
- It can help you predict the future.
- It can help you develop your company's strategic plan.
- It can help you identify process improvements and other operational efficiencies.
- It can help you measure results.

Data can do many more things as well, as we will discuss throughout the book.

Positive Potential of Data on Society

The overwhelming potential of data to positively impact society, including both the global economy and the quality of life for all of us, is massive. Think about all the benefits data can have on society globally. It can help us understand and defeat diseases and minimize impacts from injuries. It can help us anticipate and prevent crime. It can help improve educational performance and student outcomes. It can help prevent conflicts and instability. It can help reduce racial profiling and make people aware of the importance of **cognitive diversity** and harmony. It can help protect our heritage, help solve global warming, help sustain natural systems and resources, and help prevent extinctions, even our own. Let's look at a few examples of these amazing benefits.

Healthcare. In healthcare, genetic data is being used to personalize drug treatments for patients. INTelico Therapeutics is a startup company based in Arizona that uses a variety of genetic data from millions of patients to predict the effects of various drugs on the individual patient.[3]

Law enforcement. In the law-enforcement industry, data and analytics can be used to predict future crimes and to then deploy the correct set of resources proactively to try to prevent them. This process, called predictive crime mapping, uses historical data and related information about previous crimes to find patterns and locations where certain crimes may occur. Police resources can then be assigned to patrol these areas rather than randomly policing other areas.

Retail. In the retail industry, Amazon, a global retailer, uses customer data to drive sales. If you've ever shopped on Amazon's website, you will recognize that you receive product recommendations while on the site or via email. Amazon bases its recommendations on what a customer has bought in the past, the items in the customer's online shopping cart, what items the customer has ranked or reviewed after purchase, and what products the customer has viewed when visiting the site. Amazon also uses metrics such as click-through rates, open rates, and opt-out rates to further decide which recommendations to push to which customers. What has been Amazon's outcome by doing this? Amazon made data-informed decisions to invest in these capabilities, and, as a result, the company discovered that product recommendations do in fact drive sales.

Environment. In the environmental industry, data is used to fight climate change and global warming. Historical data exists on socioeconomic populations, temperatures, flood and drought statistics, and much more. That data can give insights that will help us understand global climate-change patterns and how to restore much-needed depleted resources. One company called Carbon Tracker, an independent financial think tank, is working toward the United Nations' goal of preventing new coal plants from being built in favor of alternate renewable sources of energy, like wind and solar. Carbon Tracker uses satellites to monitor coal-plant emissions and then uses that data to determine where air pollution is coming from and to convince industries, such as the finance industry, that carbon plants are not profitable.[4]

Potential Risks with Data

Having shown some examples for which data can make a positive impact, it is important to note that there are also risks associated with the increasing use of data. These risks can have a negative impact and can cost organizations millions of dollars in lost opportunities and added costs.

These risks can be organized into the following categories:

- basing decisions on data that is incomplete, incorrect, or not trusted
- basing decisions on incorrectly built and interpreted visualizations and analytics
- making biased decisions
- making ineffective decisions based solely on data

- making ineffective decisions due to the organizational culture
- incorrectly communicating decisions
- basing decisions on data that may be unethical or illegal

Basing decisions on data that is incomplete, incorrect, or not trusted. A very common scenario that occurs when an organization is trying to make a data-informed decision is that the data needed for the analysis is at some level incomplete, incorrect, or not trusted. Maybe there are no standardized data definitions or standardized calculations used for a measure. As a result, the data is not accurate nor trusted. For example, what if two separate groups within an organization calculate the organization's customer conversion rate (the rate that prospective customers turn to actual paying customers) and get different results? Which one do you believe? In this example, neither group standardized the definition and calculation of what a customer conversion is, and they both came up with their own. As a result, each group will be making decisions based on data that is not universally accepted as true within the organization. Maybe it is as simple as one of the groups missing certain channels that are actually driving those conversions. This can lead to one group making decisions that have unintended consequences, like shifting budget funds to other channels that may actually be underperforming. Once this happens, then neither group will trust the data going forward and will refuse to use it, citing the old adage "garbage in, garbage out."

Another common scenario seen is that decision-makers within an organization do not even have access to the right data needed to make appropriate decisions. Historically, organizations have had centralized data and limited access to it, so any reports sent out have tended to be static. This lack of access to full information makes it incredibly hard to drill down into the data to look for patterns and relationships. Estimates show that companies are only leveraging around 12 percent of the data they have.[5] Critical insights are likely in this data that is not being leveraged. Part of the challenge is sourcing and being comfortable with the quality of the data. Another part of the challenge is ensuring that everyone is leveraging the data using standardized, trusted, and approved methods to make data-informed decisions.

A further challenge is that many times, decision-makers aren't even aware that they don't have all the data needed to make a decision. There is no report that says I have it all or don't have it all. Therefore, decision-makers need to apply problem-solving and creative thinking to see if there is other data that could be relevant to their decision.

Below is a list of warning signs that can help you determine if your data is incomplete, incorrect, or not to be trusted:

- You are spending time manually updating your analysis.
- The numbers that your finance team report out on a monthly or quarterly basis do not add up to the numbers you see.
- You or your leaders do not share data when making decisions.
- You struggle to get help from any employee resource related to data or analytics because they are too busy on other projects.
- You are spending time having to justify things because someone else shows you a report that has incorrect data about your business and makes it look worse than it really is.

More details about **data quality** will be discussed in chapter 5.

Basing decisions on incorrectly built and interpreted visualizations and analytics. The previous risk focused on the data itself. However, even if the data is complete, correct, and trusted, people could use incorrect visualizations or analytics with the data. Individuals and organizations who are not **data literate** will be more likely to use less-than-ideal analytics and visualizations as part of their data-informed decision-making process. This could be as simple as using the wrong visualization type based on what you are trying to analyze. Or it could be more complex like excluding information (data or **context**) that is vital to making the best decision. In some cases, the correct calculation on a given measure is appropriate for the analysis, but maybe the measure itself was not appropriate to use for the current situation.

That measure may not be an accurate **key performance indicator (KPI)** that ties to organizational goals and thus may lead to unintended consequences. One famous example of this relates to snakes in India. At one time, India's government wanted to reduce the number of venomous snakes, so it decided to offer a reward for every dead cobra snake turned in. Initially, this initiative was deemed successful, as hundreds of cobras were turned in. However, citizens soon realized they could breed cobras to turn in to the government and create an income stream. Once the government learned of this, it stopped the reward program. Then, those breeders had no use for the snakes, so they set them loose, increasing the number of venomous snakes in the wild to a larger number than before the reward was put into place.[6]

Making biased decisions. In some cases, the interpretation of a given analysis could be incorrect due to a cognitive bias or an outdated mental model. **Cognitive bias** can be defined as an unconscious, systematic, and reproducible failure in information processing that gets in the way of logical thinking. A **mental model** is how an individual understands the world. However, in times of change, like during the digital revolution we are living in, the world is changing so rapidly that mental models can quickly become outdated. For example, a mental model for how to watch a movie in 1990 was very different than a mental model for how to watch a movie today. No longer do we have to either go to a movie theater or a physical store to rent a movie. Today, we can also stream movies to our TVs and phones and other devices.

Let's look at an example of a biased decision.

A stockbroker is testing an investment strategy on a large group of stocks. The broker applies each trading strategy to historical data to see how accurately the strategy would have predicted actual results. The broker tests the strategy against fifteen years of stock data. He is looking at stocks that have complete information for the entire fifteen-year period. Based on that information, the broker decides on an investment strategy. On the surface, this looks like a sound and rational decision. However, the decision included a cognitive bias called survivor bias. *Survivor bias* is an error in logic that involves focusing on a subset of data that made it past some selection criteria while ignoring others that did not. This typically happens when the data that is ignored is not visible to the decision-maker. In the stockbroker example, the broker is only looking at data for stocks that have a complete fifteen years of data. However, this focus ignores any stocks from organizations that may have gone bankrupt over that time period. That data is absolutely valid and should be included in the analysis but is overlooked due to survivor bias. Maybe that data includes clues that would change the analysis and the decision being made.

Another example of a biased decision comes from Wells Fargo, an American multinational financial-services company. In an effort to upsell existing clients, Wells Fargo introduced an incentive to encourage its employees to sell eight accounts per customer. These eight could include credit cards, savings accounts, and other financial services. As a result of the incentive, Wells Fargo employees began breaking the rules to meet their targets. Millions of unauthorized credit card and deposit accounts were opened. Ultimately, the bank was ordered to pay a $142 million settlement.[7] In this example, Wells Fargo had the right data and information, but its decision to have a KPI tracking how many of its customers had purchased all eight accounts pushed employees to provide accounts to customers that should never have been approved or opened, and the company failed to see the unintended consequences.

There are many types of cognitive bias beyond survivor bias. Bias and mental models will be discussed in greater detail in chapter 3.

Making ineffective decisions based solely on data. There are many situations in which an organization makes decisions based on data alone. However, data alone is not a magic bullet for the best decisions. Even if an organization has good data, decisions based solely on data are typically also made with assumptions. **Assumptions** are implicit or explicit thoughts that are accepted as true without any proof. If those assumptions are not correct, you will make a bad decision, regardless of the accuracy of the data. This is why it is important to both follow a process that will help challenge those assumptions and to marry the data with intuition, personal beliefs, and experiences. Data cannot replace intuition, but when data is used along with intuition, personal beliefs, and experiences, flawed decisions are minimized.

A good way to explain this risk is by looking at a common example related to car navigation systems. There are countless stories of drivers driving into lakes, off cliffs, and into other nonfunctional areas because their car navigation system told them to. In these stories, the decision-makers relied on the data and information from the system but failed to challenge their assumptions (the GPS is always accurate) and to apply their own thought processes, beliefs, and intuition (driving off the road into a lake is bad). While this is an exaggerated example, in business, it translates to an organization's decision-makers blindly trusting data to make decisions without stopping to challenge their assumptions or use their intuition.

Making ineffective decisions due to the organizational culture. Individuals and organizations often freeze and fail to make **strategic decisions**, citing a fear of making the wrong decision. This is especially true in organizations that have a culture that does not embrace failure. Decision-making is iterative, and organizations that can course correct their less-than-optimal decisions by failing fast, then fixing fast, and then learning from their failures will be the ones that succeed. Amazon bases its success not on a reactionary approach of detecting market trends but by a fast decision-making process to create such trends in the first place. Amazon CEO Jeff Bezos stressed the importance of quick decision-making in a letter to his annual shareholders in 2016:

> Most decisions should probably be made with somewhere around 70 percent of the information you wish you had. If you wait for 90 percent, in most cases, you're probably being slow. Plus, either way, you need to be good at quickly recognizing and correcting bad decisions. If you're good at course correcting,

> being wrong may be less costly than you think, whereas being slow is going to be expensive for sure.[8]

Making decisions too soon with not enough data is a mistake, but so is making decisions too late or not making a decision at all. In some situations, decision-makers can have the urge to keep collecting data and to ensure that all risks are resolved at the expense of making a decision. They are afraid to make the wrong decision. This mindset can negatively impact your business. For example, imagine you are starting a new company and planning to enter into a newly emerging tech market. You are working on the product, but in parallel, you are continuously debating the marketing strategy and have delayed the product launch as a result. During this time, other companies entered the same market with similar products and took control of the market share before you even launched.

Incorrectly communicating decisions. In many organizations, different people are responsible for building analytics and visualizations than those who actually need to consume them to make decisions. In these cases, the consumers of these analytics and visualizations can misinterpret the information, leading to incorrect conclusions and insights.

One famous example of this is when the engineers in charge of a part on the US Space Shuttle Challenger tried to get the launch stopped because they believed the part would get damaged during the takeoff, which could then lead to a massive explosion. Those engineers showed a visualization to NASA that included only a subset of the data they used to gain their insights. That visualization was then misinterpreted by NASA, who deemed that the launch was not at risk. Therefore, the launch happened, and tragically, the space shuttle exploded during takeoff. The after-action report highlights multiple lapses in process and also **groupthink**, the practice of making decisions as a group in a way that discourages creativity or diverse perspectives.[9]

Another common mistake is to not communicate the thought process for a decision. One famous example of ineffective communication was the failure of project managers and engineers to fully communicate, which resulted in the deadly collapse of a Hyatt Regency walkway in 1981. In this shocking event, two walkways within the hotel collapsed and fell onto the lobby, killing over one hundred people and injuring over two hundred others.

The results of investigations concluded that the disaster was due to the flawed design of steel rods designed to hold the walkway up. The project architect had prepared architectural drawings of the walkway and delivered them to the steel company responsible for making the steel rods. The steel company went on to build the steel rods per the specs in the design. However, the original drawings were only drafts, and that important piece of data was not communicated.[10]

Basing decisions on data that may be unethical or illegal. Target, a popular retailer based in the United States, collects a lot of data about its customers. With this information, Target can correlate each person's purchase history, demographics, and other relevant information. But what does the company do with this information, and what decisions are made from it? One example involves pregnant women. In this example, company decision-makers analyzed historical buying data for all the women in Target's baby registry. One piece of knowledge this analysis revealed was that pregnant women were purchasing large quantities of unscented lotion at the beginning of their second trimester. Similar knowledge was gleaned, and Target identified twenty-five different products that were designated as pregnancy-prediction factors and then assigned a scoring value. The model was improved over time with more data until Target was able to estimate the baby's due date down to a two-week window. What decision was the company then able to reach? It was now able to send mothers-to-be targeted advertising and coupons at specific points during their pregnancies. The model was so accurate that it even detected pregnancy in a high school girl before her own parents found out.[11] This is where one of the downsides comes into play. Is it ethical to detect someone else's pregnancy?

Sometimes, decisions are not only unethical but could also be illegal. Suppose a bank wants to determine whether or not to provide a loan to a customer. When trying to automate the decision-making process for this, the bank needs to determine parameters and desired outcomes for the decision. For this scenario, two potential outcomes could be to maximize loans that are not defaulted or to maximize profit for the bank. The bank could then feed this into a **machine-learning** model that is used to automate the decision-making process. As the model learns, it would analyze the data to determine what criteria predict the desired outcome. However, what if the criteria the model chooses end up creating a decision that is biased or even illegal? For example, what if the solution is to give out subprime loans (loans in which the interest rate is higher than the prime rate) to maximize profit? Or what if the solution results in actions that violate fair-lending laws? The model could have the bank partaking in illegal practices.

Summary and Key Takeaways

- Data has the potential to positively impact not only individuals and organizations but also society as a whole.
- Organizations that do not have a data-informed decision-making process encounter multiple challenges, including incorrect interpretations of their data, poor visualizations, poor communication and adoption of decisions, and poor decisions due to bias and not thinking about unintended consequences.

CHAPTER 2

INTRODUCTION TO DATA-INFORMED DECISION-MAKING

"We are the sum total of our experiences. Those experiences – be they positive or negative – make us the person we are . . . and those [experiences] yet to come, continue to influence and reshape the person we are, and the person we become."[12]

—B.J. Neblett

Now that we understand both the potential and the risks associated with data, let's dive in and learn how we can seize this opportunity. Let's start out by explaining what we mean by data-informed decision-making. **Data-informed decision-making** is the ability to transform information into actionable and verified knowledge to ultimately make business decisions. There is a spectrum of critical capabilities that need to be in place at an organizational level to support this.

There needs to be a data-literate workforce who understand how to read, work with, analyze, and argue with data. There needs to be a data strategy in place to ensure that the data is high quality and trusted. There needs to be a data analytics strategy to properly analyze the data. There needs to be a set of skills and practices in place and supported, including systems thinking, critical thinking with data, a cognitively diverse workforce, active listening, and the ability to communicate and tell stories with data. All of this needs to be supported by an organizational culture that embraces these capabilities and data-informed decision-making. A visual highlighting these capabilities is shown in figure 1, and they are all discussed in greater detail in the remainder of this book.

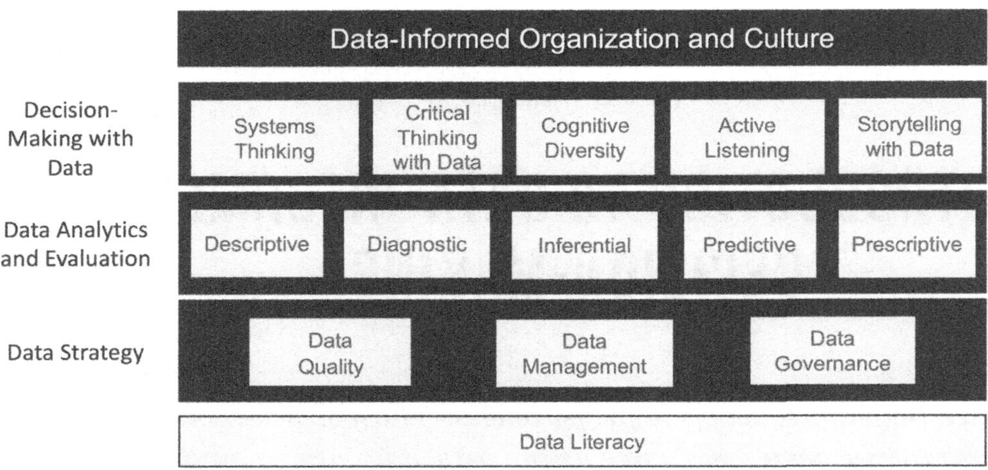

Figure 1. Data-informed decision-making capabilities

With so much potential but so many risks, how do organizations maximize the potential to make positive data-informed decisions while minimizing the risk of falling victim to any of the issues listed earlier? The answer to this question is the focus of this book and requires three things:

1. Decision-makers need to follow an overarching decision-making *process*. A data-informed decision-making process defines the high-level steps that should be systematically followed.
2. Decision-makers need to define and embrace a *methodology*. A methodology outlines what needs to be done in each step of the process, including how and why to do it.
3. Organizations need to have the right set of *skills* to allow them to follow the process and to apply the methodology accurately and successfully.

The 6-Phase Data-Informed Decision-Making Process

There are various processes and models out there that can be followed for data-informed decision-making. The one covered in this book is an overarching six-phase process that factors in approaches to minimizing all of the threats and maximizing all of the opportunities listed in the previous chapter. Following this process will help you turn your vast amount of data into insights to make data-informed decisions. This six-phase process blends together the need to ask the right questions, to source the right data in the right format, to critically appraise and analyze the data using an analytic framework, to apply your personal expertise and that of others while being aware of any unconscious bias, to communicate your decision to all stakeholders, and to then build a review framework and mechanism to monitor the decision and to iterate through the process again based on the findings.

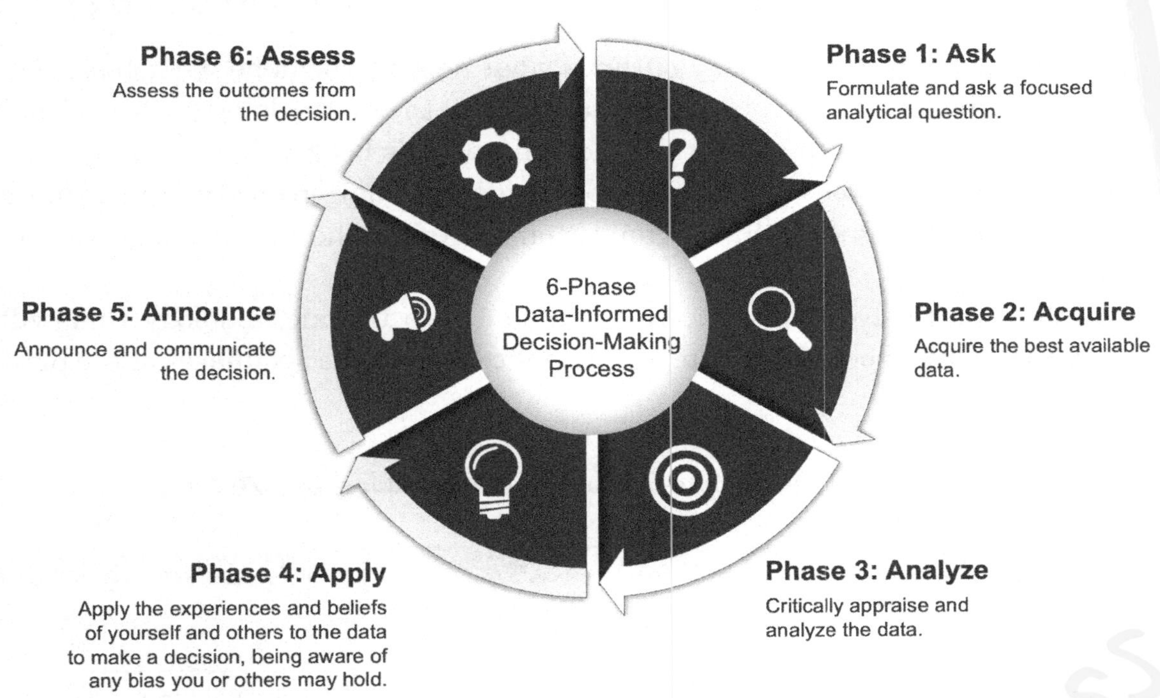

Figure 2. Six-phase data-informed decision-making process

The six phases in the process are the following:

1. Formulate and *ask* a focused **analytical question**.
2. *Acquire* the best available data.
3. Critically appraise and *analyze* the data.
4. *Apply* the experiences and beliefs of yourself and others to the data to make a decision, being aware of any bias you or others may hold.
5. *Announce* and communicate the decision.
6. *Assess* the outcomes from the decision.

Leveraging this systematic and systemic process will reduce impacts from bias, foster diversity and inclusion, minimize unintended consequences, and allow you to improve on your decisions by failing fast, fixing fast, and learning fast, including improvements to your data and measurement frameworks, increased accountability, and better data-informed decisions.

The 12-Step Data-Informed Decision-Making Methodology

As discussed earlier, a *methodology* outlines what needs to be done in each step of the process, including how and why to do it. Many times, the methodology will refer to other models or frameworks to use within each phase. This book will discuss one specific methodology with examples, but it will also provide information on other potential components that can be used within organizations to tailor the methodology specific to their culture.

The following twelve steps, shown in table 1, are the methodology that will be discussed within this book. These steps are applied within the six phases of the process, shown in figure 2.

Table 1. Twelve-step data-informed decision-making methodology

STEP	PHASE	DESCRIPTION
1	Ask	Turn business questions into analytical questions.
2	Ask	Classify the decision needed.
3	Acquire	Find and source all relevant data. Remember to think about the analytical questions systemically and to include any interrelated data that could be relevant. This means not only internal data but external data and information as well.
4	Acquire	Ensure the sourced data is trusted.
5	Analyze	Create a measurement framework to describe your data with key performance indicators (KPIs) and descriptive analytics.
6	Analyze	Use diagnostic analytics to find patterns, trends, and relationships that may exist but not be obvious to start to drill into root cause. If applicable, leverage inferential statistics to take a sample of data and make generalizations about the entire population, predictive analytics to run simulations or to test potential decisions/solutions, and prescriptive analytics to act on situations as they happen.
7	Apply	Review and orient yourself to the data and information so far, apply your personal experiences to it, and create a hypothesis.

STEP	PHASE	DESCRIPTION
8	Apply	Challenge the data, and actively look for information to see if you can disprove your hypothesis.
9	Apply	Leverage strategies to become aware of and to mitigate bias, and then make a decision.
10	Announce	Announce your decision at the right level to ALL stakeholders (direct, indirect, upstream, and downstream) by leveraging tools like reframing, the Pyramid principle, and the Rule of Three in your storytelling.
11	Announce	Provide adequate time for stakeholders to unlearn any outdated mental models and to learn new ones.
12	Assess	Set up a review mechanism to monitor the impacts of the decision after it is made and acted upon. Leverage that review mechanism, and fail/fix/learn fast, making improvements to data, measurement frameworks, accountability, decisions, and anything else relevant.

It is important to note that this six-phase process and the twelve steps in this methodology are not always a linear process. Decision-making is an iterative process. There are many situations in which you will gain insights during one phase that require you to go back to a previous phase before proceeding on. We will see examples of this later on in the book.

Other processes and methodologies exist that relate to decision-making. Some of them cover certain components of the decision-making process, but none of them cover the entire spectrum, starting with asking the right question and ending with assessing the decision. Some of the relevant tools that can be used within the methodology covered in this book are discussed in chapter 10.

Top-10 Data-Informed Decision-Making Skills

With all the recent advancements in technologies used to process and analyze data, too-much emphasis has been placed on the technology alone. However, technology is not the lifeblood of the fourth industrial revolution; the lifeblood are the people who are interacting with the technology and the data inputted and outputted from it. Therefore, it is imperative that people have the right skills to properly use this technology to make decisions. The right skills needed are a combination of both hard skills and soft skills. **Hard skills** are teachable abilities or skill sets that relate to specific technical knowledge and are easily measurable. Using Microsoft Excel and being able to speak a foreign language are examples of hard skills. **Soft skills** are personal habits or traits that shape how an individual works and how the individual works with others. Effective communication and empathy are examples of soft skills.

Organizations, including businesses and schools, are behind and need to catch up fast. The set of skills required to compete as an individual or an organization in today's world is lacking. Institutions that educate on a comprehensive set of skills as a unified curriculum are few and far between. Some will build curricula around technology and hard skills, but an organization's ability to compete relies a lot more on soft skills than hard skills. The companies that embrace and foster the culture and development of soft skills will be the ones that survive. A recent CEO survey from the company PricewaterhouseCoopers (PwC) found that 77 percent of the 1,400 CEOs surveyed highlighted soft skills as the biggest threat to today's business.[13]

So, what are the skills needed to make data-informed decisions? It is unrealistic to expect any decision-maker to have all of the required skills. Some of the skills are important for everyone to have. Others are more specialized and only needed by individuals at certain phases of the process. This is why decision-making within an organization should be a team sport.

Figure 3 shows the top-ten skills required within an organization to follow the data-informed decision-making process.

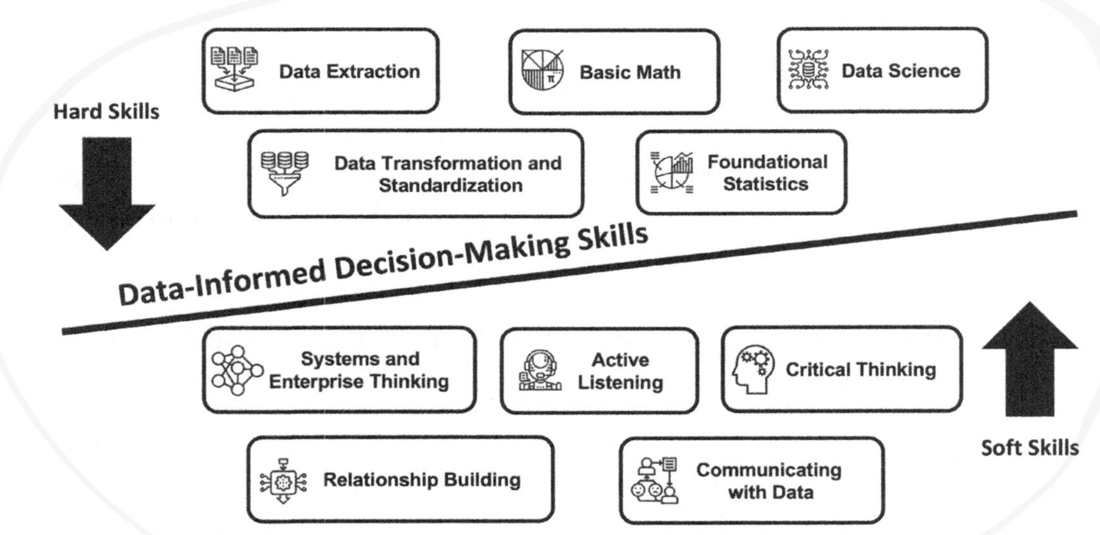

Figure 3. Top-ten data-informed decision-making skills

TOP-5 HARD SKILLS

Organizations that want to embrace data-informed decision-making require a broad set of competencies that fall under the category of **hard skills**. These are required skills to be able to start with **raw data** and then extract, transform, and standardize it.

Next, to make use of the data, everyone touching it needs to have a basic understanding of data types and attributes as well as basic math. From there, proper analysis will require decision-makers to work with individuals who have foundational statistics skills and data-science skills. All of these skills are teachable abilities that relate to specific technical knowledge and are easily measurable.

Below is a list of the top-five hard skills required in an organization to foster data-informed decision-making.

Data extraction. When an organization has an **analytical question** it needs to answer, the key is understanding what data has information that will aid in answering that question. Once this data is identified, it needs to be extracted. With some analytical questions, that may just involve taking data as is from an Excel file. For more-complex questions and situations, it may involve extracting the data information from **big-data** systems and technologies.

Data transformation and standardization. Once the data is extracted, it needs to be transformed and standardized to be made analytics ready. Research shows that up to 80 percent of the time spent making data-informed decisions is on tasks related to cleaning, standardizing, and organizing data.[14] This shows how absolutely important it is that organizations have the right skills to be able to clean, transform, profile, tag, catalog, and standardize data.

Basic math and understanding of data. For data-informed decision-making, not everyone within an organization needs to possess data-science skills, but everyone should possess basic math skills. These math skills include a fundamental understanding of data, including types of data (**quantitative** and **qualitative**), attributes of data, and various data **aggregations** (calculations used to group data) and distributions. With skills in basic math, everyone can understand and leverage **descriptive analytics**, which is a key step in the data-informed decision-making process (descriptive analytics will be discussed more fully later in the book). Descriptive analytics skills can range from someone responsible for building and maintaining a **measurement framework**, which includes critical **key performance indicators**, to decision-makers who need to apply meaning to the information they are seeing.

Foundational statistics. Statistics is a broad discipline that involves using mathematics to analyze, interpret, and present data. Foundational statistics skills are vital for an organization that wants to make data-informed decisions. The individuals who are ultimately making the decisions do not necessarily need these skills, but they need someone working with them on the decisions who can provide an understanding of foundational statistics. Foundational statistics skills require an understanding of probability and correlation, simple regression, and **inferential statistics** to ensure that things like **sample** sizes are created properly. Statistics, and how it relates to analytics, is covered in more detail in chapter 6.

Data science. While data science is not a single skill by itself, grouped together here, these skills encompass everything that an organization needs to do with **machine learning** and **artificial intelligence**, including **predictive** and **prescriptive analytics**. With the vast amount of data available to organizations today, machine-learning skills are essential to turn the data into insights to make data-informed decisions. The types of analytics used in data science are covered more fully in chapter 6.

TOP-5 SOFT SKILLS

In addition to hard skills, **soft skills** are critically important to organizations that want to embrace data-informed decision-making. Remember, soft skills are personal habits or traits that shape how an individual works and how the individual works with others. These are required skills to be able to think critically and look past symptoms to find the root causes to problems. Soft skills are required for organizations to work collaboratively to gain valuable insights by leveraging relationship building and active listening. Finally, these skills are required to be able to translate data into a story that emotionally moves and motivates an organization's stakeholders and helps them understand the decisions being made.

Below is a list of the top-five soft skills required in an organization to foster data-informed decision-making.

Systems and enterprise thinking. According to management consultant W. Edwards Deming, 94 percent of problems in business are systems driven, and only 6 percent are people driven.[15] **Systems thinking** helps decision-makers understand why people behave like they do. It is a way of looking at an organization (and the world) as a set of systems that all connect in some way. When viewing the organization this way, identifying causes versus symptoms is easier as decision-makers can consider how each part interacts with the others. Systems thinking will be covered in greater detail in chapter 5.

Critical thinking. Decision-makers need to not only understand the data available to them but also know the meaning of that data and how it should be applied to their business. Insights are not found in data but in how humans assign meaning to data. Part of the data-informed decision-making process is the ability to think critically about the data and to recognize both the complexity of the decisions and the possibility of multiple, valid positions. Decision-makers need to understand possible limitations of the data presented, and they need to be aware of and to mitigate against any **cognitive bias** they may have. Very rarely will decision-makers have a complete set of data at their disposal. Decision-makers need to accept this, avoid analysis paralysis, deal with the uncertainty, and make the best decision they can with the data that is available to them.

Active listening. During many phases of the decision-making process, people are exposed to information, whether it's requirements for the project, insights from the analysis, or feedback on the decision during the Assess phase. It is human nature to apply meaning to that information based on our own cultural and personal perspectives and to then draw conclusions. In reality, those conclusions may be based on what someone thinks someone else said, as opposed to what the person actually said. This is why active listening combined with critical thinking is vital.

Active listening involves a person not only listening to what another person is saying but also consciously making an effort to listen to the complete message being communicated. This involves paying attention and not being distracted or losing focus or interest in what the other person is saying. There are five key active-listening techniques:

1. Pay attention.
2. Let the speaker know you are listening.
3. Defer any judgment.
4. Respond appropriately.
5. Provide feedback.

Relationship building. When making a decision, it is important to consider as many aspects of the decision as possible and to work collaboratively. Two people may have access to the same data and information but have different experiences, which can lead to valuable insights not previously considered. Collaboration is critical to the data-informed decision-making process and depends on the quality of relationships among people as they work through the process together. This means that relationship building is a critical skill—from gathering requirements for analytical questions, to communicating out to all the stakeholders, to gathering feedback on the decision after it is made.

Communicating with data. Communicating decisions out to stakeholders is one of the most important skills an organization can have. An organization needs to be able to translate data into a story that emotionally moves and motivates its stakeholders and helps them understand the decisions being made. Organizations can have quality data and skilled analysts who use analytics tools to present insights and recommendations; however, if those are not communicated properly to the decision-maker or the decision-maker does not have the confidence or a consistent process to make the decision, then everything else is useless.

Appropriate and skillful communication of data includes an approach called *analytic storytelling*. This is the process of bringing data to life through a well-constructed narrative. In analytic storytelling, you use the right data, the right visualizations to support your decisions, and the right amount of storytelling to get your message across at the right level. You do not want to overwhelm or bore your audience. Most importantly, you should not only present the data but also add in the appropriate **context**. Give the audience the idea, the picture, and then the applicable details. Chapter 8 will go further into successful data communication.

Summary and Key Takeaways

- Data-informed decision-making should follow a systemic and systematic process, such as the one that will be discussed in this book.
- Data-informed decision-making requires a combination of hard and soft skills.

CHAPTER 3

THE SCIENCE OF DECISION-MAKING

"The greatest enemy of knowledge is not ignorance; it is the illusion of knowledge."[16]

—Daniel Boorstin

Data alone is not information and does not provide knowledge or wisdom or insights. There is a hierarchy that explains how we go from **raw data** to ultimately making a decision. To best understand this hierarchy, it is important to understand both the neuroscience and the psychology of decision-making. This includes understanding how the human brain processes information, how it applies meaning to social and cultural values and beliefs, and how it is susceptible to systematic errors based on limits in its capacity to process information.

Going from Data to Wisdom

One model that explains the process an individual goes through to take data and turn it into wisdom and insights is called the *DIKW pyramid*.

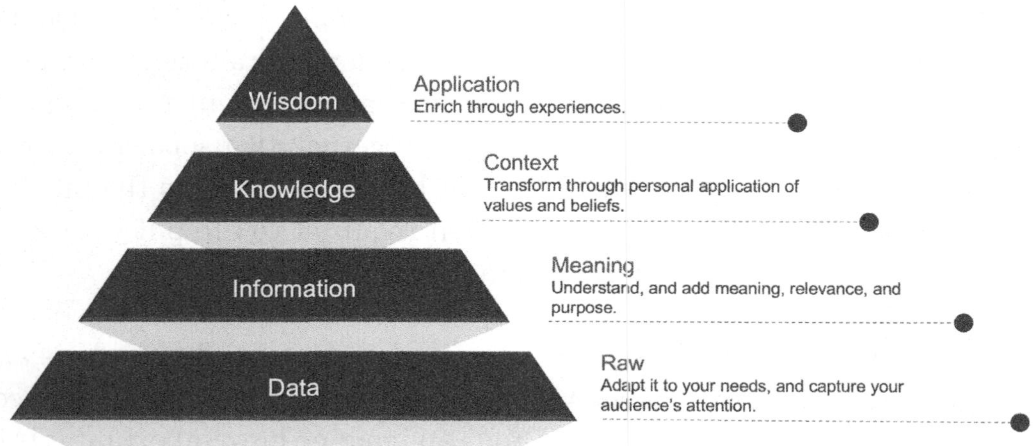

Figure 4. DIKW pyramid

The DIKW pyramid is made up of four levels, as shown in figure 4: data, information, knowledge, and wisdom. At the bottom level, you have *data*. You may clean up the data and perform other basic calculations on it, but it is just a piece of **raw data**. The next level up is *information*. Information is data that has meaning and purpose. You are analyzing the relationships and connections between the pieces of raw data.

Knowledge is the third level of the pyramid and is perhaps the hardest concept to define. One may define knowledge as sets of information that have been processed, organized, or structured in some way over time. Some explain knowledge as the synthesis of a human taking all of the various information presented and trying to derive meaning from it. Another view is that knowledge is a product of a synthesis in the human mind and exists only in the thoughts in someone's mind. This would mean that knowledge can only be shared as information and then become knowledge again in someone else's brain. However you try to explain knowledge, the thing to consider is that it answers the how or what questions.

The final level in the pyramid is *wisdom*. Wisdom is a state in which the decision-maker has taken in all the knowledge necessary and then makes an informed decision. Wisdom brings everything together and is the most important state of understanding because it is where higher-level thinking takes place. The decision-maker should be able to explain to others what is happening and, most importantly, why it is happening.

Let's look at a few examples of this process.

You're a pilot. For this first example, assume you are a pilot, and the number 10,000 flashes on your cockpit display without any context. No labels, no descriptions, no units of measurement. At this point, you have data, but it does not mean anything. Now let's add in some description. Let's say the cockpit display reads, "10,000 feet above sea level." At this point, this is information because the raw piece of data, 10,000, has been given some meaning. Now let's say you are flying over a mountain range, and you know from another piece of information that there are mountains in the range that are over 12,000 feet. At this point, you have pieced together two separate pieces of information, and you have some knowledge. What is your decision as the pilot? You decide to climb above the mountains. This decision required you to put your knowledge into action and do something. That is wisdom.

You're running a large company. That was a general example, but let's apply the concept of the DIKW pyramid to a business. Assume you are running a large company that has hundreds of different data points. You can imagine how important it is to make sure you understand the meaning (information) and context (knowledge) associated with the data to ensure that you are making the best decisions. Not only is it about coming up with the best decisions, but it is also about the speed at which you can do so. In many cases, it is the company that connects the most information together the most quickly and the one that is the most agile to adapt to new information and context as they come that makes the best decisions with the right speed to thrive. This is why evaluating and making necessary changes to chosen courses of action is a key component. Data is not a static entity, so neither are decisions based on data.

You work for a grocery store. Let's now look at a more complex example. Let's assume you work for a grocery store that stocks inventory from multiple suppliers. You have data on each product, identified by a SKU, in your warehouse, including what the product is, who the supplier is, when the product was delivered, and much more. At this stage, this data is useful to know, but there is no context around what you will do with this data. Let's now give this data meaning and context. You can **aggregate** all the data, including historical data, to see how many units of a particular product are in stock, how long they have been there, and how long you have before you need to sell the units. This is now information. With all this information together, you can make decisions on when to restock the product. You can also run promotions to sell off the product before it expires. These decisions are made based on knowing why things happen. This is knowledge. Finally, you can achieve wisdom by tracking your inventory to see if it matches up with specific times of year, holidays, or natural disasters.

You work in sales. Let's walk through one more example. Assume you work in sales and are trying to understand what is happening with your business from a financial perspective. Your company sells two products: Alpha and Beta. At the data level, you have data on the sales costs and sales revenue for both products. At the information level, you have calculated the profit margin, which is the net value of revenue minus product cost. You have determined from those calculations that the profit margin is decreasing for both products. This is really useful information, but to really make decisions, you need to know *why* the profit is decreasing. After bringing in additional data and information, you are able to determine that the profit is decreasing with product Alpha because the sales are being discounted, so the revenue generated is going down. With product Beta, you determine that the costs of some of your vendors have increased, which is eating into your profits. You now have accurate knowledge, for you know why the profit is going down in both cases. Wisdom will be the decisions you make to try to improve the profit in both cases. In this example, it is to trigger another investigation into what is causing discounting to happen for product Alpha and to find replacement vendors who are cheaper yet still provide the same quality of service for product Beta.

In these examples, you can see that we cannot simply use data to make a snap decision but must formulate an understanding, as Einstein pointed out when he famously said, "Any fool can know. The point is to understand."[17] The Alpha and Beta products example highlights that data is not information, and there is a process we need to follow and operationalize to make informed decisions from the data. It also points out the importance of the quality and accuracy of the data below it. In the example of the pilot, had the pilot's display read 13,000, his or her decision-making would have been wrong because the data was wrong, resulting in an inaccurate assessment of the situation and a likely crash. This is why data quality is so critical.

While the DIKW pyramid is a good model to highlight the process a decision-maker must go through to turn data into knowledge and wisdom, it does not highlight what can get in the way of this process. Therefore, the rest of this chapter is devoted to the neuroscience of how the brain makes decisions.

Understanding How the Brain Makes Decisions

There are multiple theories and schools of thought on how the brain stores information and makes decisions. Nevertheless, most of them agree on the same underlying principles. We will discuss these principles here.

THE UNCONSCIOUS MIND

The unconscious is a theory that helps explain how the human mind works. In earlier days, many people assumed that humans had control of their minds, that dreams were divinely inspired, and that memory was perfect. However, as science advanced, we learned more about how the mind really works. The theory that truly revolutionized our understanding of psychology was psychoanalytic theory, introduced by the Austrian physician Sigmund Freud.

In Freud's psychoanalytic theory, the mind is divided into the "conscious," "subconscious," and "unconscious" processes, often represented by an iceberg,[18] as shown in figure 5.

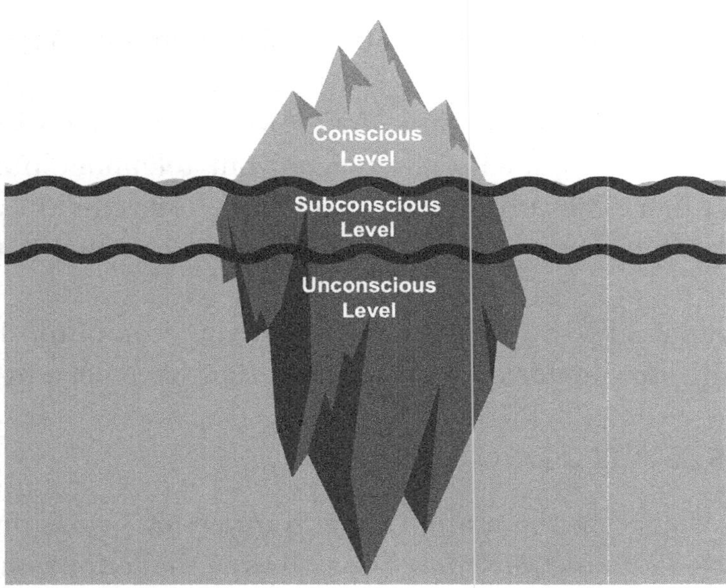

Figure 5. Freud's iceberg

Freud proposed that a person may have desires or memories of which he or she is unaware but which manifest themselves as conscious behaviors. This, he argued, is the *unconscious* mind, where most of a person's personality is determined. Freud was also the first to promote that the unconscious is the origin of what happens in dreams.

The *conscious* brain is rational, careful, analytical, slow, and deliberate, and it understands exceptions. However, it is not efficient to use the conscious brain for every single decision. Humans are exposed to eleven million pieces of information at any given point in time yet only have the capacity to process forty pieces at one time.[19] Therefore, for a majority of our smaller and quicker decisions, we use our unconscious to help make an intuition-based decision.

The *subconscious* is the region that sits between the conscious and unconscious, just below the level of consciousness. It acts like a guard, controlling what is brought to consciousness from your unconscious.

Imagine your mind is like a computer. Your conscious mind is best represented by the keyboard and monitor. Data is inputted on the keyboard, and the results are cast on the monitor. That is how your conscious mind works—information is taken in via some outside stimulus from your environment, and the results are instantly cast onto your consciousness.

Your subconscious is like the RAM in your computer. RAM is the place in a computer where programs and data that are currently in use are kept so that they can easily be reached by the computer processor. It is much faster than other types of memory, such as the hard disk or DVD.

Your subconscious works in the same way. Any recent memories are stored there for quick recall when needed, memories such as your telephone number or the name of a person you just met. The subconscious also holds your current programs that you run every day, such as your current recurring thoughts, behavior patterns, habits, and feelings.

Your unconscious is like the hard disk drive in your computer. It is the long-term storage place for all your memories and programs that have been installed since birth.

SYSTEM 1 AND SYSTEM 2 DECISIONS

Similar to Freud's theory on the mind, Daniel Kahneman's work on decision-making, discussed in his book *Thinking, Fast and Slow*, showed that our brain has two operating systems. Kahneman calls these System 1 and System 2 decisions.

System 1 decisions, which make up 97 percent of our thinking, are fast, automatic, effortless, and unconscious. These decisions are made without self-awareness or control and can be referred to as "gut-reaction" decisions.

System 2 decisions, which make up 3 percent of our thinking, are deliberate and conscious and require effort and controlled mental processing along with rational thinking. These decisions involve critical thinking, problem-solving, analysis, and reflection.

System 1 is continuously creating impressions, intuitions, and judgments based on everything we are seeing and sensing. For 97 percent of the time, we just go with the impression or intuition that System 1 generates. System 2 only gets involved when we encounter something unexpected that System 1 can't automatically process.

System 1 thinking seeks a coherent story above all else, which can lead us to jump to conclusions. While System 1 is generally very accurate, there are situations in which it can make errors of bias. System 1 sometimes answers easier questions than the real questions we asked, and it has little knowledge of logic and statistics.

One of the biggest risks with System 1 is that it seeks to quickly create a coherent, plausible story—an explanation for what is happening—by relying on associations and memories, pattern matching, and **assumptions**. And System 1 will default to that plausible, convenient story—even if that story is based on incorrect information.

According to Kahneman:

> Systems 1 and 2 are both active whenever we are awake. System 1 runs automatically, and System 2 is normally in comfortable low-effort mode, in which only a fraction of its capacity is engaged. System 1 continuously generates suggestions for System 2: impressions, intuitions, intentions, and feelings. If endorsed by System 2, impressions and intuitions turn into beliefs, and impulses turn into voluntary actions. When all goes smoothly, which is most of the time, System 2 adopts the suggestions of System 1 with little or no modification. You generally believe your impressions and act on your desires, and that is fine—usually.[20]

Relating these two systems to data-informed decision-making, because System 1 occurs automatically, errors due to outdated **mental models** or **cognitive bias** are hard to prevent. We will discuss mental models and cognitive bias in much more detail later on in this chapter. This is one reason why data-informed decision-making is a team sport. It is much easier for people to recognize other people's bias and outdated mental models than their own.

Both Freud's and Kahneman's models highlight that there are two major processes for making decisions. There is the intuition-based process in which the brain typically makes the decision unconsciously, and there is the process that is deliberate and requires conscious reasoning. Both of these will be covered throughout this book.

HOW THE BRAIN PROCESSES INFORMATION

Regardless of which type of decision you are making, there are a few things that can alter your intuition or conscious reasoning. Earlier, we mentioned that humans are exposed to up to eleven million pieces of information at any point in time.[21] Clearly, this is too much for us to process. As a result, the brain develops *a perceptual lens* that filters out certain things and lets others in based on preferences and bias adapted through life and our experiences. This lens includes **heuristics**, which are mental shortcuts that can be used during intuitive System 1 decisions. This lens also includes **mental models**, which are our explanations of how the world works—frameworks through which we view the world. Unlike heuristics, mental models are not mental shortcuts. They are created by the mind to help us make sense of the world and are used during System 2 decisions, which require deductive reasoning. Both heuristics and mental models are built upon our *perception*, a process in which we organize and interpret incoming data and information.

Have you ever noticed that when you are looking for a new car, you tend to see more car commercials or the model you are interested in on the streets more often? This is all based on these unconscious filters that allow in evidence supporting our point of view and filter out perspectives we disagree with. We perceive things differently based on those filters. These individual differences mean that we may see, hear, and interpret things differently than others. This is exactly why one of the key tenets of data-informed decision-making is to get a diverse perspective. One person's perspective could be shortsighted and focused on one element of a problem that the person is familiar with. This one element is probably not the entire story, and other perspectives are needed to see the data holistically and systemically so that the best data-informed decision can be made.

Heuristics

Heuristics, also referred to as mental shortcuts or rules of thumb, are built into a brain's perceptual lens to aid in making intuitive System 1 decisions. One of their key functions is to reduce the complexity of a problem or decision. This is done by either ignoring parts of the available information, focusing on what is perceived as most relevant, or searching for only a small subset of possible decisions and solutions. Because they rely on less information, heuristics are assumed to facilitate faster decision-making than strategies that require more information. Some suggest that this theory works because not every decision is worth spending the time necessary to reach the best possible conclusion, and thus people use mental shortcuts to save time and energy. Another interpretation of this theory is that the brain simply does not have the capacity to process everything, and so we must use mental shortcuts.

Let's look at an example. When walking down the street, you see a construction worker hauling up a piano on a pulley. Without a break in stride, you would likely choose to walk around that area instead of directly underneath the piano. Your intuition would tell you that walking under the piano could be dangerous, so you would make a decision to walk around the danger zone. You would probably not stop and assess the entire situation or calculate the probability of the piano falling on you or your chances of survival if that happened. Instead, you would use a heuristic to make the decision quickly and without much mental effort.

However, while heuristics can help speed up our problem-solving and decision-making processes, these models can also be faulty and biased. In addition, just because a heuristic (mental shortcut) has worked before, it doesn't mean that it leads to the *best* solution to a problem. Relying on an existing heuristic can make it difficult to see alternative solutions or to come up with new ideas.

We will explore a few common heuristic types in the next section. Being aware of these will help us to be more mindful of potential biases so that we can work to mitigate them.

TYPES OF HEURISTICS

There are many different classifications of heuristics. In this book, we will classify them into four groupings: *representative, availability, valuation*, and *anchoring*.

Representative heuristics. These are heuristics that rely on our existing mental models to make a decision. This is where the term *stereotyping* fits in. If we have a mental model of what a rude person is, we will have a tendency to quickly put someone into that bucket based on the information readily available. This heuristic grouping also has a tendency to judge the likelihood of an event based on previous information. For example, if you hear a meow but do not see a cat, you will most likely still think it is a cat making the sound. In many cases, it would be. But in the business world, representative heuristics can translate to making assumptions, stereotyping events and actions, and ignoring other factors, which can lead to poor decisions. Have you ever chosen whether or not to hire someone based on your first impression? Did that impression represent someone good or bad from your past?

Consider a more specific example from the journal article "Judgment Under Uncertainty: Heuristics and Biases" by Amos Tversky and Daniel Kahneman: "Steve is very shy and withdrawn, invariably helpful, but with little interest in people, or in the world of reality. A meek and tidy soul, he has a need for order and structure, and a passion for detail."[22] If you had to select one, would you think Steve is a farmer, a librarian, a physician, an airline pilot, or a salesman? Most of us would select a librarian, as the traits listed in this description are ones that—in our experiences—represent a librarian. But isn't this stereotyping? In the example, the representative heuristic is weighing the decision on how similar the description of Steve matches our experiences of a librarian more than on probability, in which there are more farmers in the world than librarians. Shouldn't this latter information be factored into the decision?

Availability heuristics. These are heuristics that judge the frequency or likelihood of an event by the ease at which relevant instances come to mind. Since the brain can recall this information, the tendency is to assume that this means it is important or more important than other potential solutions or pieces of information. However, the human brain does not work that way. Our recollection of facts and events is distorted by many factors, including the vividness of the information, the number of times we are exposed to it, and the recency of it.

For example, do you think there are more words in the English dictionary that begin with the letter r or that have r as their third letter? Most people would say there are more words that begin with the letter r. In reality, there are more words with r as the third letter. This is because we store words in memory alphabetically, so it is much easier to retrieve words that start with the letter r.

In another example, if people were asked if there were more murders or suicides in their region, most people would say there were more murders, even if the region has had many more suicides than murders. Tversky and Kahneman would say this happens because the option that has more instances in our memory will cause our brain to believe that is the option that is more numerous in general.[23] With this specific example, we see many more murders in the news than suicides, so they are more available in our memories. Thus, this makes it easier for our memories to believe there are more murders than suicides.

In business, the availability heuristic can lead to disastrous consequences. Organizations that tend to rely on information that is readily recalled in order to make decisions are only looking at part of the data needed to make data-informed decisions. Imagine if a bank that is deciding whether to provide loans were to only look at recent events in the economy and ignore historical trends. This was one of many factors that caused the economic crisis in 2008. Housing prices had been showing steady and continuous growth for the previous six years. However, using that data and ignoring the fact that there had been housing-price declines before that time period caused many people to purchase subprime loans, which then defaulted when the housing prices did, in fact, decline.

Valuation heuristics. These are heuristics that relate to how someone values something. This heuristic includes both sides of the spectrum, including relating to things overly positively or overly negatively. The negative grouping relates to the tendency to overvalue costs sustained and to overestimate the intrinsic value of the losing experience. A company may, for example, stick with a product that continues to underperform, doing so because of all of the time and money the company has spent on the product. The positive grouping include bias that relates to an overly optimistic view of the world. Individuals, for example, may skip their yearly physicals or not wear seat belts, believing they are less likely to suffer from the misfortune of sickness or car accidents. However, by definition, everyone cannot be above average, so these beliefs are overly optimistic.

Anchoring heuristics. These are heuristics that relate to the tendency to be influenced by a reference point. That reference point is called the *anchor*. The tendency is to then use that reference point as an anchor and to make adjustments up or down from that reference point. This heuristic type highlights that we are very influenced by previous values or events. Ever wonder why the sticker price on a car is always higher than what it should be? This technique tries to take advantage of this heuristic to make the adjustments below the sticker price look like a bargain. In business, we want to be careful of the opening proposals of vendors in negotiations. Anchoring is not just related to a number, however. What if the boss in an organization starts a decision-making meeting by stating an opinion? This opinion may unconsciously be used as an anchor for others in the room.

In one study detailed in "Judgment Under Uncertainty," participants were asked to quickly calculate one of the following mathematical expressions: 1x2x3x4x5x6x7x8 or 8x7x6x5x4x3x2x1. They were asked to calculate quickly (within five seconds) so that they could not actually perform the math in time but rather had to estimate the answer. The median (the midpoint of all the values) of all the participants who calculated the expression starting with 1x2 was 512. The median of all the participants who calculated the expression starting with 8x7 was 2,250.[24] Why was the latter calculation so much bigger? According to the anchoring heuristics, it was because the first calculation, 8x7, was so much bigger than the 1x2 that started the other expression, and both of those calculations were used as anchors.

Mental Models

A **mental model** is an individual's explanation of how the world works—a framework through which the individual views the world. Mental models shape what we think and how we understand. They are related to heuristics, but whereas heuristics are used during System 1 decisions, or unconscious or intuition-based decisions, mental models can be used during System 2 decisions, or conscious decisions that require deductive reasoning and problem-solving. Mental models explain someone's thought process and why different people perceive the world differently. For example, when a botanist looks at a forest, he or she focuses on the ecosystem; an environmentalist sees the impact of climate change; a forestry engineer the state of the tree growth; and a businessperson the value of the land. None are wrong, but none of them on their own are able to describe the full scope of the forest. Therefore, sharing knowledge with each other and learning the basics of the other disciplines would lead to a more well-rounded understanding that would allow for better initial decisions about managing the forest.

Just like with heuristics, mental models can facilitate the process of making good decisions, or they can negatively impact decisions. This is especially true when circumstances deviate abruptly from what you are used to—for example, when you deplane in a foreign country, and your habitual "left-right-left" traffic checking at crosswalks must reverse to "right-left-right" in order to not get hit by oncoming traffic. The good news is that in this specific situation, the different circumstances will be greatly noticeable and sufficient to trigger reevaluation of your heuristics.

However, when circumstances change slowly over time, people may not be aware that they are using outdated heuristics and mental models as part of their decision-making process. In fact, many of the mental models we formed during school and built our careers on are now outdated. Let's look at an example in business. Kodak created mass-market photography when it created the film roll. Then, the digital revolution came, and with it a paradigm shift. Kodak, aware of this digital revolution, used it to double down on its film products by investing in digital printing.[25] However, the company's mental model was focused on film products being the business. In reality, the paradigm shift meant that online photo sharing was not just a way to expand the printing business—online photo sharing *was* the new business. In this example, the organization, Kodak, was making decisions based on outdated mental models. Other examples include the previous model of working thirty years for a company as the way to prosperity or a nine-to-five job being the norm when we are now in an era of working in a virtual environment, which includes remote working and virtual communication like videoconferencing.

In other examples, the mental-model shift is visible, but the brain still requires extensive time to adapt and understand. This is because individuals need to unlearn the old models and then relearn the new models. In one famous experiment, engineer Destin Sandlin attempted to ride a backwards bike. A backwards bike is one on which the handlebars turn the bike in the opposite direction. Turning the bars to the left will turn the bike to the right and vice versa. It took Sandlin over eight months of riding the backwards bike five minutes each day before he was able to ride it without falling off. What is interesting to note is that after he mastered this skill, he was no longer able to ride a normal bike.[26]

Perception and Interpretation

Two other critical factors that impact the decision-making process are individuals' perceptions and interpretations of the data. Heuristics may provide the brain with shortcuts, but these perceptions and interpretations can impact those shortcuts, just like fallacies and cognitive bias can. At a psychological level, *interpretation* refers to the process by which we represent and understand the data that affects us.

To visualize this, take a look at the picture in figure 6:

Figure 6. The young and old lady[27]

This picture will be perceived differently depending on the person. Do you see the young lady or the old lady? In this situation, both interpretations are right. Our interpretations are subjective and based on personal factors. These factors include *experience, cultural values and beliefs, expectations and desire*, and many other influences.

Experience. Prior experience plays a major role in the way a person interprets data. For example, someone who has experienced abuse might flinch when seeing a person raise his or her hand, expecting to be hit. That is this individual's interpretation of the event (a raised hand). Someone who has not experienced abuse but has played sports, however, might see this as a signal for a high five. Different individuals react differently to the same event, depending on their prior experience of that type of event. This principle directly translates from personal stories to decisions made in business. For example, if an organization is changing business models, employees with prior experience using the same business model at other organizations would interpret related data differently than someone who has never experienced the new business model before.

Our interpretations of events will be different than someone else's. Therefore, it is important to assume that neither one is wrong or incorrect, just a different perspective that may help us to make a more informed decision.

Cultural values and beliefs. Culture provides structure, guidelines, expectations, and rules to help people understand and interpret behaviors. People with different social and cultural backgrounds have different norms and values. Ethnographic studies suggest there are cultural differences in social understanding, interpretation, and response to behavior and emotion. The definition of a bad person may be different for one culture compared to another. Similarly, social and cultural values impact how situations are interpreted and what the best decisions are for those situations. Cultural scripts dictate how positive and negative events should be interpreted. For example, Eastern cultures typically perceive successes as being arrived at by a group effort, while Western cultures like to attribute successes to individuals. Situations in which cultural differences can be seen in the workplace include, but are not limited to, whether or not to ask questions and give suggestions and feedback and how well people promote their contributions.

Culture does not necessarily have to be an individual's culture, or region of origin. It can also refer to **organizational culture**. A company's ideas, values, attitudes, and beliefs will all guide how an employee and a group think, feel, and decide. We will revisit organizational culture later on in this chapter.

Expectations and desire. An individual's hopes and expectations about data can also affect the individual's interpretation of it. In one experiment, students were assigned either a pleasant or unpleasant task by a computer. They were told that either a number or a letter would flash on the screen. In one group of students, if a letter flashed on the screen, they would have to drink an unpleasant-tasting health drink. If a number flashed on the screen, they would have to drink orange juice. In another group of students, the opposite was true. If a number flashed on the screen, they would have to drink an unpleasant drink, and if a letter flashed on the screen, they would have to drink a pleasant drink. During the experiment, the screen would actually show an ambiguous figure, which could either be read as the letter B or the number 13. When the letters were associated with the pleasant task, subjects were more likely to perceive a letter B, and when letters were associated with the unpleasant task, they tended to perceive a number 13.[28] The students' desire to avoid the unpleasant drink led them to interpret a figure in a particular way. In business, an individual's desire to do a good job, make a sale, or help a customer at all costs can lead that individual to interpret data in a particular way as well.

Similar to desires, expectations of data can also impact interpretation. A classic psychological experiment showed slower reaction times and less-accurate answers when a deck of playing cards reversed the color of the suit symbol for some cards (e.g., red spades and black hearts).[29] People's expectations about the data ("if it's red, it must be diamonds or hearts") affected their ability to accurately interpret it.

Expectations can also be influenced by the brain's filtering, as discussed earlier in this chapter. Let's take a look at the visual example shown in figure 7.

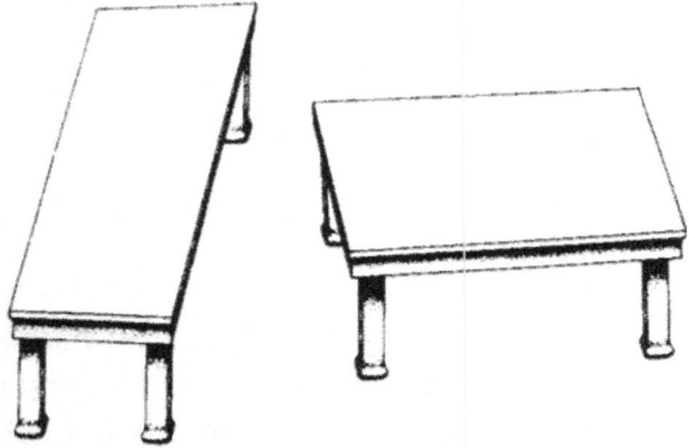

Figure 7. Which table is longer?[30]

Which table in figure 7 is longer? The one on the left or the one on the right? If you have not seen this example before, it may shock you to know that they are both the same exact length. But how can that be?

What is interesting is that this example would typically be called an optical illusion, but this perception is not created by our eyes. It is created by our brain. When we look at the picture, we have no reason to assume that there is an illusion at play, so in its **System 1 decision**, our brain doesn't even consider this possibility and simply assumes that the left table is longer. In this case, the visual expectation causes us to make an incorrect decision.

Why is this example relevant? Because we make assumptions and determinations about what is real every moment of every day. This highlights that our perceptions are deeply buried in our unconscious, which makes it difficult or near impossible to see their impact on our decision-making and on what we see as real.

Understanding Cognitive Bias

The topic of cognitive bias, or unconscious bias, was introduced earlier in this chapter. **Cognitive bias** can be defined as an unconscious, systematic, and reproducible failure in information processing that gets in the way of logical thinking. There are literally hundreds of different types of bias. In the next section, we will explore some of the most common ones that impact data-informed decision-making.

COMMON CATEGORIES OF COGNITIVE BIAS

Dan Lovallo and Olivier Sibony, professors of strategy, came up with a topology that organized biases into the following categories:[31]

- pattern-recognition and salience biases
- action-oriented biases
- interest and social biases
- stability biases

Pattern-recognition and salience biases. When we make decisions, we tend to look for patterns that match our prior experiences, or we tend to accept ideas and hypotheses when they are presented in a coherent story. Common biases that fall into this category are confirmation bias, projection bias, availability bias, absence of evidence bias, and clustering illusion.

Confirmation bias is a type of bias that involves favoring information that confirms previously existing beliefs that someone holds. This is important to be aware of because people tend to place greater importance on data that supports what they already believe. People may even seek further data that validates this belief as opposed to searching for data that may disprove their belief. *Projection bias* is the tendency to overpredict future preferences by trying to match them to current preferences. *Availability bias* is the tendency to remember and recall something that has happened recently, something you personally observed, or something more vivid and recognizable. *Absence of evidence bias* is the tendency to fail to consider the degree of completeness of the information. *Clustering illusion* is the tendency to see patterns where there are not any.

Action-oriented biases. When we make decisions, there are certain times when we either feel pushed to make an action or we feel overconfident when deciding on an action. These situations can lead us to be less thoughtful than we should be. Common biases that fall into this category are optimism bias, overconfidence bias, competitor neglect, ostrich bias, and base rate neglect.

Optimism bias is the tendency to believe that you are less likely to experience a negative event as a result of your decision, and thus you overestimate the probability of a positive outcome for your decision. *Overconfidence bias* is similar to optimism bias but relates more to overconfidence in your skills when compared to others. This can be seen when someone takes more credit for a positive outcome, rejecting the fact that it could have happened by chance. *Competitor neglect* is the tendency in business to focus on your own company's capabilities, plans, and data, neglecting data from external forces and competitors. *Ostrich bias* is the tendency to ignore dangerous or negative information when making your decision. *Base rate neglect* is a tendency to ignore an established probability in statistics when making a decision. For example, if it is a known fact that new startups fail 75 percent of the time, that should be factored into your decision if you are planning on starting a company. You should not favor your intuition over this information.

Interest and social biases. When we make decisions, there are certain times when we either have conflicting incentives, including emotional ones, or we want to avoid conflict. These situations can lead us to make biased decisions. Common biases that fall into this category are self-serving bias, self-relevance bias, groupthink, stereotyping/implicit association, affinity bias, and conformity bias.

Self-serving bias is the tendency to favor decisions that will enhance your self-esteem. *Self-relevance bias* is the tendency to encode information in the brain differently depending on the level at which the individual is implicated in the information. When people are asked to remember information related in some way to themselves, the recall rate is typically higher. *Groupthink* is the tendency to favor choices of mass populations and to strive for consensus at the cost of rational assessments of alternate decisions. *Stereotyping/implicit association* is the tendency to expect a group or an individual to have certain qualities without having any real information about the group or individual. *Affinity bias* is the tendency to gravitate toward and develop relationships with people who are more like ourselves and share similar interests and backgrounds. *Conformity bias* is the tendency to favor choices of mass populations, even over personal judgments. This can lead to groupthink, which can lead to suppression of outside opinions during the decision-making process.

Stability biases. Stability biases involve the tendency to be comfortable with the status quo. This bias type occurs more often when there is limited pressure to change. It can cause us to remain unchanged in our original thoughts and to ignore critical information. Common biases that fall into this category are anchoring bias, loss aversion and sunk cost bias, status quo bias, and ambiguity bias.

Anchoring bias is the tendency to be influenced by the first shown information. This causes tunnel vision and people failing to make adjustments to account for subsequent information. *Loss aversion and sunk cost bias* is the tendency to stick with a decision once it is made, even if the decision was not ideal, for fear of losing the effort, time, energy, or more put into the original decision. *Status quo bias* is the tendency to favor the current situation, or status quo, and to maintain it compared to making a new decision or taking a new direction. This can be due to loss aversion. *Ambiguity bias* is the tendency to favor an outcome that is more knowable compared to alternatives that are not. This bias has a major impact on decisions that involve innovation, as innovation is risky and typically has an unknown process.

EXAMPLES OF COGNITIVE BIAS IN ACTION

Example 1. Assume an organization is analyzing its sales for the last quarter and sees a remarkable increase. As a result of this spike, the organization decides to double down on its growth strategy for the remainder of the year. This means hiring many new employees. If the organization considered this recent spike only and neglected all the historical data, it will be exhibiting *recency bias*, which is a form of *availability bias*. Placing more emphasis on the latest information received and neglecting previous data will skew the analysis and the discussion. In a worst-case scenario, the historical data the organization neglected to view may have demonstrated that similar spikes have occurred before, and they all come back to the norm rather than continuing to trend upward.

Example 2. Assume an organization is deciding whether to discontinue one of its products due to increased market pressure resulting in a continuous decline in sales over the past six quarters. The product is seven years old, and the organization has invested millions of dollars in it already. If the organization decides to keep the product around, citing the investments already made in it and ignoring the data that the market is changing and the sales continue to decline, the organization would be exhibiting *sunk cost bias*. The money already spent on the product has already been incurred and cannot be recovered. Regret over this lost money should not factor into the company's decision about the future of its product.

Example 3. Assume an investment bank is deciding how to invest money. If the leader in charge of the decision starts out a meeting providing her thoughts and then asks for input, receiving just affirming nods and smiles, the group is probably falling victim to *groupthink*. There could be individuals who have concerns about the plan, but because they do not want to go against the group unity, they do not speak up regarding their concerns.

Example 4. Assume an organization that sells coffee supplies is trying to decide on its strategic goals for the coming fiscal year. (This organization has consistently been at the top of its industry for almost a decade.) Company leaders begin by reviewing key data, like their available funding and any immediate threats and opportunities, but they completely fail to look at any outside factors, such as their competition. This could also be a case of *overconfidence bias*, but in this case, they don't dismiss the outside factors and competitors; they just don't factor competition in. In this case, this organization is exhibiting *competitor neglect*. In today's world, with digital transformation, everything is changing rapidly, and failing to look outside your organization could cause serious issues. In this example, the competitor that was not looked at could be a new startup with a brand-new process for distributing coffee that could shake up the industry, leaving the more traditional organization behind.

Example 5. Assume an analyst is performing some data analysis related to his team's functions. At a high level, the analyst sees something that validates his hypothesis. At this point, if the analyst fails to look at any possible alternatives or symptoms that may be related, he would be exhibiting *confirmation bias*. What if the information the analyst found was just an **outlier** or due to another cause? If it really was due to another cause, making this decision could be very costly for the analyst's organization.

TEST YOUR BIAS

Don't believe we all have bias? Let's take a look at the experiment in figure 8, famously created by cognitive psychologist Peter Wason in 1960.[32]

If a card has a vowel on one side, then it must have an even number on the other side.

Which two cards would you turn over to test the rule?

A) A, 4 C) Q, 4

B) A, 7 D) Q, 7

Figure 8. Peter Wason psychology experiment

Which option would you choose? The overwhelming majority of people choose option A. However, the only option that allows you to break the rule is option B. With the A card, if it was flipped over and the other side did not have an even number, the rule would be broken. With the 7 card, if it was flipped over and the other side had a vowel on it, the rule would be broken. No other combination can break the rule, but also no other combination can completely validate the rule.

This example highlights that our instinct and brain unconsciously look to find data that supports the rule (or our decision), rather than disproves it. This is an example of *confirmation bias* in action.

Understanding Groupthink

Cognitive bias is not the only thing to be concerned with when trying to make a decision. If you are trying to come up with a group decision, you may encounter some psychological resistance called groupthink. **Groupthink** is the practice of making decisions as a group in a way that discourages creativity or diverse perspectives. Have you ever been in a meeting in which you thought about speaking up and then decided against it because you didn't want to appear unsupportive of the group's efforts? Or maybe you have been in a meeting in which you didn't want to speak up against the leader, but in hindsight, you realized you were not provided with all the information or the environment to really challenge the data. If so, you have experienced groupthink.

Research has shown that there are certain conditions that can increase the chances of groupthink occurring. These conditions include:

- **High cohesiveness and homogeneity within the group.** This group lacks cognitive diversity.
- **Insulation of the group.** This group does not have much contact with those outside of it.
- **Lack of systematic processes for the Acquire and Apply phases.** This group lacks repeatable, clearly defined processes (systematic processes).
- **The absence of disagreement.** Everyone in the group says they agree with all decisions. While some may not agree, they do not vocalize this.

Most **strategic decisions** within an organization are ripe for groupthink, as they are made in groups under high pressure with the need for decisions to be made quickly. Let's take a look at an example of how groupthink can play out in business. Assume there is a financial institution that manages mutual funds and has five employees, who are each in charge of a specific mutual fund. These employees have all worked together for a long time and trust each other. They meet regularly to discuss strategies. Now, assume during one of their meetings, one of the managers announces he is making a decision to invest in one specific company for his fund. That manager shares his rationale without going into too many details. Despite the lack of detail, all the other managers accept the rationale and decide to invest as well, without doing any further research. One specific manager had some concerns and saw some potential flaws in the decision, but since everyone else in the room agreed, this manager agreed as well. Fast-forward to a month later, when the stock they had all invested in drops significantly. Turns out, there were some flaws in the investing manager's decision process. However, as a result of groupthink, no one saw them or wanted to rock the boat (as in the case of the manager who did have some concerns). We will come back to groupthink in chapter 7 during the Apply phase to understand strategies to mitigate it.

The Impact of Organizational Culture on Decisions

An organization's culture can also have a major impact on decision-making. Organizational-development expert Edgar Schein defined **organizational culture** as "a pattern of shared basic assumptions that was learned by a group as it solved its problems of external adaptation and internal integration, that has worked well enough to be considered valid and, therefore, to be taught to new members as the correct way to perceive, think, and feel in relation to those problems."[33]

These shared assumptions inform employees within the organization on what to believe, how to act, how to make decisions, and what values to adhere to. They also guide employees in how they should perceive information, the company environment, and their employee roles.

At the highest level, organizational cultures can be categorized as strong or weak. *Strong* organizational cultures are ones that can more-strongly influence their employees' acceptance of a decision. *Weak* organizational cultures are ones in which individual employees rely more on personal principles and beliefs that are not widely shared within the organization. This means that the same decision can have different impacts at different organizations, depending on the organization's culture. For example, assume a strategic decision needs to be made about whether to continue doing the same process or dropping it for a completely new one. The new process will require a strong change management program. For an organization with a strong organizational culture, the decision to go with the new process may end up with a better outcome than in an organization with a weak organizational culture, in which the staff may doubt the decision and make the implementation of the decision hard. Decision-makers must consider an organization's culture as a criterion for their decisions.

According to Schein, "When one brings culture to the level of the organization and even down to groups within the organization, one can clearly see how culture is created, embedded, evolved, and ultimately manipulated, and, at the same time, how culture constrains, stabilizes, and provides structure and meaning to the group members."[34]

Summary and Key Takeaways

- The brain makes less-critical decisions really quickly by processing tons of information and applying filters to that information based on our previous experiences.
- Cognitive bias can impact our decision-making without us even knowing it. These biases can be related to having too-much information to process, having information with not-enough meaning, having to make a decision too quickly, or having hit the physical limits of our brain's capacity.
- Groups and organizations can suffer from groupthink, which will lead to suboptimal decisions.
- Organizational culture and values have an impact on decisions as well. This means that decision-makers need to factor in their organization's culture and values when coming up with their decisions.

CHAPTER 4

PHASE ONE – THE ASK PHASE

"If you do not know how to ask the right question, you discover nothing."[35]

—W. Edwards Deming

Steps Involved in This Phase

1	Turn business questions into analytical questions.
2	Classify the decision needed.

The Ask phase is the first phase of the data-informed decision-making process and has two discrete steps. First, we turn the business questions into **analytical questions**, which will help us identify which decisions need to be made. Second, we classify the decisions needed, which will help us scope out the appropriate way forward.

Visualizations alone are not enough to make data-informed decisions. They do enable and facilitate insight and action, but they will most likely only have a bottom-up view (i.e., "Here's the data; now what's the value that can be derived?"). This approach is neither user-centered nor aligned to business outcomes.

Decision-making should always start with the goal in mind. What do you think is meant by the "goal"? Is it a general motivation, such as "make more money," or an answerable question? Let's take a look at three example questions about a wine manufacturer:

1. "Can we increase profits by securing forward contracts from a region with less-expensive grapes?"

2. "What expense categories account for the greatest budget variance by region? Is there seasonality in the variance?"
3. "Are there any patterns or trends?"

Which one of these is not tied to a business goal? Did you answer number three? The third question is not a focused question and may not relate to any of your business outcomes. It is a discovery exercise that may uncover unanticipated opportunities; however, as management consultant W. Edwards Deming once said, "If you do not know how to ask the right question, you discover nothing."[36] A pattern or trend discovered without any context does not inform; it is analogous to a tree falling in a forest without an observer.

Turning Business Questions into Analytical Questions

Too often, people are asking generic questions like "How successful was my campaign?" While that may be a valid business question, it is not something that you can answer without asking more questions and getting more context.

In the "How successful was my campaign?" example, compared to what? The marketing campaigns from Q1 and Q2? The Q3 campaigns from previous years? Over what time period? This quarter compared to this quarter last year? Should we examine the ROI of the campaign? Should we analyze the responses of various factors within the campaign—for example, response rates for different channels or approaches?

You must first define what is important to your decisions and strategy. Understanding what question(s) you really need to answer is critical before you begin.

When thinking about questions to ask, consider the following: How important is the question to the business? Put questions in the right language. Answers need to be quantifiable. Create questions from your question. Understand the data required to answer the questions.

FORMULATING GOOD ANALYTICAL QUESTIONS

What do good analytical questions look like? Here are five key characteristics:

1. **Clear.** A good analytical question will be clearly stated with as little ambiguity as possible. If there are assumptions implicit in the business question, state them explicitly in the analytical question. For example, with our original business question "How successful was my campaign?", it is not clear which campaign is being referenced or how to determine what is considered successful or not.

2. **Specific.** A single business question may not be easily translated into a single analytical question. In this case, create a set of analytical questions that each address a specific aspect of the business question.

3. **Scoped.** An analytical question should have a defined scope. For instance, if the business question focuses on trends over time, the analytical question should indicate the relevant time period.

4. **Data oriented.** An analytical question should point clearly to what data will be required to answer the question.

5. **Answerable.** An analytical question should provide the analyst a clear understanding of what the answer for the question will look like, which includes the units in which an answer will be expressed. If the question is quantitative, what is a reasonable range for the answer? If qualitative, what relationship or trend is expected?

EXAMPLE ANALYTICAL QUESTION

Let's now take a look at our original business question and how we can turn it into a question suitable for analysis. To recap, the business question was "How successful was my campaign?"

To begin, let's ask a few clarifying questions:

- What qualifies as successful?
- What period are you looking at and comparing to?
- Are there various dimensions you want to compare?

Based on those questions, the following additional information is gathered. The marketing group is interested in an assessment of response rates overall and whether or not the different approaches, channels, etc. made a difference. The marketing group is also interested in how response rates varied across demographics.

From there, we are able to turn the business question "How successful was my campaign?" into analytical questions:

- What was the overall positive response rate for the Q3 marketing campaign?

- What were the differences in positive response rate (if any) among the various marketing channels?
- What were the differences in positive response rate (if any) across different demographics?

Using the first analytical question as an example, we can see how all the characteristics of a good analytical question are present. The question is *clear* and *specific*, as it explains which campaign and what criterion we need to analyze. It is *scoped* as it specifically mentions the time period (Q3). It is *data oriented* as it specifies what data is needed to answer the question (overall positive response rate). It is also *answerable*, as the question can be answered using data.

Classifying the Decision

Once a set of analytical questions has been identified, it is important to then classify the *type* of decision needed. Classification is important as it allows us to understand the next set of steps required in the process.

Not all decisions are created equal. Business decisions can fall into one of the following categories: strategic, tactical, or operational. **Strategic decisions** include policies and complex decisions that have a major impact on the business. *Tactical decisions* include procedures and typically impact subgroups within an organization. *Operational decisions* are small decisions that typically focus on the execution of existing policies and procedures. Operational decisions may seem insignificant on their own, but in aggregate, they are very important. While this book will help everyone with all levels of decisions, there is a great need in the workplace today to improve strategic decision-making. According to a McKinsey survey, 72 percent of senior executives said they thought bad strategic decisions either were about as frequent as good ones or were the prevailing norm in their organization.[37]

There are also two types of decisions based on how often they occur. There are **non-programmed decisions**, which are one-off decisions that are not part of a routine, and there are **programmed decisions**, which are reoccurring decisions. Nonprogrammed decisions tend to include strategic decisions like whether to acquire another company. Programmed decisions tend to include operational decisions like what to price your offerings or which promotions to run.

Another classification was coined by Jeff Bezos, founder of Amazon, and relates to whether the decision can be easily reversed. He has stated that decisions can be either Type 1 or Type 2. **Type 1 decisions** are irreversible decisions, like quitting a job or changing a product direction, and **Type 2 decisions** are decisions that you can always revert back from if they end up not being ideal, like executing a specific marketing campaign or changing a vendor in your supply chain.

Type 1 decisions are typically made in leadership meetings, whereas Type 2 decisions are traditionally made within small groups or by individuals who have shown good judgment in the past.

According to Bezos:

> As organizations get larger, there seems to be a tendency to use the heavy-weight Type 1 decision-making *process* on most decisions, including many Type 2 decisions. The end result of this is slowness, unthoughtful risk aversion, failure to experiment sufficiently, and consequently diminished invention. We'll have to figure out how to fight that tendency.
>
> And one-size-fits-all thinking will turn out to be only one of the pitfalls. We'll work hard to avoid it . . . and any other large organization maladies we can identify.[38]

In this same letter to shareholders, Bezos also highlighted the concern with organizations using Type 2 decision-making on what should be Type 1 decisions: "The opposite situation is less interesting and there is undoubtedly some survivorship bias. Any companies that habitually use the light-weight Type 2 decision-making process to make Type 1 decisions go extinct before they get large."[39]

For example, imagine an individual made a very quick decision without looping in other key leaders in the organization (Type 2 decision) to lay off 20 percent of the company workforce (a Type 1 decision). The decision to lay off workers is not reversible, and it can cause disastrous consequences if it is not treated like a Type 1 decision.

Classifying a decision that needs to be made by its category (strategic, tactical, or operational), its frequency (nonprogrammed and programmed), and whether it's a Type 1 or Type 2 decision will help you to determine what level of time needs to be invested in the decision-making process and what individuals need to be brought on board. The practice is a valuable one.

Summary and Key Takeaways

- Business questions are not good questions for decision-making. They need to be transformed into analytical questions.
- Analytical questions need to be clear, specific, scoped, data oriented, and answerable.
- Not all decisions are created equal. Decisions should be classified in order to understand the investment required to come up with their answers.

CHAPTER 5

PHASE TWO – THE ACQUIRE PHASE

"All things appear and disappear because of the concurrence of causes and conditions. Nothing ever exists entirely alone; everything is in relation to everything else."[40]

—The Buddha

Steps Involved in This Phase

3	Find and source all relevant data. Remember to think about the analytical questions systemically and to include any interrelated data that could be relevant. This means not only internal data but external data and information as well.
4	Ensure the sourced data is trusted.

Once you have your analytical questions, you will need to acquire the data to help you answer the questions and make a decision—and to ultimately execute and take action on that decision. There are two aspects of the Acquire phase. The first is to find and source all relevant data. Remember to think about the analytical questions systemically and to include any interrelated data that could be relevant. This means not only internal data but external data and information as well. The second aspect of the Acquire phase is to ensure that your sourced data is trusted. This requires you to have a proper data strategy in place that includes data quality, collection, governance, and management.

Finding and Sourcing All Relevant Data

To start with, let's look at how to find and source all relevant data that is directly referenced in your analytical questions. Start by looking for the nouns in your analytical questions.

Here are our three example analytical questions from the previous chapter:

1. What was the overall positive response rate for the Q3 marketing campaign?
2. What were the differences in positive response rate (if any) among the various approaches?
3. What were the differences in positive response rate (if any) across different demographics?

The following is the data needed to help answer those three example questions:

1. The offers, channels, and creative efforts that were used to deliver the offer to each prospect
2. Each prospect's response
3. Demographic information on each prospect

As you search for the best available data, realize that you will be starting with **raw data** but that data may go through various stages of transformations and aggregations. This process will require you to have a sound **data strategy** in place so that the data is trusted and means the same thing to everyone. But first, how can we find and source the data we need to answer our analytical questions?

TAKING A SYSTEMS PERSPECTIVE

The data directly referenced in the analytical questions may not be all of the data needed to properly make a decision. With many decisions, there are hidden forces and causes that could impact the decision. Enter **systems thinking**. Systems thinking moves away from looking at data and events to identifying underlying structures that drive the data. While this book is not a book solely on systems thinking, this section is designed to provide you with an introduction to what it is, why it is important, and what general tools can be used to apply it.

Sir Isaac Newton's third law of motion states that "every action has an equal and opposite reaction."[41] This concept of balance applies not only to the physics of motion but also to all things in nature, in our lives, and in business. Nature and its ecosystem are intended to be balanced. Our lives and our organizations should also be balanced. To help with balance, it is great to think systemically. Thinking systemically helps you to think of the big picture and to balance short- and long-term perspectives when making decisions. In addition, systems thinking is essential when trying to solve critical business problems. Business problems occur when a system is out of balance. Many times, decision-makers assume the root cause is something directly related to where the problem resides. However, in most cases, the root cause is far away from the actual problem that is observed. Decision-makers who think linearly have a hard time seeing these root causes that are multiple levels away. This is why it is vitally important to understand the systems within your organization.

A *system*, as defined by organizational theorist Dr. Russell Ackoff, is a set of two or more elements that satisfy the following three conditions:

1. The behavior of each element has an effect on the behavior of the whole.
2. The behavior of the elements and their effects on the whole are interdependent.
3. While subgroups of the elements are formed, each has an effect on the behavior of the whole, and none has an independent effect on it.[42]

A system, therefore, is a whole that cannot be divided into independent parts. The essential properties of a system taken as a whole derive from the interaction of its parts, not their actions taken separately.

This can be visualized using any of several diagrams, including events-patterns-structure icebergs, behavior-over-time graphs, causal loop diagrams, connected circles diagrams, and system components diagrams. In this book, we will explain systems perspectives using *causal loop diagrams* and *system components diagrams*.

Suppose our problem is that we need a lot of coffee each day to wake up. As a result of drinking a lot of coffee, we end up having trouble sleeping. Having trouble sleeping then makes it hard to wake up, which then reinforces the need to start out the next morning with more coffee. This is called a *reinforcing loop* because each action reinforces the other (which is why the causal loop diagram in figure 9 includes an "R" in the middle to highlight that it is a *reinforcing* loop and why each line in the diagram includes an "S" next to it to highlight that the relationship is driving in the *same* direction, meaning that as your coffee intake goes up, so does your trouble sleeping). We can see from this perspective that one way to break the cycle is to figure out how to get more sleep.

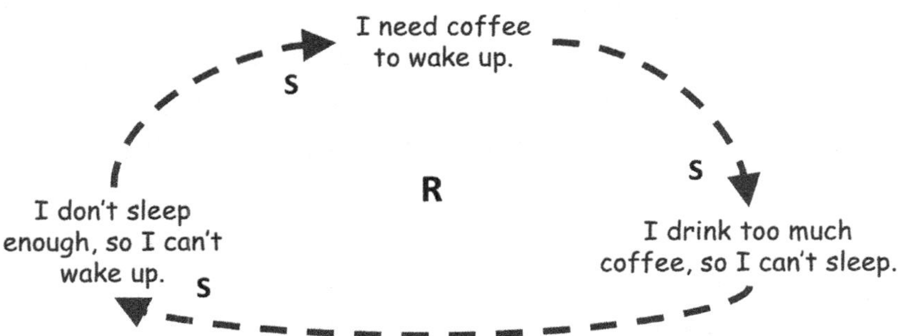

Figure 9. Basic reinforcing loop

The other type of loop is called a *balancing loop* because the actions balance each other (which is why the loop visual in figure 10 includes a "B" in the middle to highlight that it is a *balancing* loop and why the line depicting the relationship between indulgence and stress includes an "O" next to it to highlight that the relationship is driving in the *opposite* direction, meaning that as indulgences go up, stress goes down). For example, suppose you have a lot of stress in your life. As a result, you indulge in a guilty pleasure to help calm down, like smoking or drinking alcohol. The result of that action is lowered stress. The cycle balances itself out—at least in the short term.

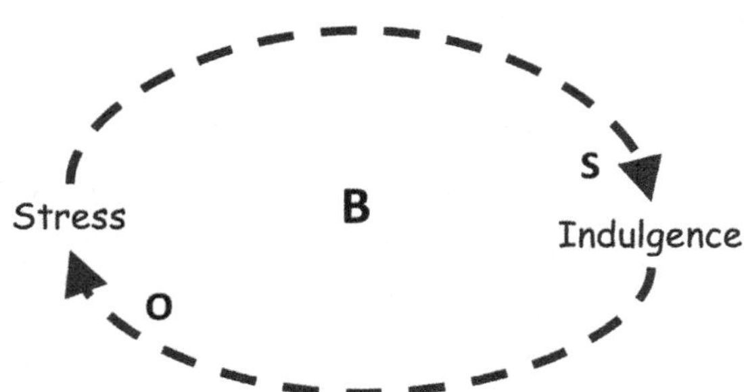

Figure 10. Basic balancing loop

In the long term, however, the impacts of the smoking or drinking as a coping strategy will cause a negative action on your wellness. As a result, your productivity will suffer, and your stress will increase as a result. In this case, the causal loop diagram will show both loops interacting with each other, as displayed in figure 11.

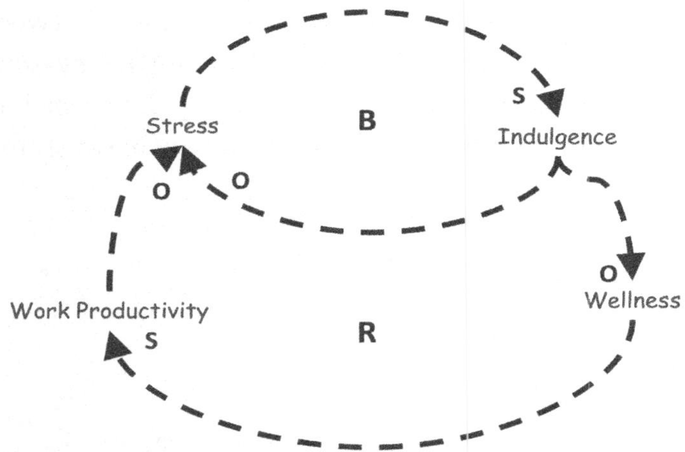

Figure 11. Causal loop diagram with multiple loops

Now let's look at an example related to business. Suppose a company is currently seeing an increase in customers not renewing their subscription (customer churn) and wants to determine why and what to do to course correct. Where can the company start? There are several potential reasons why the churn is happening. To think about the problem systemically, the company can start by drawing a *system components diagram* like the one shown in figure 12.

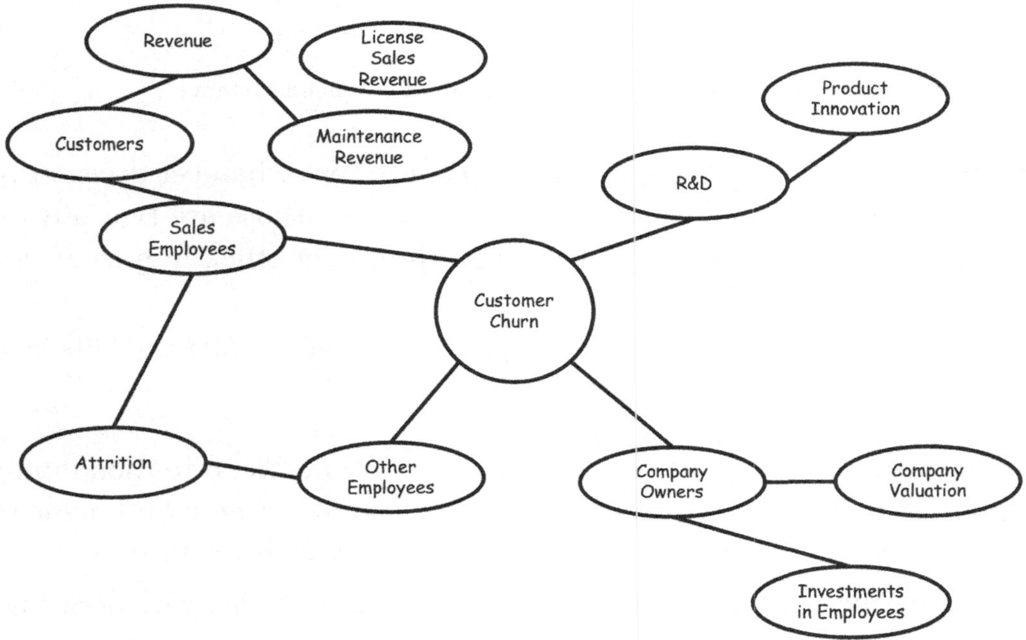

Figure 12. System components diagram

The company can then identify the interconnectedness between the various components to see how they relate to each other and the entire system. This can be done using a causal loop diagram (figure 13). In the causal loop diagram, loops can be balancing or reinforcing. The ultimate goal is to make sure the entire system is balanced.

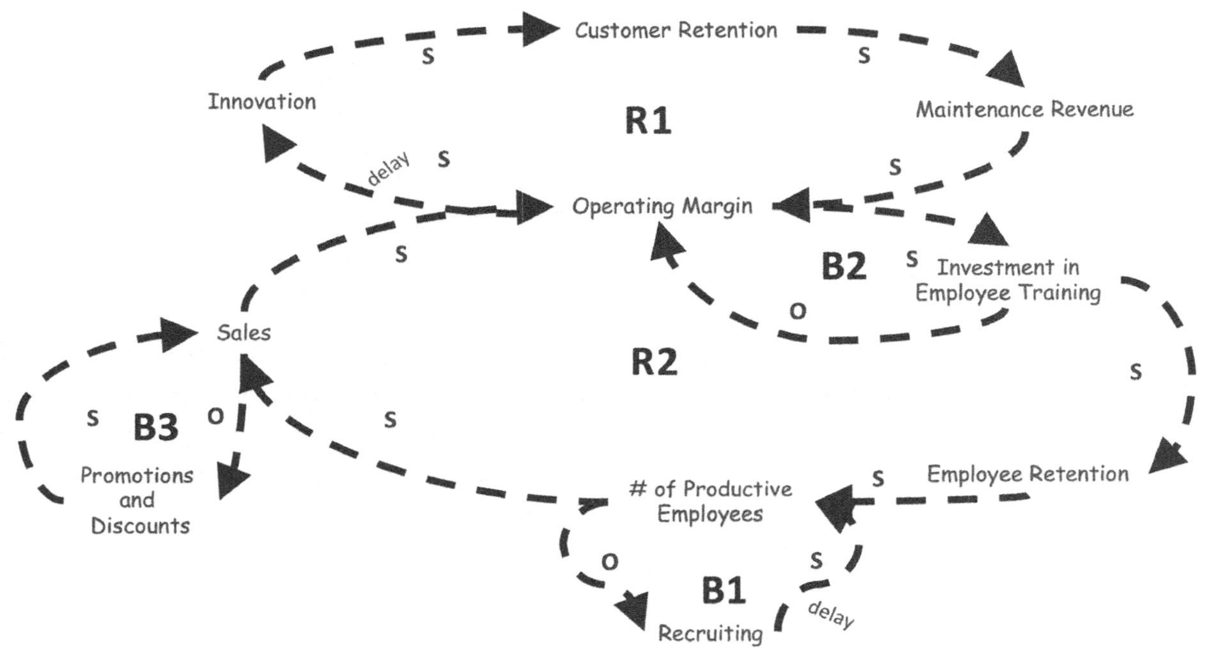

Figure 13. Causal loop diagram of balanced system

When making decisions, it is important to ensure that whatever decision you make does not upset the balance of the system. When it does, those are typically called unintended consequences. There are times when things get stuck in a reinforcing loop, which can cause imbalance.

In our customer-churn example, let's look at the causal loop diagram, as shown in figure 13, and the reinforcing and balancing loops:

1. The company has an issue with customer retention. The retention numbers continue to decline. As a result, the company's revenue from maintenance drops as well since the customers who leave no longer pay maintenance.
2. When the maintenance revenue goes down, the company's operating margin drops as well.

3. When the operating margin goes down, the company needs to cut investments, and product innovation goes down.
4. As innovation goes down, this further reinforces the issue of customer retention, as customers no longer have a need to continue paying maintenance for the product, and customer retention continues to go down. This completes a reinforcing loop (R1 in the figure). At this point, the system is imbalanced. The actions in this loop reinforce the problem rather than balance it. In order to bring balance back, the company must look at actions that will balance out part of that loop. We will come back to this shortly.
5. As a result of the operating margin going down, innovation is not the only element impacted. Investment in employee training and development is impacted as well.
6. When investments in employees goes down, employees leave, and employee retention goes down.
7. When employee retention goes down, the number of productive employees goes down.
8. When the number of productive employees goes down, the sales revenue goes down as there are less employees than needed to hit the company's sales quota.
9. When the sales revenue goes down, the operating margin continues to go down. This completes a second reinforcing loop (R2 in the figure).
10. As mentioned in step 4, to offset reinforcing loops, organizations need to look for solutions to balance the system. In this example, when the number of productive employees goes down, recruiting efforts pick up to find replacements.
11. When recruiting efforts increase, after a delay, the number of productive employees increases. This completes the first balancing loop (B1) and helps to reverse the direction of the R1 and R2 loops.
12. When investment in employee training goes down, operating margin goes up (as there are less expenses). This completes the second balancing loop (B2).
13. When sales revenue goes down, management increases promotions and discounts.
14. When promotions and discounts increase, sales revenue increases as a result. This completes the third balancing loop (B3).

This is, of course, an oversimplification of the system, as there are probably many more components, both internally and externally, but you can see the importance of understanding the system and how an impact on one component will impact another component.

Using this approach, the company in our example can identify the problem (customer churn), understand the system and interconnectedness of all the components, and then look at possible decisions to improve the problem and how they may impact or alter the system.

With this example, here are three potential options for decisions:

1. Look for more ways to sell technology digitally using a no-touch model to increase sales without the overhead of sales employees.
2. Potentially look to recruit continuously and even over recruit so that we have less of a delay with lower sales employees than the target.
3. Approve a lower operating-margin target temporarily while trying to drive innovation with the product.

THE IMPORTANCE OF USING A VARIETY OF DATA SOURCES

Data triangulation is the process of gathering and validating information from two or more sources. Triangulation increases the probability of making a good decision because you are looking more holistically and systemically at the data related to the decision. It also helps you eliminate bias by not relying solely on one source of data. For example, you may acquire data that provides information on a specific measure, but that data source fails to explain the root cause of what is impacting that measure. By using just this one source, you could end up taking action on symptoms and not root causes of the problem.

When acquiring data to help make a decision, in addition to thinking systemically, you should look at multiple sources of information, including qualitative and quantitative data. **Quantitative data** is numerical information that can be measured or counted, like sales totals or the number of seats sold for a concert. **Qualitative data** is descriptive information about characteristics that are difficult to measure or that cannot be expressed numerically. Qualitative data can be put into categories like gender and sales regions. You will learn more about qualitative and quantitative data in chapter 6. As it relates to data triangulation, you may be trying to answer a question that requires you to think systemically by using qualitative data like surveys, interviews, and focus groups.

For example, if you have uncovered that your organization has higher-than-planned attrition (employees leaving), you will need to understand why. You should consider things like exit interviews and focus groups as part of the data you should acquire to help answer that. Collecting this type of qualitative data is slightly different than collecting data that is stored in a database. It requires you to transform the unstructured data using a technique called *coding*. Coding creates structure that you can then use during the Analyze phase to look at themes. In the example of exit interviews, one of the questions could be "Why did you leave?" You could then classify the replies into various codes such as compensation, promotion, and culture. These codes can then be analyzed, as discussed in chapter 6.

It is important to note that data triangulation is not just about verifying existing information. There are multiple insights you can obtain from triangulation. Other data can be used to corroborate the same results and decisions you have already suggested from using another data source. Other data sources can be used to elaborate on the previous results, potentially helping to clarify root causes or providing other useful and necessary insights into other dimensions of the data. Other data sources can complement previous results. This means that the results from the multiple sources may be different, but when put together, they build coherent insights that can help you make better decisions. Other data sources can also provide contradictions, in which there are conflicts between the results. This is not a bad thing, however, as it is important to acknowledge conflicts early in the process before making and acting on your decisions.

THE IMPORTANCE OF DISCUSSING DATA WITH PEOPLE

Billionaire investor Ray Dalio talks about the importance of triangulation in his book *Principles*. He states that you should triangulate decisions with "highly believable" people[43]—those with an established track record who can clearly explain their point—willing to have a thoughtful disagreement to enhance the quality of the decisions being made. Avoid valuing one's own believability more than is logical. Practice distinguishing between people who are credible and who are not and how to tell the difference. When disagreements arise, start by trying to agree on the principles used to make the decision, and explore the merits of the reasoning behind each principle.

SOURCES OF INSIGHT

Professor Patrick Noonan provides another method to triangulate data. His approach, called the *sources of insight*,[44] aims to triangulate data (evidence), theory, and intuition to provide better facts, reasoning, and judgment about potential decisions. The data can be both quantitative and qualitative. The theory portion of the data relates to any data that is seen as best practice, industry standard, or similar. For example, if we are trying to analyze our sales-forecasting accuracy (how accurate our sales revenue is projected from the start of a month to what the actual sales revenue is at the end of the month), acquiring data from an analyst firm that explains what the industry average is for sales-forecasting accuracy is critical. In addition, we should not ignore intuition. Intuition is a really important part of data-informed decision-making, along with the other sources of data and insights. Sources of insight will be discussed in more detail in chapter 8 in relation to how to communicate a decision.

Ensuring That Data Can Be Trusted: Having a Data Strategy

The second part of the Acquire phase requires decision-makers to ensure that the data is trusted and that the consumers of the data find the data trustworthy. This can be accomplished by having a well-thought-out and well-executed **data strategy**. A data strategy is the essential foundation for any company looking to make better data-informed decisions. According to Chief Data Officer Leandro DalleMule and Professor Thomas H. Davenport, a data strategy is a "coherent strategy for organizing, governing, analyzing, and deploying an organization's information assets that can be applied across industries and levels of data maturity."[45] This strategy needs to include processes for understanding *data quality* and for the *effective collection, governance, and management of data*. Without this foundation, companies have no framework or processes to ensure effective data usage. This lack of process decreases productivity and increases technology spend and debt. The remainder of this section will focus on what should be included in an organization's data strategy.

Think about the following questions regarding your organization:

- Do we know what data we have available?
- Do we know where that data is?
- Do we know what people are doing with it?
- Do we have consistent definitions of the data for all?
- Do we have good-quality data?

In order to be able to answer yes to those questions, you must have an understanding of data quality and proper data collection, governance, and management. Once you have this foundational-level data strategy in place, you can be assured that your organization has quality data to start with.

DATA QUALITY

Data quality refers to the overall level of quality, or utility, of data. Poorly collected or managed data can easily result in poor data quality, which will then result in faulty business decisions. Poor data quality includes situations in which you have duplicate data, incomplete data, inconsistent formats, or a lack of accuracy. To better understand how to avoid these issues, let's take a closer look at the characteristics of quality data. Quality data is *accurate, complete, consistent, unique,* and *timely*.

Characteristics of Quality Data

Data accuracy. Data *accuracy* refers to whether the data is correct and accurately represents what it should. It also encompasses the validity of the data. Data *validity* is determined by whether the data measures what it is intended to measure. For example, suppose you are running a survey, and the survey changes. If the data-collection process, like the form itself, does not get updated, the data you are collecting now is invalid. Or, suppose you work in an organization, and the regions used to segment your customers geographically change. As soon as that happens, your data collected is invalid and needs to be updated.

Data completeness. Data *completeness* refers to whether there are any gaps in the data between what was expected to be collected and what was actually collected. Data requirements should be clearly specified based on the information needs of the organization and the data-collection processes matched to those requirements. For example, if your organization is trying to track sales based on various demographics or against certain competitors and this is part of your organization's strategy, if those fields are either optional or nonexistent on the CRM (customer relationship management) system, you will not have a complete view of the data to help your decisions.

Data consistency. Data *consistency* refers to whether the types of data coming in align with the expected versions of the data that should be coming in. This may seem like data completeness; however, while these two can be similar, they are also quite different. Data should be recorded and used in compliance with relevant requirements, including the correct application of any rules or definitions. This will ensure consistency between periods and with similar organizations, measuring what is intended to be measured. For example, suppose you are analyzing sales across regions, and your form allows the sales reps to enter the cities the deal is taking place in as free-form text. What will happen as a result is you will have a field of data that has inconsistencies. For example, some people may enter "New York City," others may enter "NYC," and others may just enter "New York." These inconsistencies will impact the downstream value of your data, and your ability to make data-informed decisions from it will be at risk. Solutions to this can range from not using free-form fields to using fuzzy search-matching software as part of your data management. Fuzzy search-matching software will find strings that approximately match a pattern, to account for when users misspell a word or use an abbreviation.

Data uniqueness. Data should be *unique* and captured only once, even though it may have multiple purposes. Having multiple versions of the same raw data will lead to problems downstream. This is a type of data fragmentation that is very common in businesses. With data teams strapped for resources, many departments and individuals create their own data sets or databases. Over time, these do not follow the same requirements and processes for data quality and governance and can easily lead to inaccuracies, which create misinformation, which leads to poor decision-making. Imagine an example in which the sales department builds a dashboard that includes their own data set about their customers, and the customer-support department builds their own dashboard that leverages their own data set about the same exact customers, rather than building on the same one that sales uses. Over time, these two data sets can easily become out of sync and lead to misinformation.

Data timeliness. Data *timeliness* refers to the expectation of when data should be received for the information to be used effectively. The expectation and reality do not often align, leading to ineffective use of the data and a lack of data-driven decisions. This timeliness refers not only to the first access but also to the frequency of updates. If an organization's strategy is to check trends in sales month over month but it is only receiving and checking quarterly sales data, the data is not timely.

As you can see, if any of these characteristics are absent or disorderly, data quality will suffer and so will your decision-making.

DATA COLLECTION

Data collection is the process of gathering and potentially measuring data from a variety of sources. Data-collection processes should adhere to all the characteristics described earlier for data quality. This applies not only to the raw data but also to any calculations or metrics created from the raw data. Assume you have fragmented data and are working on a report that shows the "attach rate" of consulting to a license deal. In general, attach rate defines how many consulting hours are attached to a license deal. What is your definition of attach rate? Could it be different than someone else's version of the attach rate? Will there be multiple reports showing attach rate within the company that have different calculations for them? This can lead to misinformation and a lack of consistency, which will lead to a lack of trust in the data.

DATA GOVERNANCE AND DATA MANAGEMENT

Data governance is the overall practice of managing your data with guidance to make sure that the data aligns with the company's goals. To use an analogy, if data were water, data quality would ensure that the water is pure and not contaminated. Data governance would make sure that the right people with the right tools were responsible for the right parts of the overall water system to ensure that the water is safe to drink. **Data management** is the implementation of the processes, policies, technology, and training to ensure that those within an organization can achieve its data-governance goals.

Data management and governance are vast topics and beyond the scope of this book, but at a high level, they should encompass people, processes, and technologies. The data-governance framework should assign ownership and responsibility for the data. Data management should then implement the processes and policies for managing data. Those processes and policies should leverage the technologies and training that will support the people and processes to ensure the data's quality and that it aligns with the organization's strategy and what it would like to use the data to help answer.

Data, like all corporate assets, requires managing to ensure that its maximum benefit is achieved by the organization. However, many organizations do not have a proper data-management strategy in place. Let's compare managing data to another organizational asset: money.

Managing money in a business context means recognizing that money is a strategic asset that can be used to drive growth. The reason companies care about knowing everything about their money, including where it is, how much there is, and where it came from, is so they can strategically use this asset. Data needs to be understood the same way. A company should know where its data is, how much of it there is, and where it's coming from, and leaders within the company need to care so that they can deploy that data in their own projects that align with their strategy. Thinking about data this way also makes data management and data collection a value-generating activity, as opposed to a chore.

Summary and Key Takeaways

- When trying to acquire the right data to help answer your analytical questions, it is important to think about all relevant sources of data. Ensure that you are thinking systemically to understand all potential connections at all levels of the organization as well as from external factors.
- When making decisions, it is important to ensure that whatever decision you make does not upset the balance of the system.
- Organizations need to focus data strategy on business outcomes that help exploit their data and turn it into knowledge to create value.
- Ensure that the data you have sourced is trusted and reliable. This can be accomplished by corroborating your data using techniques like triangulation. It can also be done at the organizational level with the implementation of a proper data strategy that includes data quality, data collection, data management, and data governance.

CHAPTER 6

PHASE THREE – THE ANALYZE PHASE

"What gets measured gets improved."[46]
—Peter Drucker

Steps Involved in This Phase

5	Create a measurement framework to describe your data with key performance indicators (KPIs) and descriptive analytics.
6	Use diagnostic analytics to find patterns, trends, and relationships that may exist but not be obvious to start to drill into root cause. If applicable, leverage inferential statistics to take a sample of data and make generalizations about the entire population, predictive analytics to run simulations or to test potential decisions/solutions, and prescriptive analytics to act on situations as they happen.

At this point in the process, you have identified your analytical questions, and you have acquired the data to help answer those questions. Now, you are entering the phase in which you will leverage **analytics** to start to make sense of and to apply meaning to your data. There are two aspects of the Analyze phase. The first is to create a **measurement framework** to describe your data using **key performance indicators (KPIs)** that relate to your analytical questions. To accomplish this, you will have to use a type of analytics called **descriptive analytics**. Then, you will need to drill down deeper into your data to find patterns, trends, and relationships that may help answer your analytical questions and explain why something is happening. This process will use a type of analytics called **diagnostic analytics**. Then, depending on your analytical questions, you may need to dive even deeper into the advanced types of analytics, including **inferential statistics**, **predictive analytics**, and **prescriptive analytics**, to make predictions, test potential decisions, and ultimately act on your decision. It is not required that everyone making data-informed decisions needs to know how to use the advanced types of analytics. However, it is important that they know their capabilities and what to ask others in the organization who do have these analytics skill sets. Each of these specific analytics types will be discussed in greater detail in this chapter.

Understanding Analytics

Analytics can be defined as the process of transforming raw data into insights. The analytics process leverages data and math to find meaningful patterns and to uncover new knowledge locked within the data. Analytics is not limited to a specific field of business and can be used by everyone to make data-informed decisions. Does that mean that every decision-maker using analytics must be a statistician, mathematician, or data scientist? Not at all. What it means is that individuals must understand the fundamentals of data, data analysis, and the tools and techniques that are used to inform decisions.

Should individuals use random analytical methods that do not consider the type of data they are evaluating? No, individuals must understand which analytical techniques should be applied based on the type of data they are using and the decision they are trying to make. Analytics can take many forms. They range from basic math techniques all the way to a combination of statistics, probability, and powerful programming languages to gain valuable insights and to deliver them in the form of visualizations.

ANALYTICS AND STATISTICS

A lot of people overlap the terms analytics and statistics. While they are related, they are not the same thing. Statistics is the heart of analytics. **Statistics** is a branch of mathematics that deals with collecting, processing, analyzing, and interpreting quantitative data (numerical information that can be measured or counted). Statistics is commonly used to gain an understanding of a larger data set by analyzing a **sample** of the data. For example, when a poll is conducted with a random sample of customers of a store, statistics will be used to try to infer insights about the entire **population** (all customers of the store).

Many decisions made in analytics are based on statistical results. In those cases, the decision-makers do not need to know how to perform statistical analysis, but they do need to understand what to ask a statistician and how to interpret the results.

With modern-day technology, statistics has begun to play a key role in the success of many corporations. However, the true power of statistics was first witnessed when an analyst used it in baseball by taking player data from a team and using it to predict if the team would win. To win, the team needed to score more runs than its opponent. The analyst of this team used several different strategies to recruit a team with a low payroll that would yield the most wins. The approach reviewed many metrics to determine which of those metrics had a positive correlation to winning the game. The conclusion was that on-base percentage and slugging percentage had the most direct influence. This insight was new, and these metrics were not things that teams typically looked at in detail when determining which players they would recruit to their team. These strategies were eventually recorded and published in a book called *Moneyball*.[47] Statistics was previously used in sports by many analysts, but in this case, quantitative analysis was implemented and introduced to a broader community. Today, many sports teams have personnel with analytics and quantitative training who predict the team's performance, both in field and in a business perspective as well. Now this approach is also being leveraged by every company that would like to make better data-informed decisions. For example, retailers use analytics to perform targeted advertising. Banks use analytics for risk management. Manufacturers use analytics for supply chain management.

ANALYTICS STRATEGY AND FRAMEWORK

Now that we know that analytics can help us make data-informed decisions, let's focus on the types of analytics we can use: descriptive analytics, diagnostic analytics, inferential statistics, predictive analytics, and prescriptive analytics (as shown in figure 14). In many cases, you will not pick a single analytics approach but rather use a combination of analytics approaches that work together in a flow.

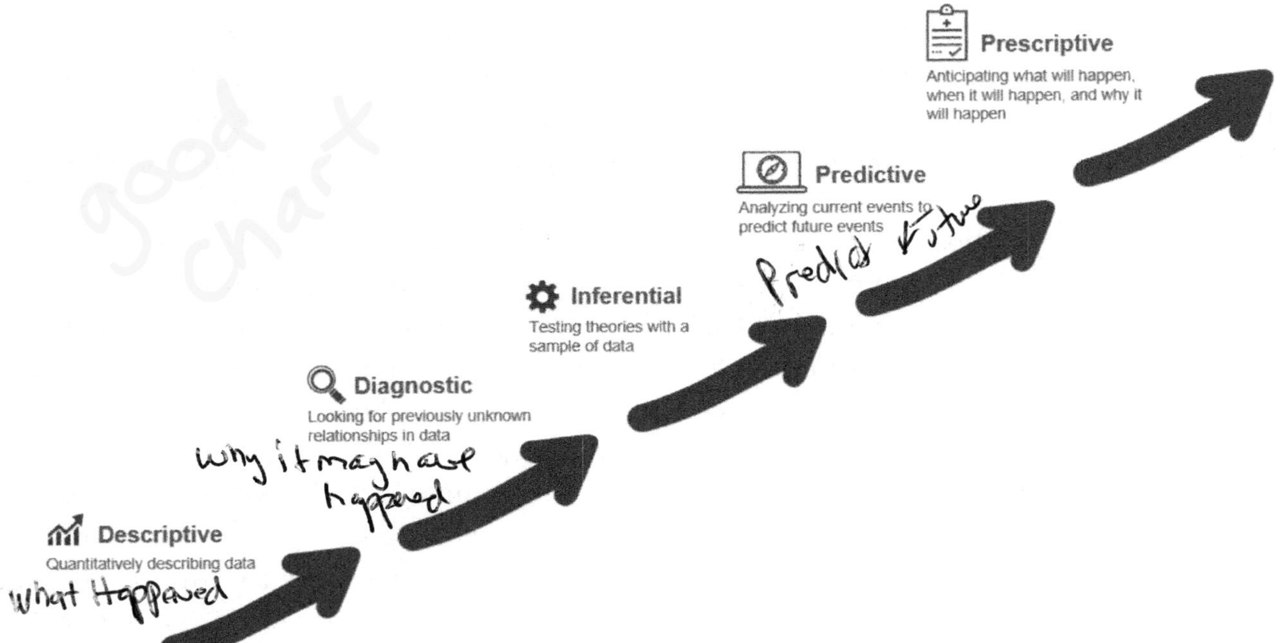

Figure 14. Levels of analytics

Typically, an analysis starts with **descriptive analytics**, a type of analytics designed to give you an overview of your data, both quantitative and qualitative. Both quantitative and qualitative data are critical when it comes to decision-making. Quantitative data analysis is based on numbers and statistics. This type of analysis is measured, not observed. The median, standard deviation, and other descriptive metrics play a major role in quantitative data analysis. (These terms will be discussed in greater detail later on in this chapter.) Qualitative data analysis uses data that is not defined by numbers, such as interviews and surveys. This type of analysis is observed rather than measured. Qualitative data must be coded so that items may be grouped together intelligently. When using qualitative data during descriptive analysis, you are typically looking at descriptive metrics like frequencies (number of occurrences over a period of time).

Next, there is **diagnostic analytics**, which can be used to find connections and unknown relationships in your data. From here, depending on what you want to do, you may look at performing inferential statistics or predictive analytics. While not used in every decision, if the data being analyzed is a **sample** or subset of a larger **population** of data, **inferential statistics** can be used to help draw conclusions about that larger population. Inferential statistics is the basis for data mining and machine learning, and examples for its use include marketing to customers, finding new markets, improving operational efficiency, and analyzing supply chains. **Predictive analytics** analyzes data from past events to make predictions about future events. This analytics type is used in forecasting sales data, detecting fraud on credit card purchases, or predicting future buying patterns to develop decision options and recommendations. Finally, there is prescriptive analytics. **Prescriptive analytics** builds on the predicted outcomes from predictive analytics and then makes recommendations on one or more courses of action to take.

To better understand these levels of analytics, it may be helpful to use the analogy of a medical visit. Descriptive analytics helps us understand what happened. This is similar to when you go to a medical visit and your vitals are taken. These vitals tell your doctor information like your temperature, blood pressure, pulse, and weight. Your doctor may also have results from basic blood work, like your cholesterol, and a list of symptoms that you have communicated. Diagnostic analytics helps us understand why something happened. During your medical visit, diagnostics are the process the doctor follows to determine the root cause of your symptoms. The doctor will ask you more questions about your symptoms and may order additional tests. Predictive analytics helps us understand what will happen. Based on your vitals and symptoms, the doctor could predict your potential health outcomes. For example, if your cholesterol and blood pressure are high, the doctor could predict that you may have some major heart issues in the near future. Prescriptive analytics helps us understand what action to take. Based on the doctor's predictions of future health outcomes, the doctor may prescribe medications like cholesterol-lowering drugs or changes in lifestyle.

The remainder of this chapter will go into each of these stages of analytics in more detail.

Using a Measurement Framework for Descriptive Analytics

The first step in the Analyze phase is to create a measurement framework to describe your data. A **measurement framework** is a visual representation of the data that is being used to answer your analytical question. Typically, a measurement framework will use descriptive analytics to show an overview of the data using **key performance indicators (KPIs)**. This overview should give you an understanding of what is happening in your business. This measurement framework is commonly implemented using a data analytics and visualization tool. When it is implemented, the measurement framework is commonly referred to as a *dashboard*.

In figure 15, we are showing a measurement framework implemented in a dashboard that was created using a product called Qlik Sense. The framework includes a company's key performance indicators, including expenses, revenue, and accounts receivable. It also shows some comparisons, like a breakdown of various expense types, a comparison of revenue by product line, and a breakdown of any accounts overdue by customers. The dashboard also shows comparisons over time, like whether expenses are trending upward compared to the last time period.

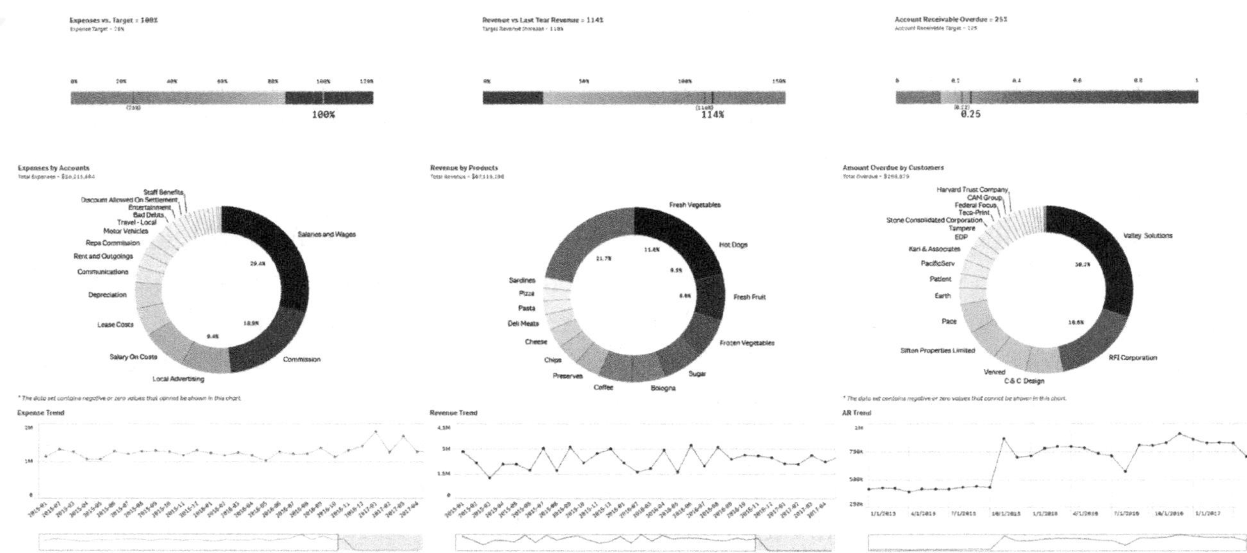

Figure 15. Sample dashboard

A measurement framework is key to data-informed decision-making because it means decision-makers know when a business area (a key performance indicator) improves, gets worse, or just changes. When someone is alerted to a change in a given KPI, it can become a trigger point or alert to start an initial investigation.

Additional benefits to using a measurement framework are that it provides transparency in analytics and reporting, a consistency of measurement, and an objective measurement. And, most importantly, it starts the process to provide a link between activities and outcomes.

To understand how KPIs are selected for inclusion in a measurement framework, it is important to first understand the difference between measurements, metrics, and KPIs. *Measurements* are data at a given point in time. They do not have context, much like the data level in the DIKW pyramid discussed in chapter 3. Examples of measurements within organizations can be customer visits, retail sales, and advertising spend. A *metric* is a data point in **context**—for example, customer visits compared to last quarter or retail sales this week compared to last week. *KPIs* are metrics that tie to a strategic objective of the organization.

There are two types of KPIs that should be included in a measurement framework: leading and lagging. **Leading indicators** can be thought of as drivers, and **lagging indicators** can be thought of as outcomes. Since lagging indicators are outcome oriented, they are typically easy to measure, but in turn they are hard to improve or influence. Leading indicators are typically input oriented and are easy to influence. However, most organizations spend too-much time focusing on lagging indicators and not-enough time brainstorming appropriate leading indicators. Leading indicators are essential as they will help you to understand potential negative impacts on your business before it is too late.

Selecting KPIs should not be done haphazardly or without some thought. If the KPIs chosen are not the right ones, measuring them won't just be useless; it will also be harmful. The wrong KPIs can have unintended consequences: They can wreak havoc on organizational processes, demoralize employees, and undermine productivity and service levels. If the KPIs don't accurately translate the company's strategy and goals into concrete actions that employees can take on a daily basis, the organization will suffer. While the company may end up being efficient, it will be efficient in the wrong things and ultimately ineffective.

Let's look at an example. For many organizations, profit and revenue growth are goals. Profit and revenue are lagging indicators that are easy to measure. But how do you actually reach those goals? What other factors influence them? This is again where systems thinking comes into play. In this example, there are a variety of leading indicators. Leads created and leads converted to opportunities are good examples.

A *logic model*, also called a *program logic model*, is a tool used for assessing the impact achieved by an organization's application of resources to one of its programs. Logic models are very useful in helping organizations focus on what to include in their measurement framework. Logic models are discussed in greater detail in the "Tools, Frameworks, and Models" chapter.

Now that we have learned a bit about measurement frameworks and KPIs, let's dive into descriptive analytics in more detail to understand how to implement a measurement framework for our analytical questions.

Descriptive Analytics

As mentioned earlier in the chapter, **descriptive analytics** provides an overview of the data. This analytics type helps answer the question "What has happened?" A business learns from past behaviors to understand how they will impact future outcomes. Descriptive analytics is leveraged when a business needs to understand its overall performance at a macrolevel and to describe those aspects. Components of descriptive analytics include *describing the data, organizing the data,* and *visualizing the data*.

DESCRIPTIVE ANALYTICS TERMINOLOGY

Before we go any further into descriptive analytics, let's look at some related terminology.

Outlier. An outlier is a number that lies outside of most of the other numbers in a set.

Mean. The mean, also referred to as the arithmetic mean, is the average of all the numbers in a given set of numbers.

Median. The median is defined as the middle of a sorted list of numbers in a set. The median is a better description of the data if there are lots of outliers.

Mode. The mode is defined as the most common number in a set of numbers.

Variable. A variable is a characteristic, number, or quantity that can be measured. In a general sense, it can be seen as a column of data.

Quantitative data. Quantitative data, also called numerical data, is numerical information that can be measured or counted.

Qualitative data. Qualitative data, also called categorical data, is descriptive information about characteristics that are difficult to define or measure or that cannot be expressed numerically. Qualitative data can be put into categories like gender and sales regions.

Raw data. Raw data is data that is collected from a source and not cleaned, transformed, or edited in any way.

Aggregate data. Aggregate data is data that has been summarized using an aggregation (a cluster of things that have been brought together) such as sum, mean, or median, to name a few.

DESCRIBING THE DATA

Data has different types and classifications, and those types and classifications are important to know when it comes to describing and ultimately analyzing the data. Figure 16 depicts a taxonomy of data types.

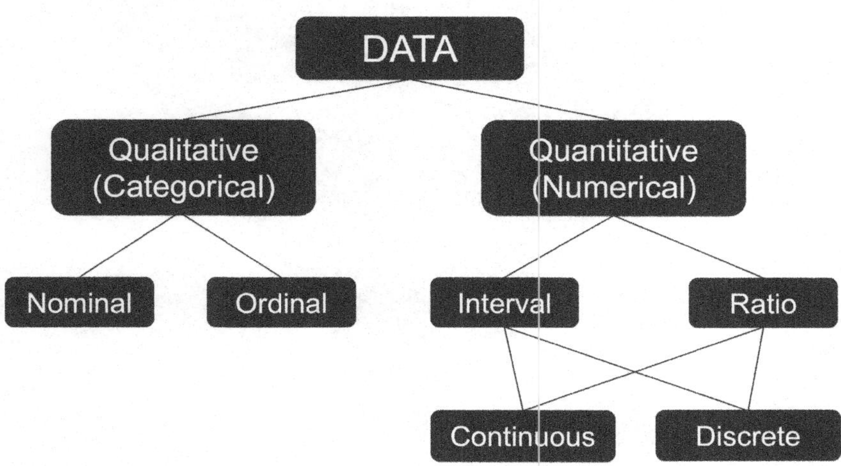

Figure 16. Data types taxonomy

At the highest level, data can be described as either qualitative or quantitative. **Qualitative data** is also called **categorical data**. (You may see both terms used interchangeably within this book.) Examples of qualitative data include gender, sales region, marketing channel, and other things that can be divided into different groups or categories. **Quantitative data** is sometimes also called *numerical data*. Examples of quantitative data include height, weight, age, and other things that can be measured numerically.

At the next level down the taxonomy, qualitative data and quantitative data can each be broken down into two main subcategories. Qualitative data can either be nominal or ordinal, and quantitative data can either be interval or ratio. These four types of data (nominal, ordinal, interval, and ratio) are commonly referred to as the *four scales of measurement* or the *four levels of measurement*. However, there is one additional level and classification that we need to discuss. Both interval and ratio can be further broken down and classified as either continuous or discrete.

From an analytics perspective, each of the four levels of measurement builds in complexity from the previous measurements. In addition, each level of measurement includes aspects of the levels before it. For this reason, sometimes you will see the levels of measurements depicted as an inverted pyramid, as shown in figure 17, with the most basic level of measurement (nominal) on the bottom and the most complex level of measurement on the top (ratio).

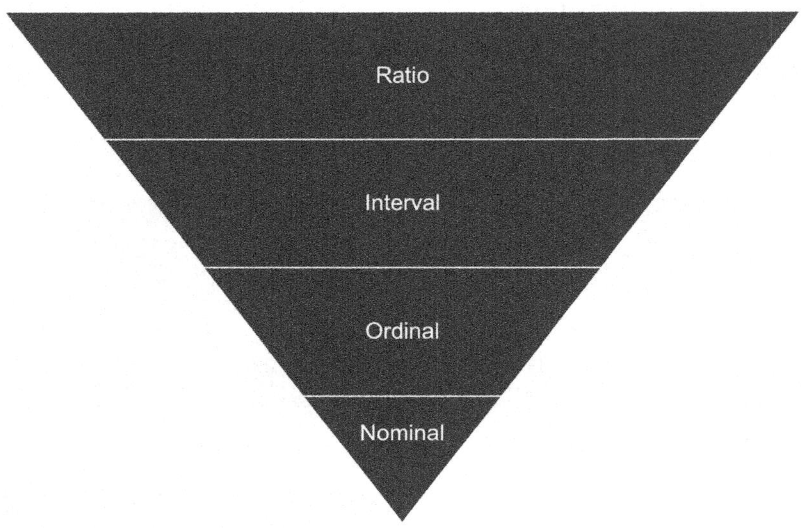

Figure 17. Four levels of measurement

Nominal data is qualitative data that has no sense of sequential order—for example, gender, makes of a car, or types of fruit. **Ordinal data** is qualitative data that does have a sense of order and can be ordered in a sequence—for example, rankings from one to five or from good to better to best. Worthy of noting is that even though one of the rankings options in this example is using numbers, they are not numerical data values in mathematics (quantitative data) but codes for groups or categories of data, which makes them qualitative.

With quantitative data, the best way to explain interval and ratio data requires us to learn about "absolute zero." **Absolute zero** is a point at which there is no measurement. A common way to ascertain absolute zero is to ask whether a value of zero means none with the specific **variable**. For example, if the variable is cash in your savings account, the value zero means none. However, if the variable is the temperature in Fahrenheit, the value zero does not mean none. It has a value. Now, back to interval and ratio data. **Interval data** is quantitative data that has no absolute zero. With interval data, you can add and subtract, but you cannot multiply and divide. For example, if the weather is eighty degrees Fahrenheit one day and seventy degrees another day, that difference (ten degrees) is the same difference in temperature in another location that has fifty degrees one day and forty degrees another day. **Ratio data** is quantitative data with an absolute zero. With ratio data, you can not only add and subtract but also multiply and divide. For example, someone who weighs two hundred pounds can be said to be twice as big as someone who weighs one hundred pounds.

Table 2 summarizes the differences between the four levels of measurement with respect to which mathematical operations can be performed.

Table 2. Four levels of measurement comparison

STATEMENT	NOMINAL	ORDINAL	INTERVAL	RATIO
Order of values in the variable is established	No	Yes	Yes	Yes
Can perform addition and subtraction (the difference between values in the variable can be evaluated)	No	No	Yes	Yes
Can perform multiplication and division (the variable contains an absolute zero)	No	No	No	Yes

Figure 18 will help determine which level of measurement a given variable is.

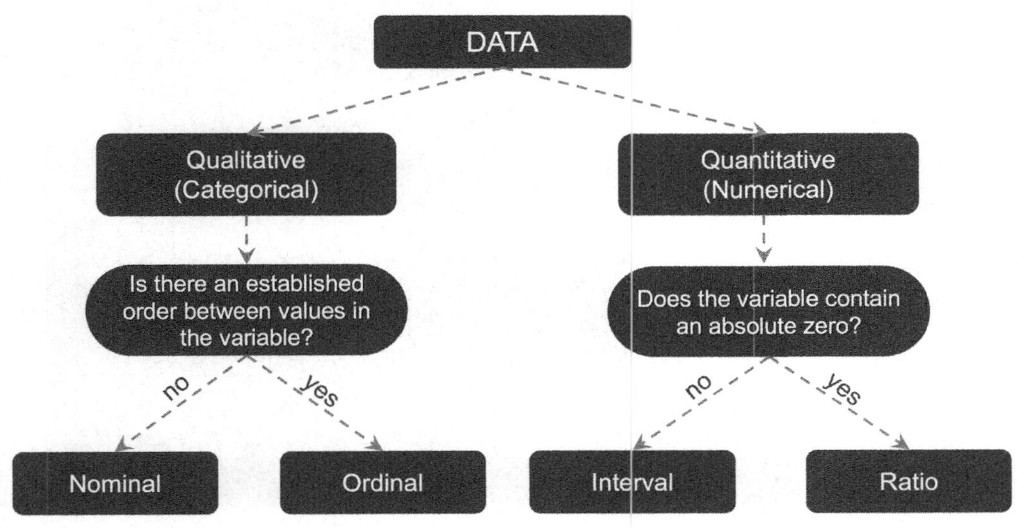

Figure 18. Flowchart for four levels of measurement

Quantitative data (interval and ratio) can also be classified as either discrete or continuous (figure 16). It is important to know the distinction between these two, especially when we discuss visualizing data later on in this chapter. **Discrete data** is quantitative data that can be counted and that only takes specific values, typically whole numbers. For example, you cannot have 1.5 store locations. **Continuous data** is quantitative data that is not confined to specific values like discrete data is—for example, a person's height is classified as continuous data because a person can be five feet and five inches.

ORGANIZING THE DATA

Now that we understand how to classify data based on its level of measurement, we can move on to how we should organize the data to aid in our analysis. The first step in organizing data is to understand how a given **variable** is distributed. A *distribution* will visually show you the frequency of values within the variable. For example, if we work for a retail company, we may want to understand our customers' demographics better. Figure 19 depicts a distribution of the ages of a retail company's customers.

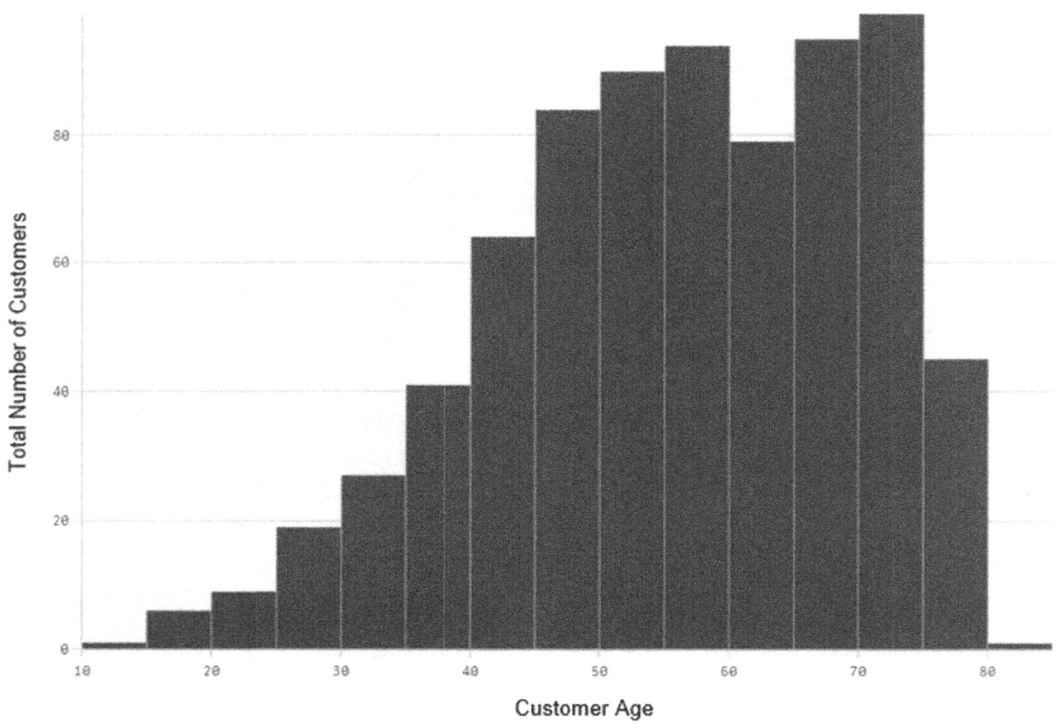

Figure 19. Distribution of customer ages

We can get a ton of useful information from this one single visualization. The vertical bars represent increments of five years. We can visually see there is one customer between the ages of ten and fifteen and another over eighty years old, and the majority of customers fall between ages forty-five and seventy-five.

This distribution is said to be skewed left, as there are fewer observations to the left. There are many other distribution types (uniform, long-tailed, and bimodal, as a few examples), but the most important one is called normal distribution. When a data set is said to be **normally distributed**, it means that extreme values and **outliers** are expected to be rare and that the average is a good estimate of the majority of the values in the distribution. A normal distribution is symmetric and has a bell-shaped look, as shown in figure 20.

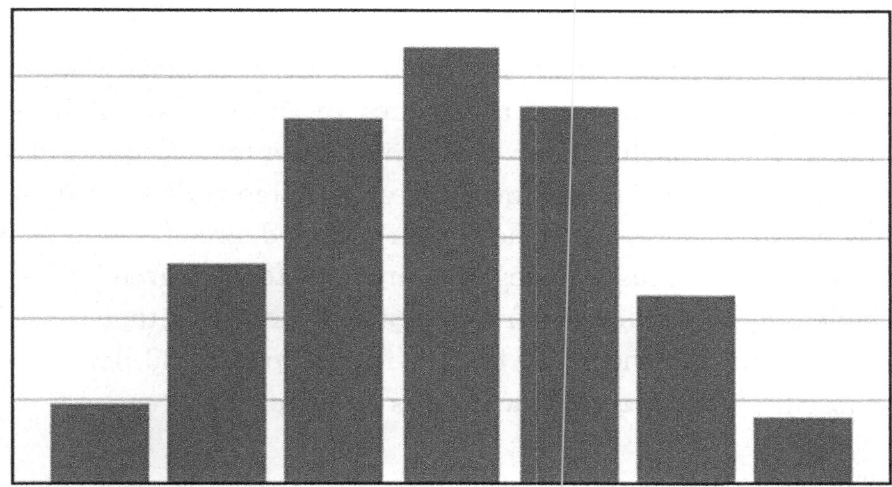

Figure 20. Normal distribution

This is a really important concept to tuck away as we progress further into inferential statistics and predictive and prescriptive analytics.

While distributions are good at providing a visual description of the data, there are many times when organizations would ideally like to have one single measure that they can use to summarize an entire variable. Perhaps what they want to know is the average customer age, the most popular customer age, or similar. What if the variable is not customer age but total purchases at their store for the day? To summarize that variable, they may want to see the average purchase per transaction for the day or the total of all purchases for the day. The measures used to provide this information are called descriptive analytics, as they help describe the data.

There are four common types of descriptive analytics:

1. **Central tendency.** This type of descriptive analytics is used if the variable is quantitative. Central tendency is useful when we want to show something like the average of a variable—for example, the average number of support tickets closed in a day by our support team.

2. **Dispersion (also called the measures of spread).** This type of descriptive analytics is used if the variable is quantitative. Dispersion is useful when we want to know how spread out our variable is—for example, when we want to know the range (difference between the largest and smallest value) of ticket prices for an upcoming concert.

3. **Frequencies and percentages.** This descriptive analytics type looks at the frequencies and percentages of the values in the variable if it is qualitative. These analytics are useful when we want to summarize qualitative variables. For example, assume there is a qualitative variable called "level of education," which has possible values of "below high school degree," "high school degree," "bachelor's degree," "master's degree," and "doctoral degree." We could analyze this variable and determine the frequency and the percentage of each value. For example, we could say there are twenty-five people, or 30 percent of the population, whose highest level of education is a master's degree.

4. **Total.** This type of descriptive analytics looks at the sum of the values in the variable if it is quantitative. This is useful when we want to see the totals of a variable—for example, the total sales for a store on a given day or the total amount of money returned to a store on a given day.

Figure 21 shows these four common types along with appropriate calculations for each. Not every calculation shown in the figure is discussed in this book, only the most common.

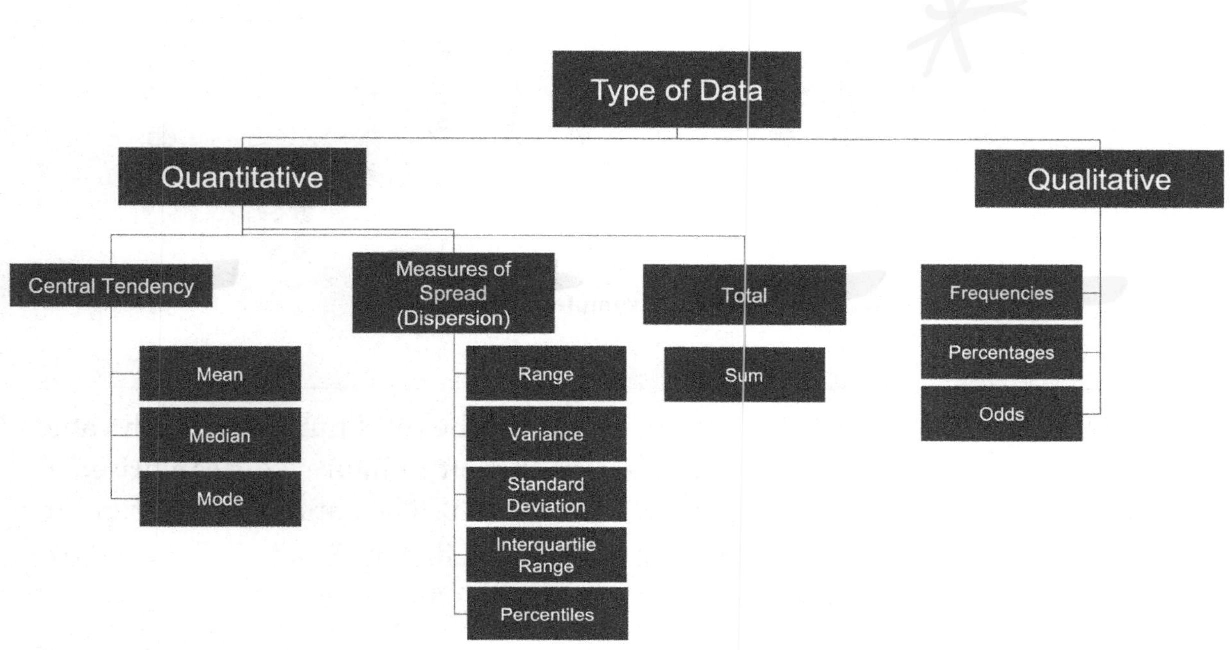

Figure 21. Types of descriptive analytics

Central Tendency

The **central tendency** is a value that describes the center of a given variable. The center of the variable is commonly referred to as the average. However, there is a level of complexity behind the central tendency as there are actually three separate measures that can be used: the *mean*, the *median*, and the *mode*. The right one to use depends on the type of data (nominal, ordinal, interval, ratio) your variable is and the analytical question you are asking. It is an important part of the descriptive analytics process to know which measure to use based on the given situation.

Mean. The mean is the most commonly used measure of central tendency. When people share the average of something, they are typically using the mean without even knowing it. The **mean** is the sum of the values within a variable divided by the total number of items in the variable. The mean is only valid for data that is quantitative (interval or ratio). The mean is also influenced by outliers. **Outliers** are individual values that differ greatly from most other values in a set. Take a look at the two examples shown in figure 22. The example on the right has identical values to the example on the left except the value of nine was replaced with a value of fifty-seven. In this case, fifty-seven is considered an outlier as its value is greatly different compared to the other values.

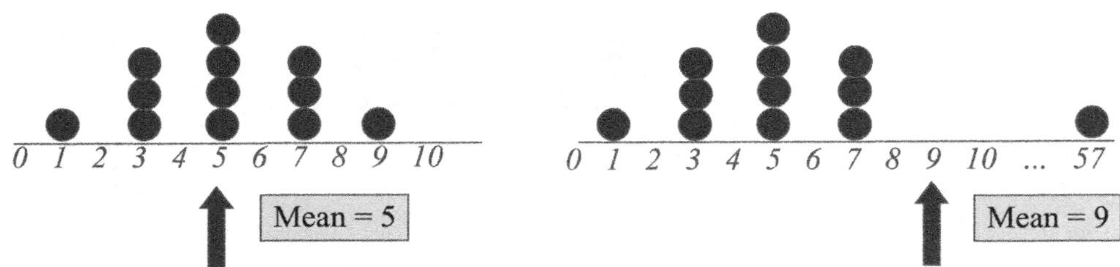

Figure 22. Examples of mean

> **Note:** The visuals used in this section represent the total number of each value in the data set. For example, the data set on the left in figure 22 is comprised of the following values: 1, 3, 3, 3, 5, 5, 5, 5, 7, 7, 7, and 9. The data set on the right in figure 22 is comprised of the following values: 1, 3, 3, 3, 5, 5, 5, 5, 7, 7, 7, and 57.

The outlier has a major impact on the mean value. In the left example of figure 22, the mean is five, and in the right example, with the outlier of fifty-seven, the mean jumped all the way up to nine. Using the mean in this situation may not be ideal as one value is skewing the entire variable. To resolve this, when you have outliers, such as the one in figure 22, you should use the *median* measure.

Median. The **median** is determined by sorting the data set from the lowest to highest values and then taking the data point that is in the middle of the sequence so that there is an equal number of points above and below the median.

If there is an even number of data points in the data set, then there is no single point at the middle, and the median is calculated by taking the mean of the two middle points. In the example in figure 23, there are eighteen total data points: 1, 1, 1, 1, 2, 2, 2, 3, 4, 6, 6, 7, 7, 7, 8, 8, 8, and 8. Eighteen is an even number, so the median is calculated by taking the mean (average) of the two middle points (4 and 6), which is 5.

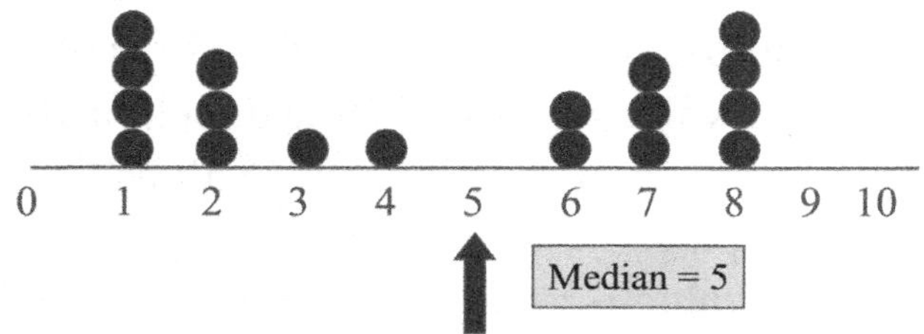

Figure 23. Example of median

The median is often used when the data contains a few outliers that could greatly influence the mean and distort what might be considered typical. Using the same example data from the earlier mean section, we can see in figure 24 that the median for the right example is five (compared to the mean of nine).

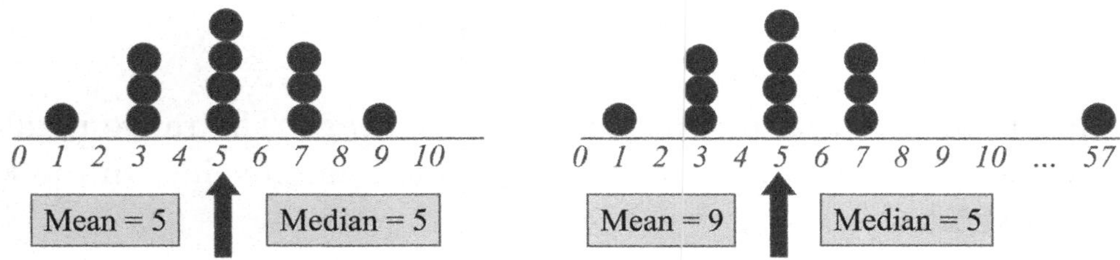

Figure 24. Median and mean

This scenario is often the case with home prices and with income data for a group of people, as this data is often very skewed. For such data, the median is often used instead of the mean. For example, in a group of people, if the salary of one person is ten times the mean, the mean salary of the group will be higher because of the unusually large salary. In this case, the median may better represent the typical salary level of the group.

Mode. The **mode** is the most frequently occurring value in the data set. A data set can have more than a single mode. The mode can be very useful for dealing with qualitative data. For example, if a sandwich shop sells ten different types of sandwiches, the mode would represent the most popular sandwich.

Table 3 highlights the various data types mentioned earlier and what measure of central tendency can be used.

Table 3. Measures of central tendency by data type

MEASURE	NOMINAL	ORDINAL	INTERVAL	RATIO
Mode	Yes	Yes	Yes	Yes
Median	No	Yes	Yes	Yes
Mean	No	No	Yes	Yes

Dispersion

While the measures of central tendency are really useful at summarizing the data, they can be misleading without knowing something about how the data is dispersed. The **dispersion**, also called the **measures of spread**, measures the spread of the data and explains the variability within the data. Using a measure of dispersion will help provide a more complete description of the data in a variable. Two common measures of dispersion include the *range* and *standard deviation*.

Range. The simplest measure of dispersion is the *range*. The range is calculated by taking the difference between the maximum and minimum values in the variable, as shown in figure 25.

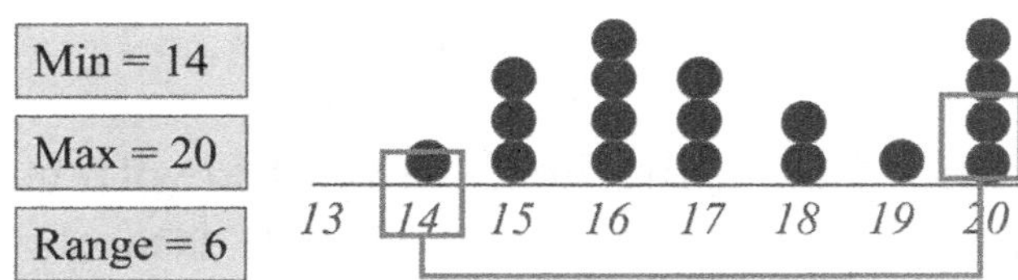

Figure 25. Range

Standard deviation. The range only provides information about the minimum and maximum values and does not say anything about the values in between. For that, a better measure of dispersion is the standard deviation. **Standard deviation** measures how widely data values are dispersed from the mean. The following steps show how the standard deviation is calculated:

1. Calculate the mean of the variable.
2. Calculate the variance. The variance is calculated by subtracting the mean from each number in the variable and then squaring the result. Then you calculate the mean of that new set.
3. Calculate the square root of the variance.

The greater the dispersion from the mean, the higher the standard deviation for a given variable. This means that a lower value of the standard deviation for a variable indicates that the values of that variable are spread over a relatively smaller range around the mean (as shown on the left side of figure 26). A larger value of the standard deviation for a variable indicates that the values of that variable are spread over a relatively larger range around the mean (as shown on the right side of figure 26).

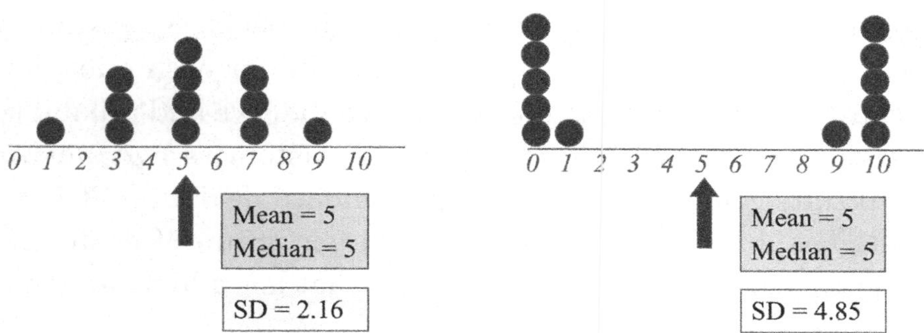

Figure 26. Standard deviation

Below are the steps used to calculate the standard deviation from the left example in figure 26:

1. **Calculate the mean of the variable.** In the example on the left in figure 26, there are twelve total data points: 1, 3, 3, 3, 5, 5, 5, 5, 7, 7, 7, and 9. Therefore, the mean is:

   $(1 + 3 + 3 + 3 + 5 + 5 + 5 + 5 + 7 + 7 + 7 + 9)/12 = 60/12 = 5$

2. **Calculate the variance.** The variance is calculated by subtracting the mean from each number in the variable and then squaring the result. Then you calculate the mean of that new set.

   $(1 - 5)^2 = (-4)^2 = 16$
   $(3 - 5)^2 = (-2)^2 = 4$
   $(3 - 5)^2 = (-2)^2 = 4$
   $(3 - 5)^2 = (-2)^2 = 4$
   $(5 - 5)^2 = (0)^2 = 0$
   $(5 - 5)^2 = (0)^2 = 0$
   $(5 - 5)^2 = (0)^2 = 0$
   $(5 - 5)^2 = (0)^2 = 0$
   $(7 - 5)^2 = (2)^2 = 4$
   $(7 - 5)^2 = (2)^2 = 4$
   $(7 - 5)^2 = (2)^2 = 4$
   $(9 - 5)^2 = (4)^2 = 16$

   $(16 + 4 + 4 + 4 + 0 + 0 + 0 + 0 + 4 + 4 + 4 + 16)/12 = 56/12 = 4.67$

3. **Calculate the square root of the variance.**
   $\sqrt{4.67} = 2.16$

Let's see how standard deviation can be helpful in business. Assume you are analyzing feedback from a customer survey. If the results for each question come back with a low standard deviation, you will have some confidence and reliability that these results can be used to infer how a larger group of customers may answer the same question. If the results come back with a high standard deviation, it is hard to infer that these results could be representative of a larger group of customers. In other words, it is harder to make decisions with the data that has a high standard deviation.

Frequencies and Percentages

When working with qualitative data, we can use the measure called *count* to determine the *frequency*. Count will add up the total number of values in the variable. *Unique count* or *distinct count* will add up the total number of unique values in the variables. For example, if you work in a restaurant and you want to analyze coffee sales, you can use count. If you want to see how many unique types of coffee were sold, you can use unique count. In the example depicted in figure 27, there are a total of twenty coffee sales (count), and those sales are comprised of four coffee types (unique count).

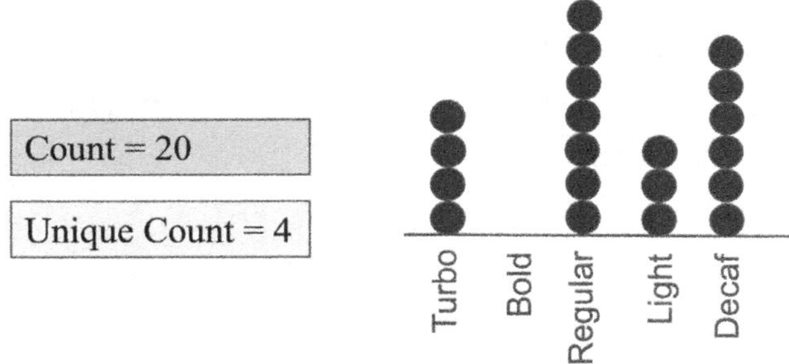

Figure 27. Count and unique count

We may also want to use *percentage* as a way to summarize data. Percentage will tell us how much of one specific value is in the variable. For example, if our analytical question requires us to analyze the market share of our product and whether it has gone up or down, we will need to use the percentage to determine what percent market share we have currently. Going back to the coffee sales as another example, if your analytical question requires you to analyze the sales of your coffee by type, you will need to use the percentage to determine each coffee type's percentage of sales, as shown in figure 28. The use of percentage will help you to determine if certain products—in this case, certain coffee types—are outselling others, and it could be an opportunity to visit the underperforming products and make a decision to try to increase the sales, maybe with a marketing campaign.

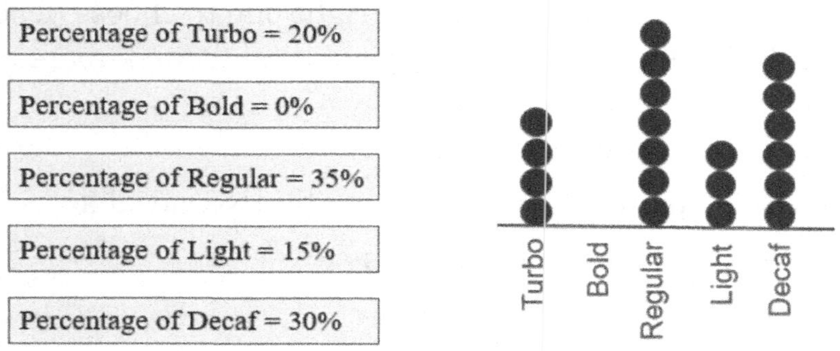

Figure 28. Percentages

Total

The last measure we will look at as part of organizing data is a sum. Whereas the count measure will add up the total number of values if the variable is qualitative, the *sum* measure will sum up the total of all the values if the variable is quantitative. For example, if we wanted to look at the total money received from sales of coffee, we would use the sum aggregation. In this example, the total money received is a quantitative value, so we use the sum. In the previous example in which we looked at the total number of coffees sold, we were not looking at the money but at the total number of orders by coffee type, which is a qualitative (categorical) variable. The sum tells us the total money received, and the count tells us the total number of coffee orders by type.

VISUALIZING THE DATA

The next step after understanding how to describe and organize data is learning how to visualize the data for descriptive analytics. There are hundreds of visualizations to choose from. In this book, we will focus on the core visualizations that should exist in most software applications. These are histograms, line charts, distribution charts, box plots, scatter plots, frequency tables, bar charts, pie charts, tree maps, KPI charts (also called text visualizations), and gauge charts. These visualization types will be shown in more detail in the rest of this section.

As part of descriptive analytics, there are many things you may want to visualize. We will focus on the top three: *visualizing distributions and comparisons, visualizing patterns and relationships,* and *visualizing summary measures.*

Visualizing Distributions and Comparisons

A *data distribution* is an arrangement of values that shows the frequency of their occurrence. When trying to visualize a distribution of your data, there are a variety of appropriate visualizations you could use. The right one to choose depends on the data types and number of variables you want to visualize and/or compare:

- distribution of one quantitative variable
- distribution of one quantitative and one qualitative variable
- distribution of two quantitative variables
- distribution of one qualitative variable
- distribution of two or more qualitative variables

Distribution of one quantitative variable. Two visualization types that can visualize distributions of a single quantitative variable are histograms and line charts. A *histogram* displays how a given variable is distributed into various categories or bins. The visual plots the frequency, which is the number of values that exist within each bin, depicted as vertical bars. A *line chart* also displays the frequency of each value in the variable, but it uses a point on the y-axis to visualize the number of values rather than a bin. Commonly, each point is then connected using a line.

For example, if we have a variable that shows the age of our customers and we want to understand the distribution, we can show it in a histogram or a line chart, both shown in figure 29. Line charts are better suited to use when there are more data points.

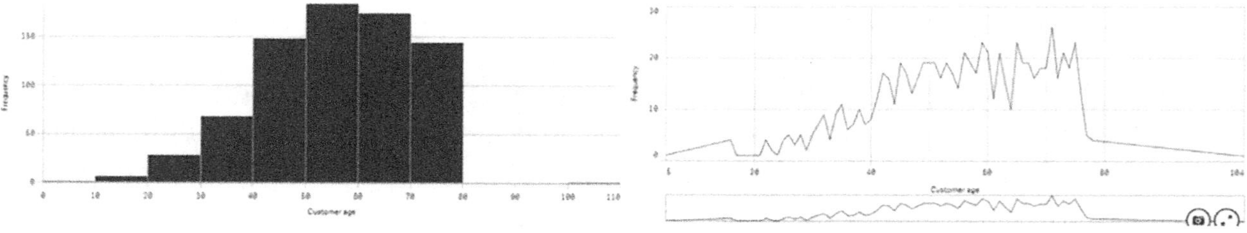

Figure 29. Distribution of one quantitative variable

Distribution of one quantitative and one qualitative variable. When you want to look at a distribution in which one of the variables is quantitative and the other is qualitative, you can use a distribution chart or a box plot. For example, assume you are looking at the total amount of sales per customer for each store region for a given year. You can use a *distribution chart* to visualize the data, as shown in figure 30. In this example, the distribution chart is comparing the range (maximum and minimum values) and the distribution of sales per customer for each of the four store regions. The gray background for each store region represents the range, and the black circles represent each specific customer transaction.

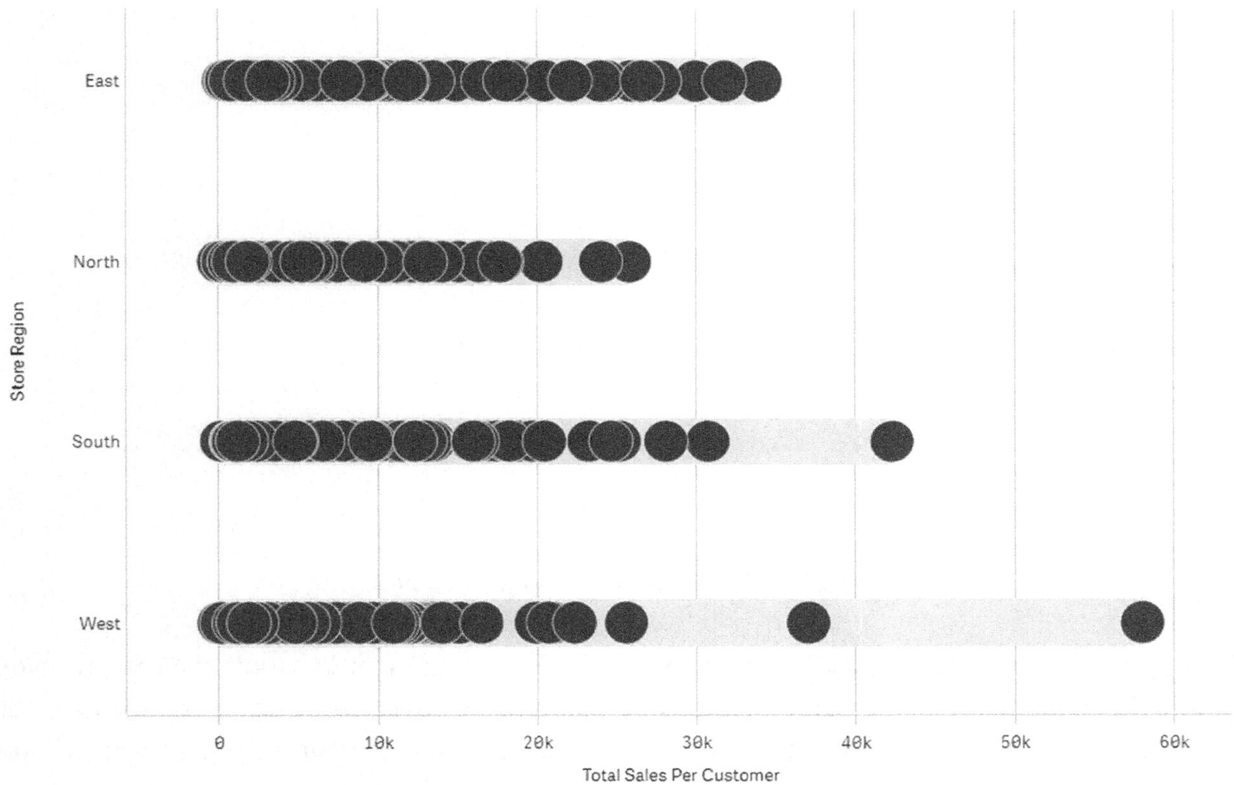

Figure 30. Distribution using a distribution chart

A more-robust visualization to show this could be the *box plot*, as shown in figure 31, as it includes more-descriptive analytics like the mean, which is depicted as the vertical line in the middle of each box, and the standard deviation, which is depicted as the lines extending out of each box. Box plots are very configurable and can include many other descriptive analytics too.

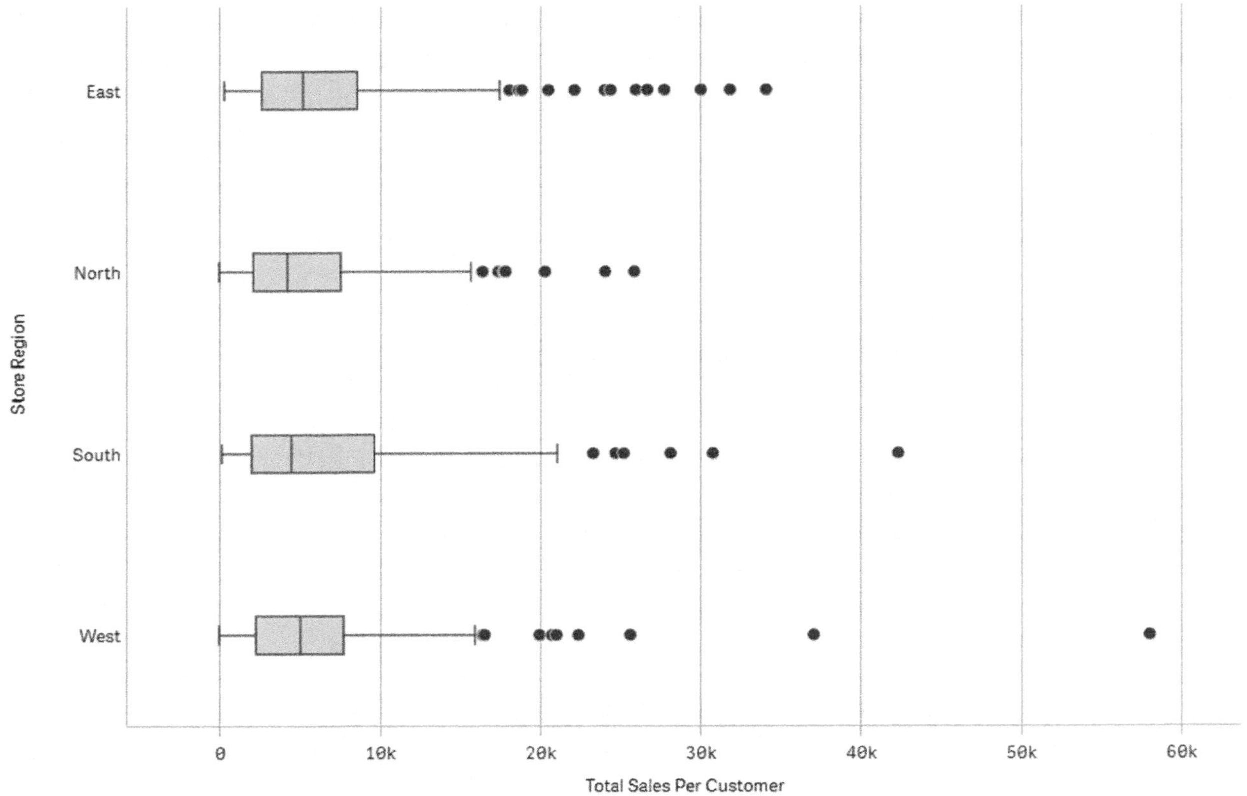

Figure 31. Distribution using a box plot

Distribution of two quantitative variables. When you want to look at a distribution when there are two quantitative variables, you can use a *scatter plot*. For example, assume you are looking at cars and want to look at the distribution of both their sticker price and their horsepower. You can plot one on each axis of the scatter plot, as shown in figure 32.

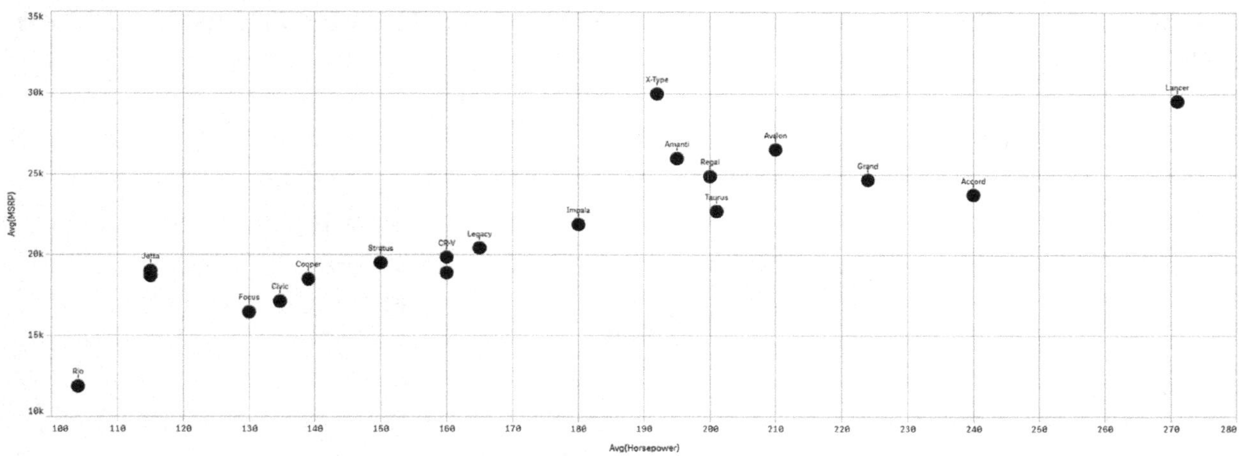

Figure 32. Distribution using a scatter plot

Distribution of one qualitative variable. When you want to look at a distribution when there is one qualitative (or categorical) variable, you can use a frequency table, bar chart, or pie chart. For example, if we are analyzing data from a retail chain with 754 stores organized into four regions, we may want to show the total number of stores per region. In this case, we will compare the regions using the count aggregation (which counts the number of items in a specific category) to show frequency in a *frequency table* and a *bar chart*, as shown in figure 33.

Store Region	Total Stores
East	185
North	189
South	188
West	192

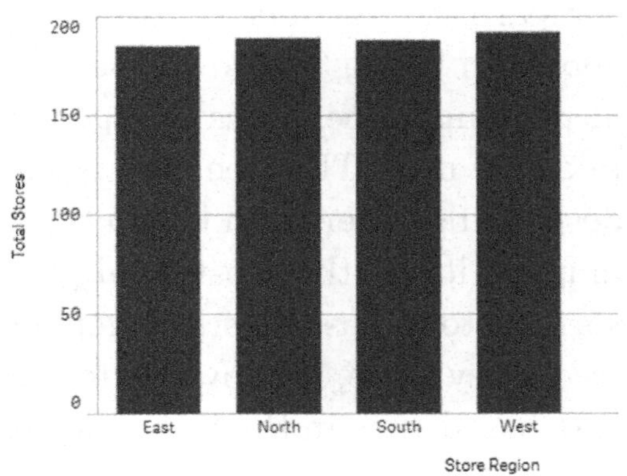

Figure 33. Distribution using a frequency table and a bar chart

If we want to show percentages, rather than frequencies, we could use a *pie chart*, as shown in figure 34.

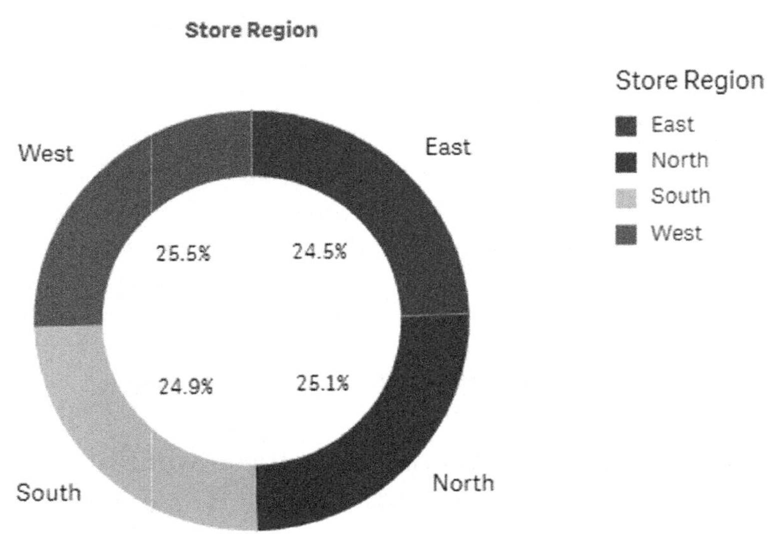

Figure 34. Distribution using a pie chart

Distribution of two or more qualitative variables. When you want to look at a distribution when there are two or more qualitative (or categorical) variables, you can use a *frequency table* or a *tree map*. For example, assume we wanted to visualize and compare the frequency of passengers on the Titanic based on their class and gender, as shown in figure 35. We can see from the frequency table on the left the total number of passengers per class and gender. The same information is visualized on the right in a tree map. The tree map is sorted to first display the total passengers per class in descending order from left to right. This is why third class is on the far left of the tree map, as it has the most total passengers. Then, within each class, the tree map will sort the total passengers by gender. While the tree map is a similar visualization to the frequency table, it allows us to visualize and compare the sizes more quickly than the text-based view in the frequency table.

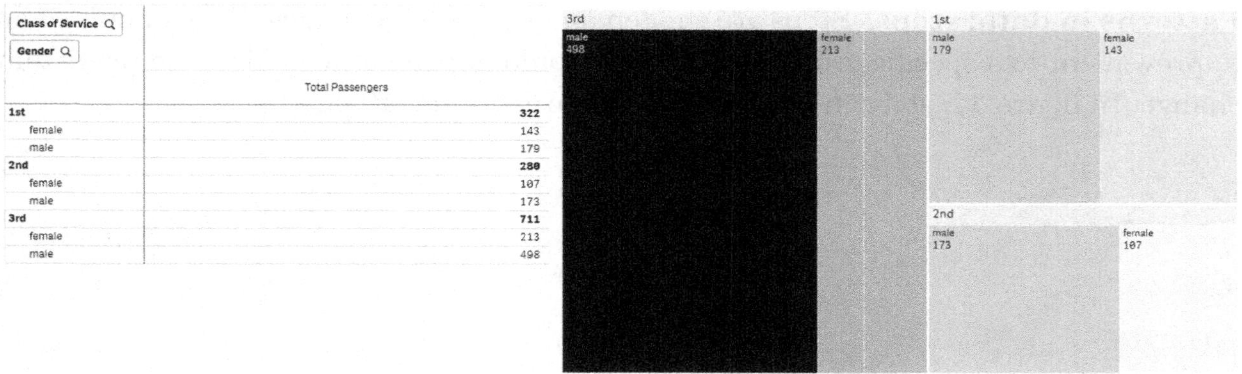

	Total Passengers
1st	**322**
female	143
male	179
2nd	**280**
female	107
male	173
3rd	**711**
female	213
male	498

Figure 35. Distribution using a frequency table and a tree map

Visualizing Patterns and Relationships

With descriptive analytics, you may want to *look for patterns in your data, visualize data across multiple dimensions,* and *look for possible relationships between variables.* When trying to visualize potential patterns and relationships within your data, there are a variety of appropriate visualizations.

If you want to visualize patterns over time, you can use a line chart. A line chart is useful in highlighting the relative changes between individual data points through the slope of the line. Patterns of change in the slope of a line can be interpreted to tell us more about the analysis. There are three main categories of patterns: *trends, steps,* and *spikes*.

Patterns in data: trends. Trends show an overall movement in one direction. The movement may have some ups and downs between individual data points, but there is an overall flow. The trends can be ascending or descending, as shown in figure 36.

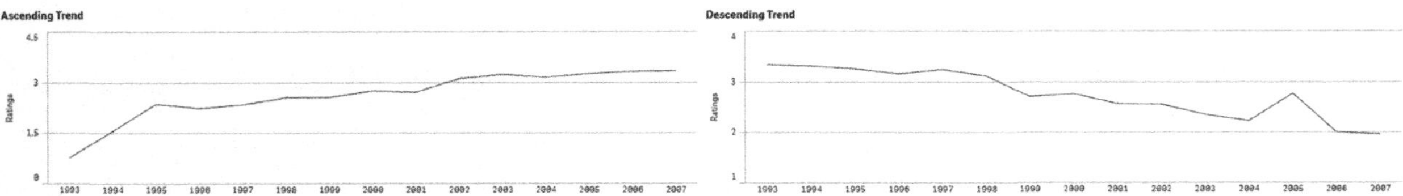

Figure 36. Visualizing trends

Patterns in data: steps. Steps are sudden and persistent changes. For example, if an improvement to a specific process is made, it would happen as a sudden and persistent change. In figure 37, you can see a step between 1998 and 1999.

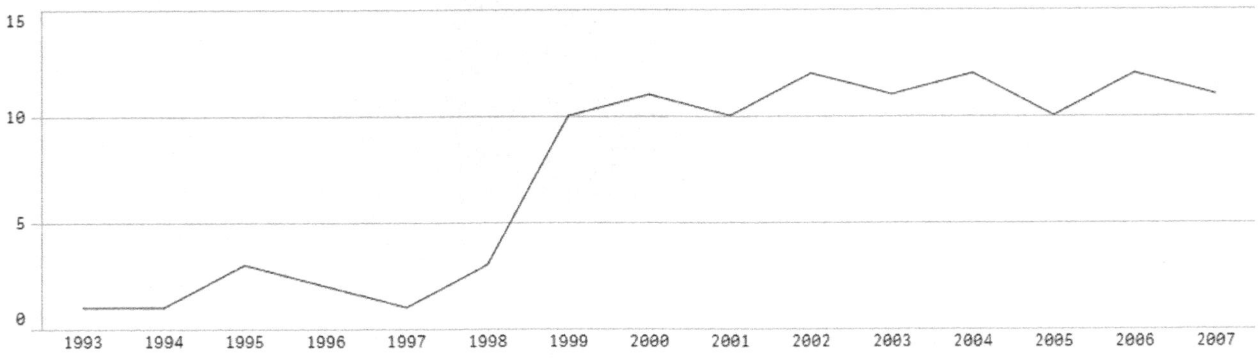

Figure 37. Visualizing steps

Patterns in data: spikes. Spikes are short-term changes. These changes can be due to a known event (imagine a sales promotion for one month impacting the sales for that month), or they can be due to unusual and unknown events, which should be further investigated. You can see a variety of spikes in figure 38, including between 1999 and 2000 and 2001 and 2002.

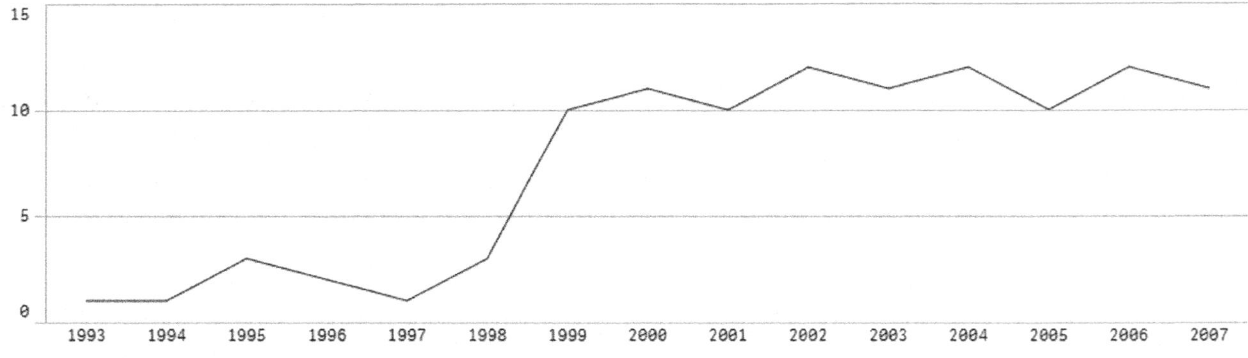

Figure 38. Visualizing spikes

Data across multiple dimensions. Line charts can also be used to visualize **aggregate data** across multiple dimensions. For example, assume we wanted to show the trends in sales over each year but broken down by the specific priority of the sales order: urgent, high, medium, low, and not specified, as shown in figure 39.

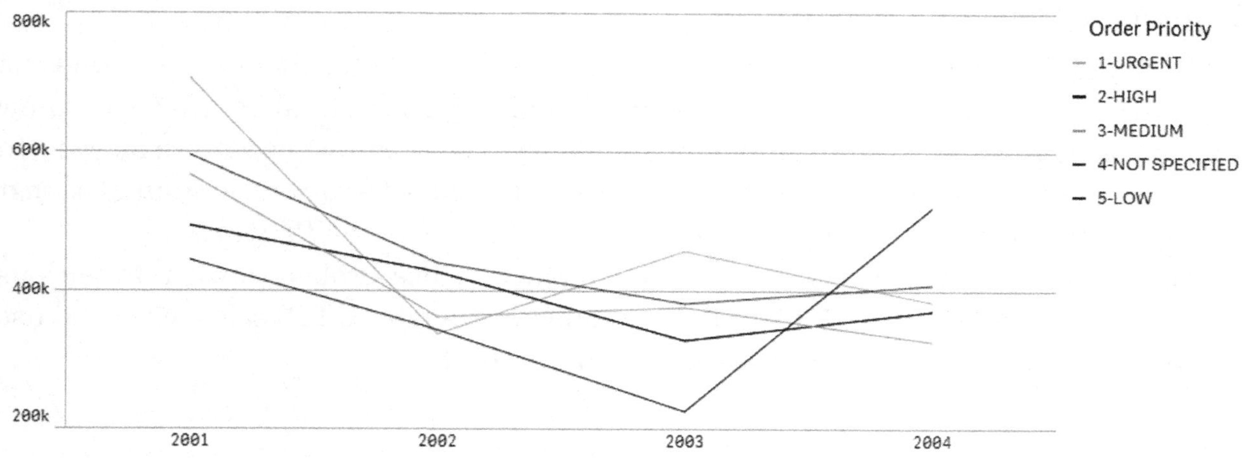

Figure 39. Visualizing data across multiple dimensions

Relationships between variables. If you would like to determine potential relationships between variables, you can plot the variables on a scatter plot. We saw an example of such a scatter plot earlier in this chapter in figure 32. Assume we are looking at cars and want to look at the relationship between a car's sticker price and its horsepower. We can plot each variable on each axis of the scatter plot to see if there is a relationship, as shown in figure 40. In this example, we can hypothesize that the higher the horsepower, the higher the sticker price. We can test this hypothesis later using diagnostic analytics or inferential statistics.

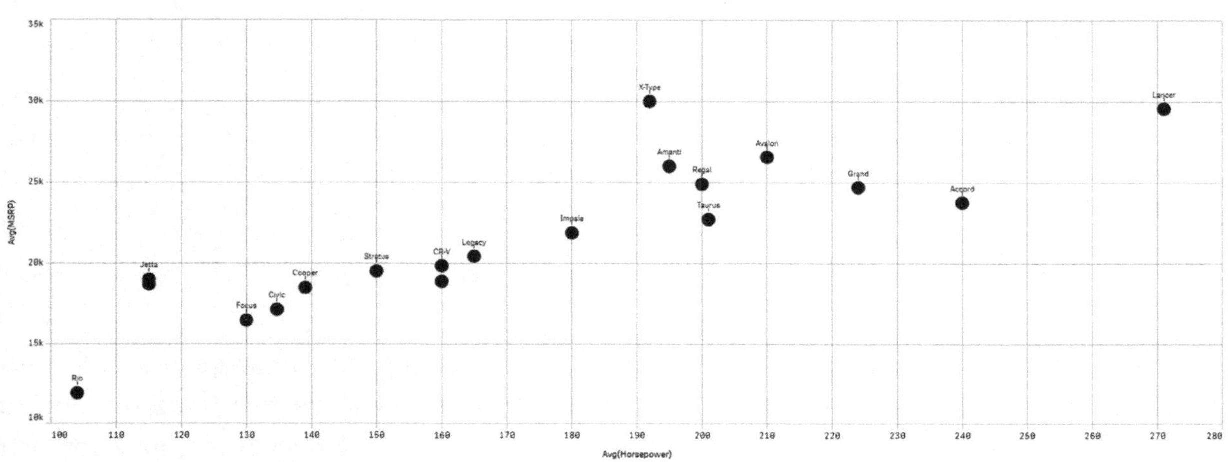

Figure 40. Visualizing relationships between variables

Visualizing Summary Measures

When trying to visualize summary measures about your data, there are a variety of appropriate visualizations. We have seen examples earlier of tables that can show various measures like mean, median, or frequency. Those can be used here as well. In addition, most software tools allow you to write out values to various measures as text to display. In some tools, they are called *text visualizations*, or *KPI charts*.

For example, if we wanted to show a company's sales broken down into various measures, like year-to-date (YTD) sales and quarter-to-date (QTD) sales, we could use a text visualization, or KPI chart, as shown in figure 41.

Brand Analysis

Sum of Total Sales	Sum of MTD Sales
$2,849,960.33	$2,849,960.33
Sum of YTD Sales	**Sum of WTD Sales**
$2,849,960.33	$2,849,960.33
Sum of QTD Sales	
$2,849,960.33	

Figure 41. Visualizing summary measures

Measures do not always have to be positive values either. Suppose we want a visualization to show the market-share movement from last year to this year, and it is down 7 percent, as shown in figure 42.

Market Share Compared to Previous Year

-7%

Figure 42. Visualizing a KPI

If you want to visualize progress toward a goal, you can use a *gauge chart*. For example, if we want to describe where we are in our progress toward hitting our quota, we can show that in a gauge chart as a percentage or as actual values, as shown in figure 43.

Figure 43. Visualizing progress toward goals

LIMITATION OF DESCRIPTIVE ANALYTICS

The limitation of descriptive analytics is that it cannot allow you to make any sort of conclusions beyond the set of data that is being analyzed. Descriptive analytics only gives you the ability to describe what is shown before you. You cannot draw any specific conclusions based on any hypothesis you have. However, you can use what you learned in this step and apply it to another analytics type, like diagnostic, inferential, or predictive, to draw conclusions. These types of analytics will be discussed later on in this chapter.

Example: Analyzing Expense Reports

A good example of where descriptive analytics is limited and where diagnostic analytics adds value would be in analyzing expense reports. Imagine you are analyzing expense reports from the past month that include the average amount of money spent on meals per night. Using just descriptive analytics, you can find patterns in the expenses, such as a small number of expense reports including much bigger or smaller expenses for meals and a large number of expense reports including the average amounts for meal expenses, as shown in figure 44.

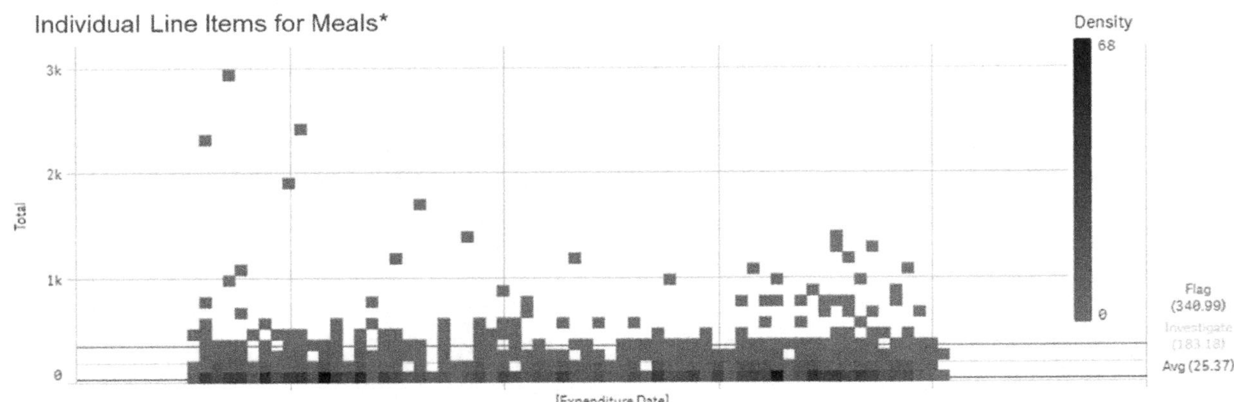

Figure 44. Expense-report analysis

Unfortunately, descriptive analysis doesn't give you the ability to go beyond this set of data. For example, you wouldn't be able to determine what the averages of the next one hundred expense reports submitted would be, and you wouldn't be able to drill down into the larger expense reports to analyze them further. For this, you would need to move up the analytics framework to diagnostic analytics.

Drilling into Data with Diagnostic Analytics

Diagnostic analytics, also called *exploratory analytics*, is an approach to analyzing data in which an individual takes a bird's-eye view of the data and tries to make some sense of it. With descriptive analytics, you are looking at key metrics of each variable of data independent of each other. With diagnostic analytics, you are looking at all of your data together to get a feel for it and then using your judgment to determine what the most important aspects of the data are and how they may relate to each other. Whereas descriptive analytics helps to answer *what* happened, diagnostic analytics starts the hypothesis into *why* it may have happened. This questioning is absolutely critical when making data-informed decisions.

Diagnostic analytics is not really a set of methods or calculations but more an approach to viewing your entire data to try to investigate outliers, patterns, and relationships. The key components of diagnostic analytics include visualizing your data in various visualizations; being able to drill down into various categories of your data; investigating patterns, anomalies, and outliers; and, finally, determining if there are any potential relationships between the variables in the data.

Let's look at a few examples of diagnostic analytics in action.

EXAMPLE: ONLINE ORDERING OF CAR PARTS

In our first example, we will look at an online company that sells car parts. The company has created a dashboard and measurement framework to allow its executives to see the values for their KPIs. As one of those indicators, the company looks at the total amount of online sales that are made for parts that are out of stock. When an order is placed with parts that are out of stock, the company needs to quickly work with its supplier to order more and then quickly ship the parts to the warehouse so that it can then fulfill the order and ship the part to the customer. This could potentially add another 5–7 days' delay to the order before the customer gets his or her parts. This is important for the company to know as customers who need replacement parts quickly may stop using the company as a vendor if the parts are routinely out of stock. However, the company has to limit its in-stock inventory to be able to keep its costs of warehousing down.

During one review of the measurement framework, the leaders of the company realize that customer purchases that are out of stock are close to 60 percent, as shown in figure 45.

Percentage of Purchases That Are Out of Stock

57.8%

Figure 45. Measurement framework – percentage of purchases out of stock

This high number causes company leaders to go from this descriptive analytic to diagnostic analytics to drill down to take a deeper look at what is driving this number. The leaders first decide to investigate which parts have the most out-of-stock orders, so they create a bar chart to visualize this, as shown in figure 46.

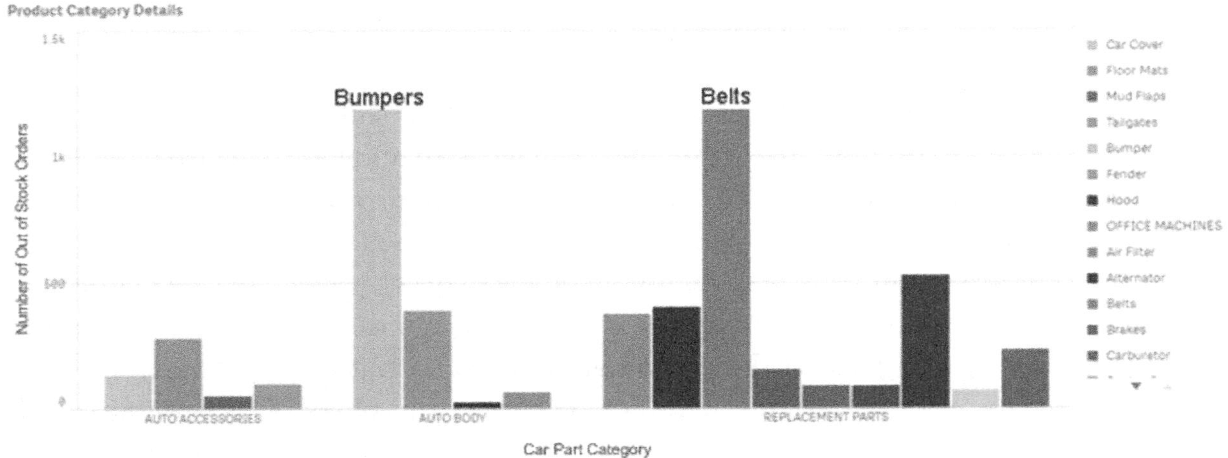

Figure 46. Out-of-stock car part categories

With this chart, they are able to see that bumpers and belts are the products having the most out-of-stock purchases. Does this information help the company leaders? Yes, but they then use their experience and highlight that those are popular items, and the total out-of-stock purchases may not be helpful without comparing that to the total purchases for those items that are in stock. Therefore, the leaders update the bar chart to visualize the percentage of orders in which the item was out of stock, as shown in figure 47.

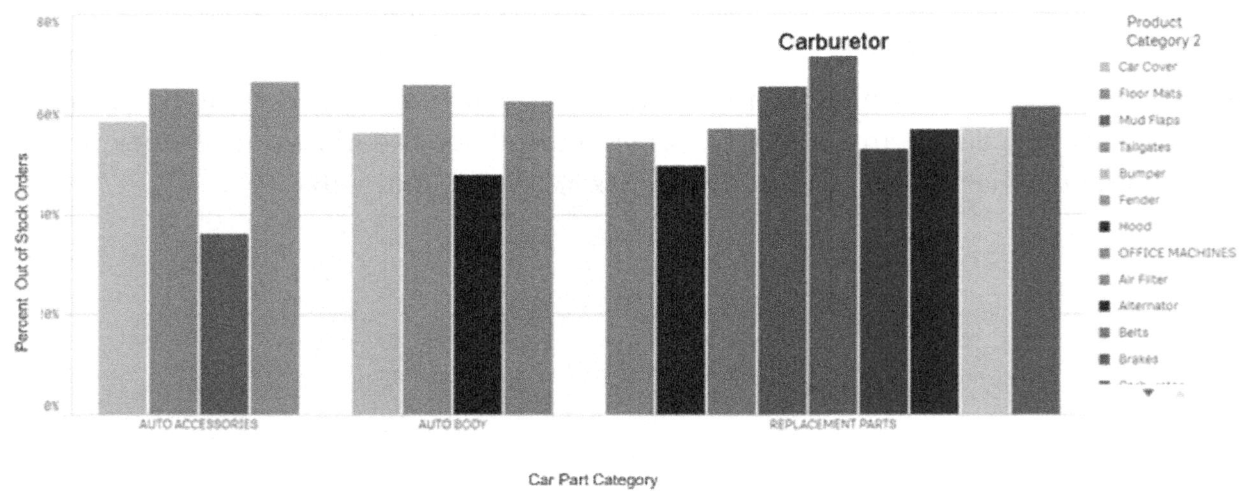

Figure 47. Percent out-of-stock car part categories

From this visualization, they can see that the item with the highest out-of-stock percentage is the carburetor. Again, the team applies their experience and highlights that carburetors, unlike some other parts, tend to be needed pretty urgently when they are ordered. Therefore, they try to test this theory out and decide to visualize the breakdown of order priorities for out-of-stock carburetor orders only, as shown in figure 48. By doing this, the team is drilling deeper into the data to try to gain more insights to make a data-informed decision.

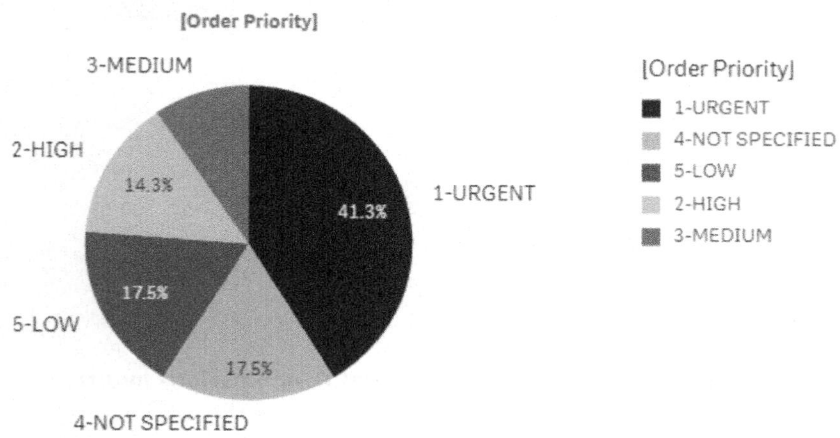

Figure 48. Order priorities

It turns out that 41.3 percent of all carburetor orders in which the item was out of stock are urgent orders. The team can then use this information to make a decision about whether or not they should keep more carburetors in stock. Of course, this is an oversimplified example, and certainly there is not just one type of carburetor that is needed for all cars—which would factor into the decision too—but you can see the value of drilling into the data to get more details beyond the measurement from the measurement framework.

EXAMPLE: A SOUP COMPANY'S LOSS OF MARKET SHARE

In our next example, we will look at a food company that sells canned soups under the name Brayden's Own. Through the company's dashboard, which uses its measurement framework, company leaders are able to see that their market share is still very high at 39.5 percent. However, the measurement framework also looks at market-share movement from a month-to-month basis, and company leaders see that this month their soup brand has dropped 10 percent in market share. In the visualization shown in figure 49, the various soup brands are displayed on the horizontal axis (sometimes called the categorical axis), and the change in market share for each soup brand is depicted as its own bar on the vertical axis (sometimes called the value axis).

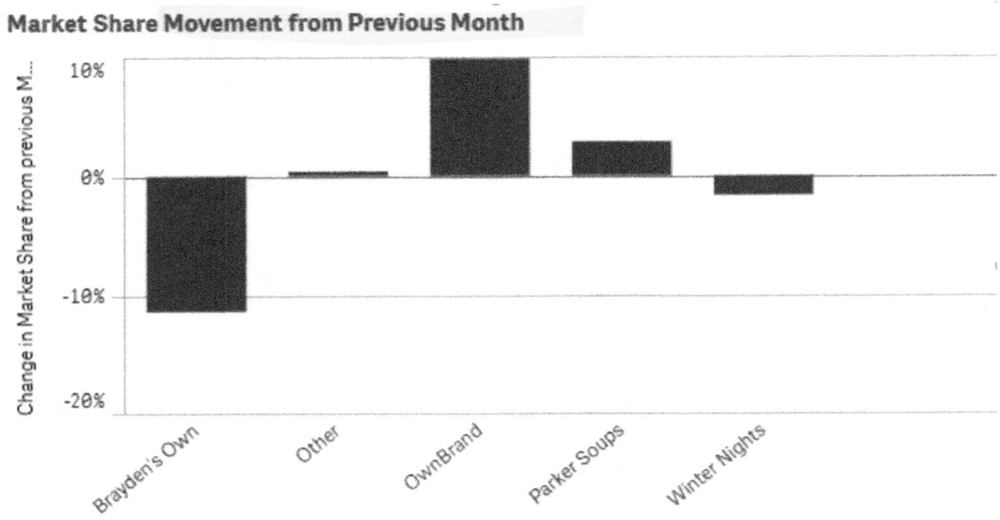

Figure 49. Market-share movement from previous month

Company leaders would like to drill down and understand this drop in more detail. They know from previous meetings that this loss of market share has not happened before, so this is not part of an existing downward trend. They do sell their soup through a variety of channels, so they decide to look at the market-share movement from the previous month to see if any channels stick out, as shown in figure 50.

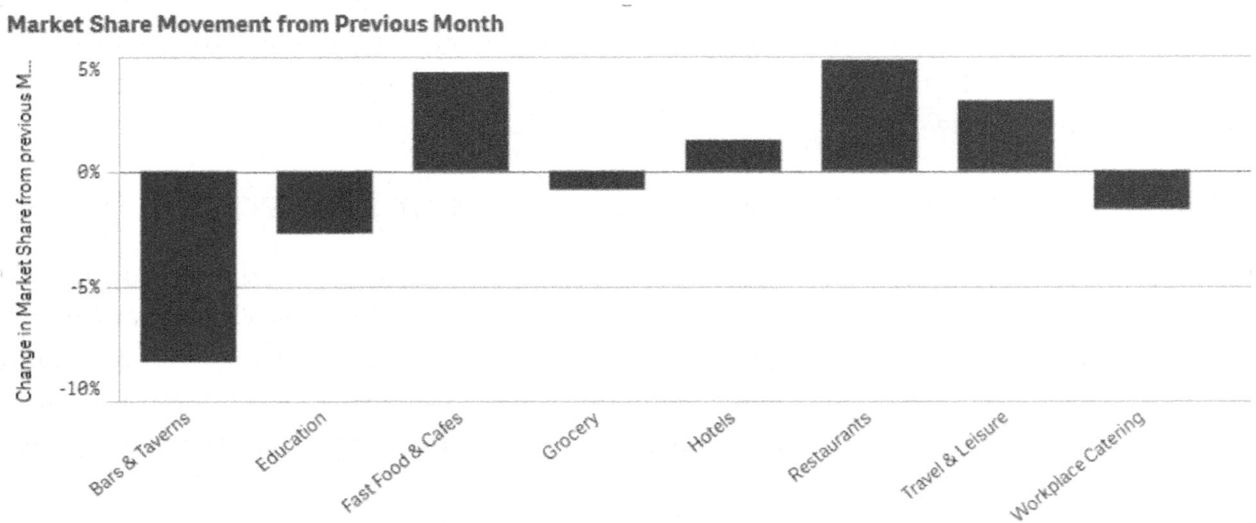

Figure 50. Market-share movement from previous month by channel

Sure enough, the leaders are able to see that the biggest drop in market share came via the Bars & Taverns channel. At this point, they decide to bring in the person responsible for that channel to ask more-specific questions about what is happening and to understand why the drop happened. In this example, just like in the previous car-parts example, diagnostic analytics was used to help make a data-informed decision. In this specific soups example, diagnostic analytics did not provide an answer to why the market share was declining, but it did provide insights into where to investigate further.

Inferring from Samples of Data Using Inferential Statistics

While descriptive and diagnostic analytics describe the data and start to create a hypothesis into why something is happening, it is not always sufficient to draw conclusions and make decisions from them, especially when you are analyzing a sampling of data. **Inferential statistics** allows you to use subsets of an entire population to make generalizations and predictions from them, including forecasts and estimates.

While there are many software tools out there that will help users perform inferential statistics, this skill is not for everyone. This is one of the skills for which an organization should rely on a trained resource to accomplish. The purpose of this section is to highlight that these capabilities exist and how they can be used to improve decision-making. We will not be discussing the mathematics behind each of the capabilities mentioned.

INFERENTIAL STATISTICS VERSUS DESCRIPTIVE ANALYTICS

Let's look at some examples highlighting the different outcomes you can gain from descriptive analytics and inferential statistics.

- **Golfers.** Golfers would use descriptive analytics to find their average score for the past twelve months. They would use inferential statistics to estimate their chance of winning a match based on their current season average and the average of their opponents.

- **Retail stores.** Retail stores would use descriptive analytics to determine the average weekly sales of a given product. They would use inferential statistics to predict, based on last year's sales, the forecasted amount of sales this year for the same product.

- **Politicians.** Politicians would use descriptive analytics to know the number of votes they received from each district during an election. They would use inferential statistics to estimate their chance of winning the election based on exit polling.

INFERENTIAL STATISTICS TERMINOLOGY

Before we go any further into inferential statistics, let's look at some related terminology.

Variable. A variable is a characteristic, number, or quantity that can be measured. In a general sense, it can be seen as a column of data.

Dependent and independent variables. A dependent variable is a variable that depends on the values of the independent variable. The dependent variable represents the output or outcome. Typically, it is the dependent variable that is being studied in inferential statistics to see if the independent variable causes an effect on it. For example, say we want to see if there is a relationship between marketing spend and sales revenue. In this test, the independent variable is the marketing spend, and we want to see what impact it has on the dependent variable, which is the sales revenue.

Population. A population is the entire pool from which a sample is drawn. Samples are used in statistics because of how difficult it can be to study an entire population.

Sample. A sample is a subset of the population we care about. For example, it may not be possible to survey every single customer from a retail store, so the retail store would survey a sample. The population would be all customers from that retail store.

Significance level. Significance level is a decision criterion that specifies the degree of certainty with which you want to make your judgment.

Statistically significant. A statistically significant result is one that cannot be explained by chance or random error.

Binary. A binary variable is a variable that can only have two values—for example, a variable that has the values true or false.

Normal distribution. Data can be distributed in many ways. When the distribution of data is around the central value (mean, median, or mode), with 50 percent of the data below the central value and 50 percent above the central value, it is said to be normally distributed. Normal distributions allow statisticians to make inferences about the data with a high degree of probability, so understanding if the data is normally distributed is a critically important part of inferential statistics.

TYPES OF INFERENTIAL STATISTICS

In general, there are three reasons to use inferential statistics, as shown in figure 51:

1. To *review the relationship* between two variables within your data—for example, to see if there is a relationship between the amount of marketing spend and sales revenue
2. To *compare means* between two samples of your data—for example, to see if there is a **statistically significant** difference in sales revenue between two locations
3. To *compare proportions*—for example, to see if there is a statistically significant difference in buying habits between two separate cities, based on a random survey of citizens of each city

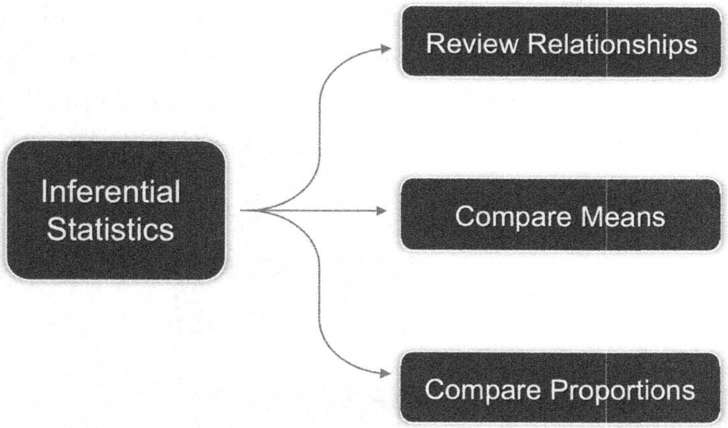

Figure 51. Reasons to use inferential statistics

In this book, we will focus on using inferential statistics to *review the relationship between variables* and to *compare means.*

Reviewing Relationships between Variables

When you are trying to review a relationship between two variables, depending on the type of data for each variable, there are a variety of methods you can use:

- **Two categorical variables.** When looking at relationships between two **categorical** variables (nonnumerical data for which the values can be one of several categories), *chi-square* can be used to calculate whether or not those variables are related to or independent of each other—for example, to see if there is a relationship between product preference and region.

- **Two continuous variables.** When looking at relationships between two **continuous** variables (numeric variables that are not confined to specific values), you can use *correlation* and a type of regression called *linear regression.* Correlation will tell you if there is a relationship between two continuous variables. If there is, you can then use linear regression to predict values for one variable based on the other. For example, correlation can be used to see if there is a relationship between sales revenue and marketing spend. If a relationship exists, linear regression can be used to predict the value of sales revenue based on marketing spend.

- **One binary and one continuous variable.** When one variable is **binary**, meaning it only has two values, and the other variable is continuous, you can use another form of regression called *logistic regression*—for example, to see if there is a relationship between whether someone logged into a product in the past ninety days and whether or not the person renews her or his subscription for that product.

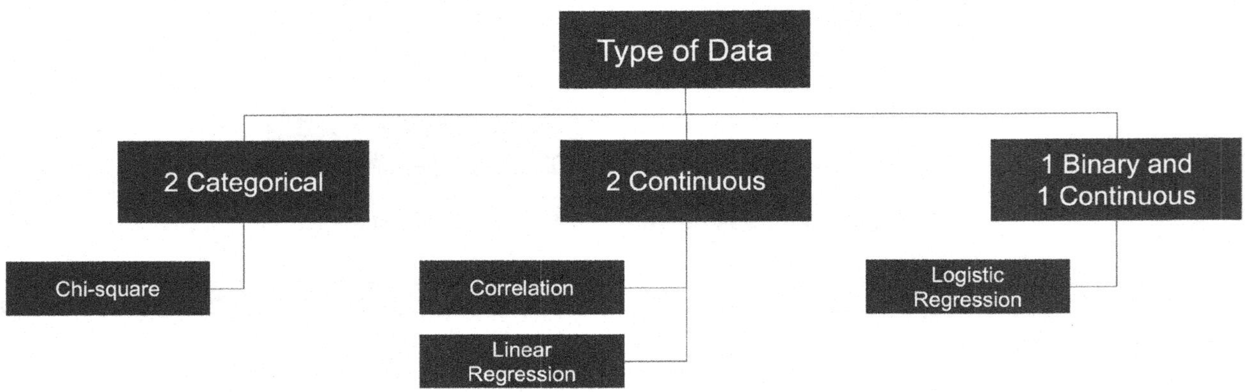

Figure 52. Methods for determining relationships between variables

CHI-SQUARE (RELATIONSHIPS BETWEEN TWO CATEGORICAL VARIABLES)

Let's look at an example of a *chi-square* test. There are actually many tests that fall under the chi-square umbrella. The specific one we will look at is called the chi-square test of independence. Suppose a sales manager wants to know if certain types of a new product brand will sell better in certain locations. To help answer this question, the company surveys three hundred of its existing customers, who are split between the two store locations, and asks them their preference between two product brands.

A table can be used to show the data (see figure 53).

Location	Product Brand	
	A	B
Totals	**90**	**210**
1	40	90
2	50	120

Figure 53. Sales by product and location

By viewing this table, we can see that preferences for Product Brands A and B vary between Location 1 and Location 2. While the table makes it appear that there is a difference between preferences of the two products and locations, this could just be pure coincidence. If you plan on making decisions based on this assumption, this is when you should definitely use inferential statistics. The chi-square test will help to determine if the variation is due to random chance or if there really is a relationship between the variables. If there is a high probability that these results were due to random chance and the organization does not use inferential statistics and makes a Type 1 (irreversible) decision, this decision will likely end up hurting the organization. For example, maybe the company decides to increase inventory of the product at the store where it seems to be preferred more, but this ends up not being a reality. Instead, this decision causes the company to overstock an item that doesn't sell out, which adds overhead costs and negatively impacts the company's profits.

In another example, that same organization may want to look at whether gender plays a part in the purchasing decision for Products A and B. Therefore, they'd be comparing the two categorical variables of products and gender, as opposed to products and location. (Remember, **categorical data** is nonnumerical data for which the values can be one of several categories.)

The chi-square test is typically calculated using a data or analytics software program as the formula is rather complex to calculate manually. We will not cover the calculations in this book.

CORRELATION AND REGRESSION (RELATIONSHIPS BETWEEN TWO CONTINUOUS VARIABLES)

When looking at a relationship between two continuous variables (numeric variables that are not confined to specific values), you will want to determine if there is a correlation. A *correlation* is a relationship between two variables. Let's take a look at an example. Suppose our organization wants to determine if there is a positive correlation between marketing spend in a given month and sales revenue. To determine this, we first need to have a hypothesis as to which variable depends on the other. In our example, we may believe that sales revenue depends on marketing spend. This means that the sales revenue is the **dependent variable**, and the marketing spend is the **independent variable**.

The correlation statistical test will return something called a correlation coefficient. The value for this correlation coefficient will be between -1 and 1. A value closer to -1 will be a negative correlation, and a value closer to 1 will be a positive correlation. A negative correlation means that there is a negative relationship between the two variables. In our example, that would mean that as marketing spend increases, sales revenue would decrease, and as marketing spend decreases, sales revenue would increase. A positive correlation means that there is a positive relationship between the two variables. In our example, that would mean that as marketing spend increases or decreases, sales revenue would increase or decrease with it. The closer the value is to -1 or 1, the stronger the correlation. The closer the results are to 0, the weaker the correlation. In our example, the correlation coefficient returned is 0.94 (figure 54). This tells us there is a strong positive correlation between marketing spend and sales revenue.

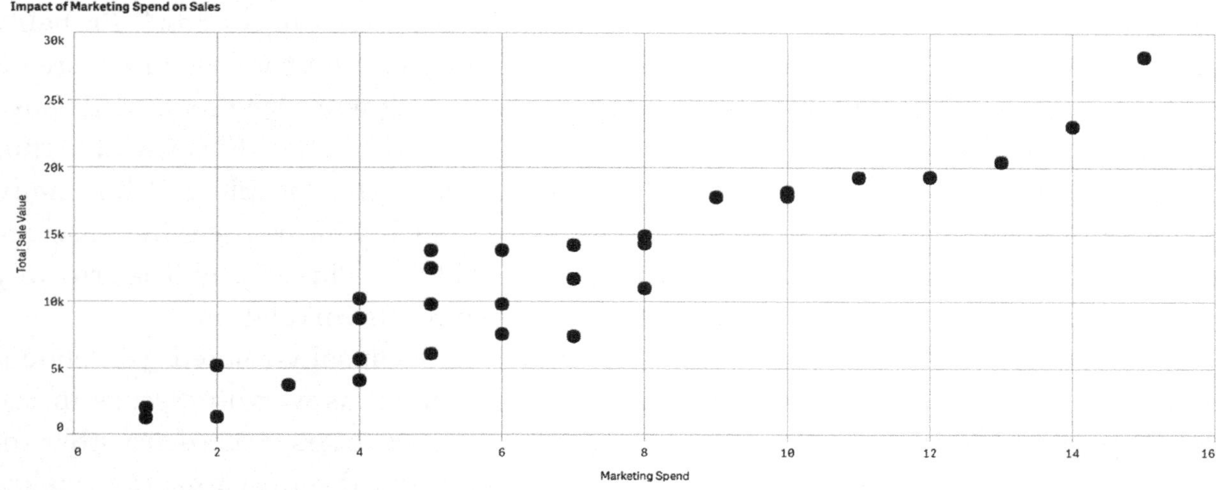

Correlation Coefficient

0.94

Figure 54. Positive correlation

Once you have defined a strong correlation, you can then do things like predictions. In our example, suppose we want to predict what the sales revenue would be if we spent even more on marketing than we did before. For this, we can use what is called a *regression model.* A regression model is a statistical approach used to investigate the relationship between two or more variables and to predict future values of the **dependent variable**. When the two variables are continuous (quantitative data that is not confined to specific values), the type of regression model used is called a *linear regression.*

Correlation does not imply causation. As part of your analysis, you should make sure you understand the difference between a correlation and a causation. If your two variables have a *correlation*, it means they have a relationship. This does not necessarily mean that one variable causes the other variable to happen. When one variable causes the other, that is called *causation*, and it is said that those variables are causally related. When it is determined that two variables are related but one does not cause the other, it is called a *spurious correlation*. This could be the case if the relationship is due to coincidence or if there is another variable that is truly the causal variable for both variables. For example, over the past ten years, the price of your product has increased. So, too, has the number of subscribers to your product. Does that mean that if you increase your prices even more, you will get more subscribers? Probably not. In another example, assume there is a correlation between the sale of ice cream and the number of drownings. Does this mean that selling more ice cream will cause more people to drown? Not likely. In this case, there is most likely a third variable that is impacting both—the temperature. If the weather is hotter, people will buy more ice cream and will also want to go swimming more, which will, in turn, increase the number of drownings compared to drownings on a cold day. This is why it is critically important to find the root cause and to not act on a spurious correlation.

To ensure that your correlated variables are actually causally related, you should apply your experiences and common sense to the problem, as we will discuss in the next chapter. In addition, you should test multiple variables to see if there are other relationships that could be causing the correlation to appear. If an organization makes a decision and acts on a spurious correlation, especially with Type 1 decisions that are hard to turn around, the organization may suffer disastrous consequences.

LOGISTIC REGRESSION (RELATIONSHIPS BETWEEN ONE BINARY AND ONE CONTINUOUS VARIABLE)

If the dependent variable is binary (meaning it has only two possible values) and the independent variable is continuous (a numeric variable that is not confined to a specific value), you can use *logistic regression* to perform predictions. For example, a bank may want to predict if its customers would default on their loans. To predict this binary outcome of yes or no, the model will include some predictor variables regarding the loan that the bank thinks would impact whether a customer would default. These predictor variables help model the probability of the loan default.

For example, some potential predictor variables for this example could include personal details such as the customer's age, employment status, and income. It could also include credit history like the number and value of past loans, including whether any were delinquent, and behavioral data around spending patterns and repayment patterns. The logistic regression model will take all that information as input and then predict whether the potential borrower would default or not on the loan if approved, as shown in figure 55.

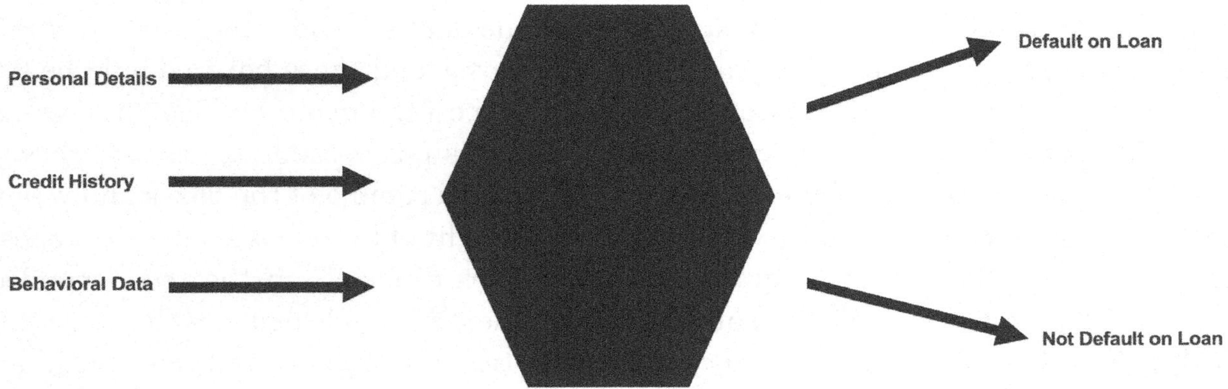

Figure 55. Sample logistic-regression model

Comparing Means

There are many cases in decision-making for which you will want to compare means for two populations or samples, or potentially the same sample at different times. You may want to look at the results of a change in process from before to after; compare if your new sales employees are hitting the right target of sales revenue; or look at whether two separate locations have statistically significant differences in sales. You can always review the differences in a table, but to do this properly in order to make a decision, you will need to determine by using statistical tests whether there was a statistically significant change. **Statistically significant** is a determination that the statistical results cannot be explained by chance or random error.

Comparing means is typically done using a statistical test called a *t-test*, but the exact technique you use depends on what type of data you have, whether the data is normally distributed, and how that data is grouped together. You will notice that one criterion is whether the data is **normally distributed**. This is why it is critically important as part of descriptive analytics to understand the data and how it is distributed. If your data has lots of outliers, it will not be normally distributed, and many of these tests cannot be used. To review distribution, read the "Organizing the Data" section earlier in this chapter.

The four major ways of comparing means from data that is assumed to be normally distributed are a *one-sample t-test*, a *paired-samples t-test*, an *independent-samples t-test*, and *ANOVA*.

One-sample t-test. Let's start by looking at a *one-sample t-test*. You would choose this test when you want to compare means between one data set and a specified constant. For example, suppose a manufacturer is making boxes and those boxes should be 0.9 pounds in weight. It is common to test boxes coming off the manufacturing line to ensure that they conform to the specifications, but it is not possible to test every box. Enter one-sample t-tests. The manufacturer can take a sample of the boxes and weigh them. The manufacturer can then take the mean weight of those boxes and use a t-test to see whether that mean weight from the samples differs from the recommended weight (0.9 pounds) with 95 percent confidence. The 0.9 pounds figure is the constant. If the t-test determines the difference to be statistically insignificant, then the manufacturer can safely assume, with 95 percent confidence, that the manufacturing equipment is working properly. If the difference is determined to be statistically significant (not explained by chance or random error), then the manufacturer can safely assume, with 95 percent confidence, that the manufacturing equipment is not working properly.

Paired-samples t-test. If you are not comparing the mean against a constant but are having one group tested at two different times, you would want to use a *paired-samples t-test*. In other words, you have two measurements on the same item, person, or thing. The groups are "paired" because of the intrinsic connections between them, meaning they are not independent—for example, comparing a company's customer-satisfaction score before and after a change in process was made.

Independent-samples t-test. If you want to compare the means of two independent sets of data, you would use the *independent-samples t-test*. For example, you would use this test if you want to compare the sales from one store location to the sales from another one.

ANOVA. A statistical test called *ANOVA*, short for analysis of variance, is the best option when you have more than two levels of an independent variable. For example, if your independent variable is "average annual per capita sales" of your product and your data contains three regions (America, Europe, and Asia), with ANOVA, you can test to see if there is a statistically significant difference in average annual per capita sales between the regions.

If your data is not normally distributed or if you do not know how your data is distributed, you can't use any of the tests just mentioned for the comparison of means.

Instead, you must use what is called a *nonparametric test*. With nonparametric tests, there is no need for the distribution to be normally distributed. For independent samples, use the *Mann-Whitney U test*. For paired groups, use the *Wilcoxon signed-rank test*. For tests of more than two levels of independent variables, use the *Kruskal-Wallis test* rather than ANOVA.

Whereas inferential statistics is useful for decision-makers to make inferences from samples of data, it is not typically used for making predictions. If you are trying to make future predictions from your data, you will want to leverage predictive analytics.

Predicting Future Actions by Leveraging Predictive Analytics

Our next group of analytics is predictive analytics. **Predictive analytics** is the study of data from the past to predict behavior for the future. It uses a combination of several different techniques and models to understand the existing data and to make future predictions. A predictive analytics model is a mathematical model that captures some important trends found in historical data. The predictive analytics will then apply that model to current data to predict what will happen. Sometimes, the event of interest will be in the future, but predictive analytics doesn't have limitations, and it can be implemented for any type of unknown in the past, present, or future—for example, for detecting fraud before it happens. Predictive analytics helps an organization become proactive, which enables the organization to make decisions based on the data and not on a hunch.

TYPES OF PREDICTIVE ANALYTICS

There are so many different types of predictive analytics techniques. In this book, we will focus on the ones that are most commonly used by businesses to make decisions: *linear programming, break-even analysis, crossover analysis, cluster analysis, simulations, decision trees, Markov analysis,* and *sentiment analysis*. The scope is not to teach you how to implement these approaches but rather to make you aware of what they are and when to use them. These are techniques that you would need a data scientist to implement or a software product to abstract the complexities.

Linear Programming

Linear programming, also called *linear optimization*, are models to help optimize a given variable—for example, to find the shortest path from one building to another; to figure out an investment strategy to maximize profit; or to determine a schedule that includes all your work, family events, and hobbies. In all of these examples, there is a decision to make, whether it is a path, a strategy, or a schedule, and there are different ways to make that decision. In this case, we are looking for the shortest path, a strategy to maximize profits, or the most efficient schedule.

Let's look at one example in more detail. Let's assume you work for a company that produces electronics like phones and tablets. The company can make from thirty to sixty phones per day and twenty to forty tablets. It can make at most eighty total units in one day. These restrictions, or limitations, are called constraints. The profit on a phone is $100, and the profit on a tablet is $175. Linear programming can help you determine the optimal mix of phone and tablet production to maximize profit.

Figure 56 highlights what a visualization might look like as part of an analysis using linear programming. The visualization draws one line for each constraint. The shaded region is called the feasible region, and any number of tablets and phones within that region is a feasible solution. The point at which both lines intersect is considered the optimal point, or optimal solution.

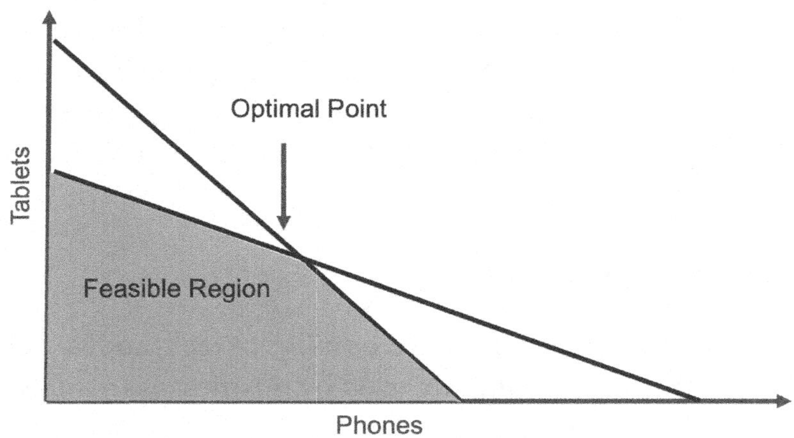

Figure 56. Linear programming

Break-Even Analysis

Break-even analysis is a modeling technique used for profitability analysis to choose the point for both units of something produced and sold at which the total cost and total revenue are equal, or breakeven.

Let's take a look at an example shown in figure 57. Suppose you are thinking about starting a new company to produce coffee pods for individual coffee-maker machines. The initial investment in the company for equipment and a workspace is $50,000. The labor and material costs are $3 per pack of forty-eight coffee pods. Assuming you are selling each pack of coffee pods at a price of $15 per pack, break-even analysis can be used to determine what volume of demand is necessary to break even.

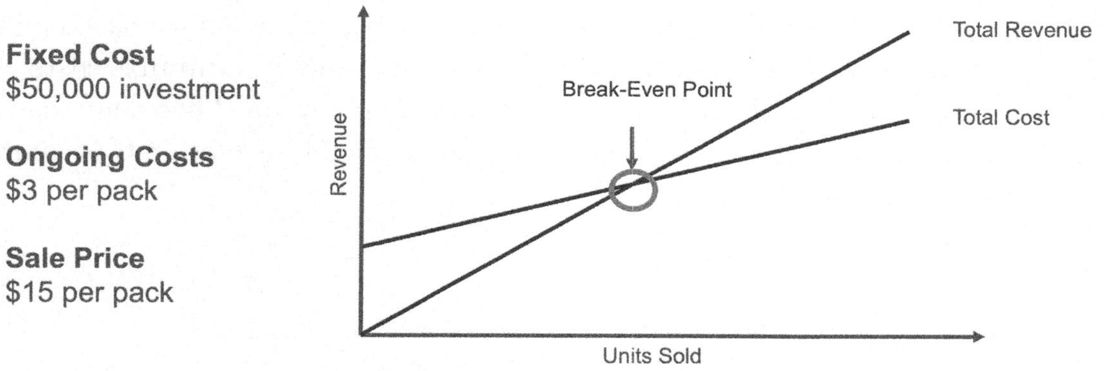

Figure 57. Break-even analysis

Crossover Analysis

Crossover analysis is similar to break-even analysis except you are not calculating a volume at which you are profitable but are choosing an option from multiple options that will influence some output, like minimizing cost or maximizing profit. Whereas break-even analysis will provide you a single answer as to when you are breaking even, crossover analysis will take into account multiple options and calculate which one will provide you with the lowest cost.

To follow on the example from break-even analysis, assume your new company has a few options in how it will manufacture coffee pods. Some of the equipment is faster than others, but it's more expensive, and each piece of equipment also requires differently sourced materials to build the pods. Therefore, each of the three options has separate fixed costs (machines) and variable costs (materials to build the pods), as shown in table 4.

Table 4. Crossover analysis

	OPTION A	OPTION B	OPTION C
Fixed costs	$45,000	$90,000	$200,000
Variable costs (cost per case of pods)	$8.00	$7.00	$5.50

Option A has the lowest fixed costs but the highest variable cost, and Option C has the highest fixed cost but the lowest variable cost. There is a decision to be made about which option to choose. Crossover analysis can be used to help you minimize cost. You can see in figure 58 that the lowest-cost process changes depending on the volume of pods produced. As a result, the decision made would need to factor in sales projections, as a different option would be selected depending on the volume of sales expected. The vertical lines on the chart indicate where the preferred option changes based on units sold. To the left of the first vertical line, Option A is the choice to minimize costs. When enough units are sold to reach the first vertical line, then Option B becomes the choice to minimize costs. Finally, to the right of the second vertical line, Option C becomes the choice to minimize costs.

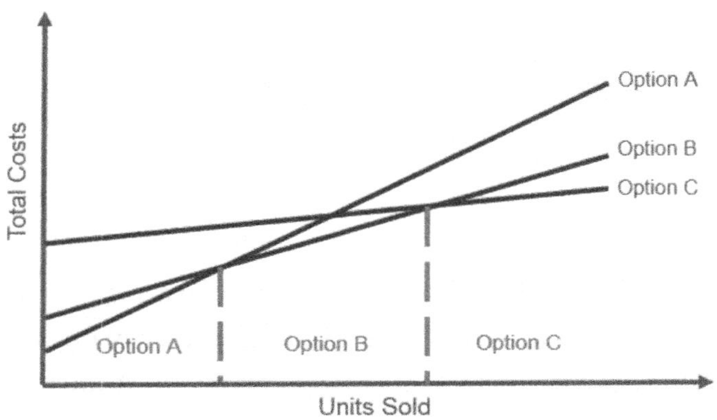

Figure 58. Crossover analysis

Cluster Analysis

Cluster analysis is the task of grouping a set of objects in such a way that objects in the same group, called a cluster, are more similar to each other than to those in other clusters.

Let's look at a few use cases. An insurance company will use cluster analysis to identify groups of auto insurance holders with a high average claim cost. A city planning or real estate company can use cluster analysis to identify groups of houses according to their house type, value, and geographical location. Clustering can be based on geography too. Surveyors can use cluster analysis to identify areas of similar land use. An online retailer can use cluster analysis to recommend similar products to what the online purchaser is considering purchasing. In figure 59, a marketing department is trying to segment its customers into six clusters based on how recently they have made a purchase and the value of their purchase. Each cluster is given its own color. The department can use cluster analysis to help discover those six distinct groups in its customer base and then use this knowledge to develop targeted marketing programs for each of the groups.

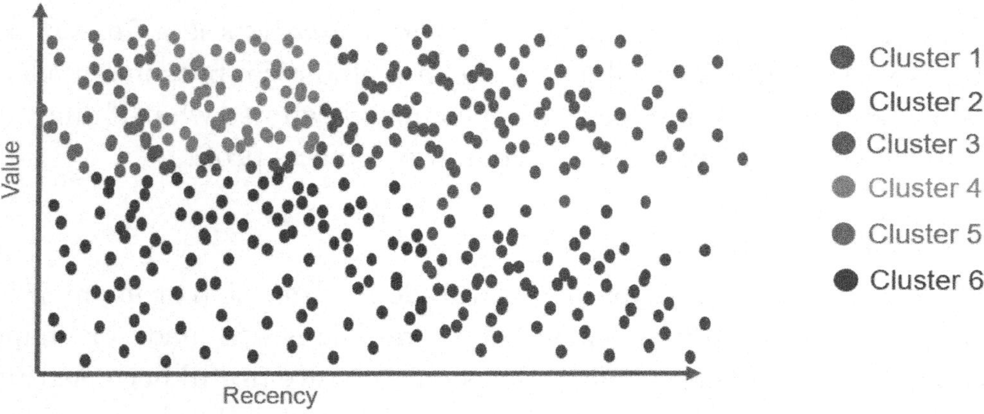

Figure 59. Clustering

Simulations

Simulations are used by decision-makers to provide potential solutions to complex problems. A *simulation* is basically an imitation—a model that imitates a real-world process or system. In business, decision-makers are often concerned with the operating characteristics of a system. One way to measure or assess the operating characteristics of a system is to observe that system in actual operation. However, in many types of situations, the cost of direct observation can be very high. Also, changing some of the relationships or parameters within a system on an experimental basis may mean waiting a considerable amount of time to collect results on all the combinations that are of concern to the decision-maker.

In business, a simulation is a mathematical imitation of a real-world system. A simulation can also be considered to be an experimental process. In a set of experimental runs, the decision-maker actively varies some of the parameters or relationships in the system, playing a "what-if" scenario. If the mathematical model behind the simulation is valid, the results of the simulation runs will imitate the results of the real system if it were to operate over some period of time.

Let's look at an example. Suppose a food truck earns an average of $300 in profit per day, but the food-truck owner expects daily sales to vary somewhat. All the food that doesn't sell spoils and is a complete loss. Using a simulation, the food-truck owner could study the effects of various business decisions based on the performance of a key metric, like daily profit. For example, the owner could test the profit impact of the decision to start each day with a lower inventory of food. It could be that the owner could make higher profits with a smaller inventory, even though he may run out of inventory some days.

There are multiple types of simulations. *What-if analysis* is a form of simulation that involves selecting different values for the probabilistic inputs in a model and then computing possible outputs. For example, a company can use what-if analysis to alter a variable, like demand of a product, to see how it impacts profit.

Decision Trees

A *decision tree* is a pictorial description of a well-defined decision problem. It is a graphical representation consisting of nodes (where decisions are made or chance events occur) and arcs (which connect nodes). Decision trees are useful because they provide a clear, documentable, and discussible model of either how the decision was made or how it will be made.

The tree provides a framework for the calculation of the expected value of each available alternative. The alternative with the maximum expected value is the best-choice path based on the information and mindset of the decision-makers at the time the decision is made. This best-choice path indicates the best overall alternative, including the best decisions at future decision steps, when uncertainties have been resolved.

Here is an example. A real estate company is faced with a choice of three possible decisions:

1. **Option A—a large investment to improve existing buildings.**
   This option could produce a substantial payoff in terms of increased revenue, but it will require an investment of $1 million. After extensive market research, it is believed there is a 40 percent chance that a payoff of $2.5 million will be obtained, but there is a 60 percent chance that it will only be $750,000.

2. **Option B—a smaller-scale project to redecorate existing buildings.**
   At $300,000, this option is less costly, but it will produce a lower payoff. Research data suggests a 30 percent chance of a gain of $1 million but a 70 percent chance of it being only $300,000.

3. **Option C—continue the present operation without change.**
   This option will cost nothing, but it also will not produce any payoff. Existing building clients will not be happy, and it will become harder and harder to rent the spaces out when they become free.

A decision tree, as shown in figure 60, can be used to visualize the decision steps to ultimately get to a decision—in this case, which option should the real estate company decide to implement?

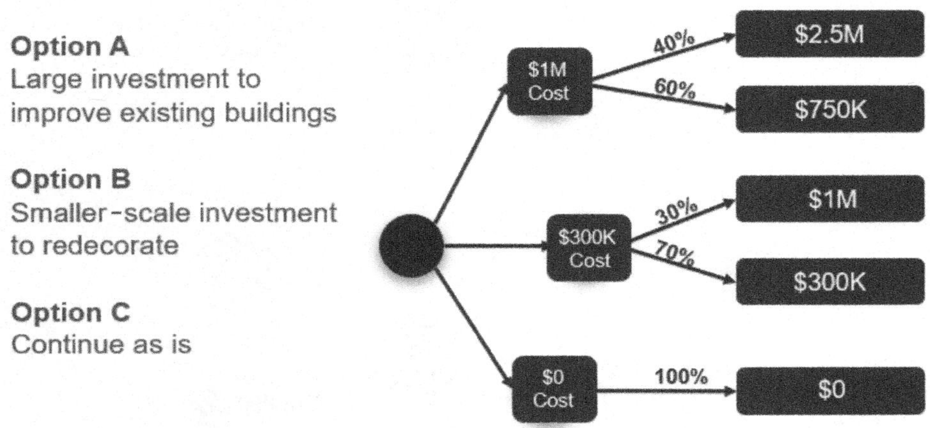

Figure 60. Decision tree

Markov Analysis

Markov analysis is a technique that determines the probability of future occurrences of an event by analyzing presently known probabilities of those events. The Markov analysis process involves defining the likelihood of a future action, given the current state of a variable. Once the probabilities of future actions at each state are defined, a decision tree can be drawn and the probability of a result can be calculated, given the current state of a variable. Markov analysis has a number of applications in business to help companies make data-informed decisions. For example, a company that makes coffee currently has 25 percent of the market. Data from the previous year indicates that 89 percent of its customers remained loyal that year, but 11 percent switched to a competitor. Also, 85 percent of that competitor's customers remained loyal, but 15 percent of the competition's customers switched to this company. With the assumption that the trend continues, Markov analysis can help determine the company's share of the market in the future.

Another example of Markov analysis's use, as shown in figure 61, is to predict the number of defective pieces that will come off of an assembly line, given the operating status of the machines on the line. The 1s represent a defect, and the 0s represent no defect. The numbers shown next to each are the probabilities.

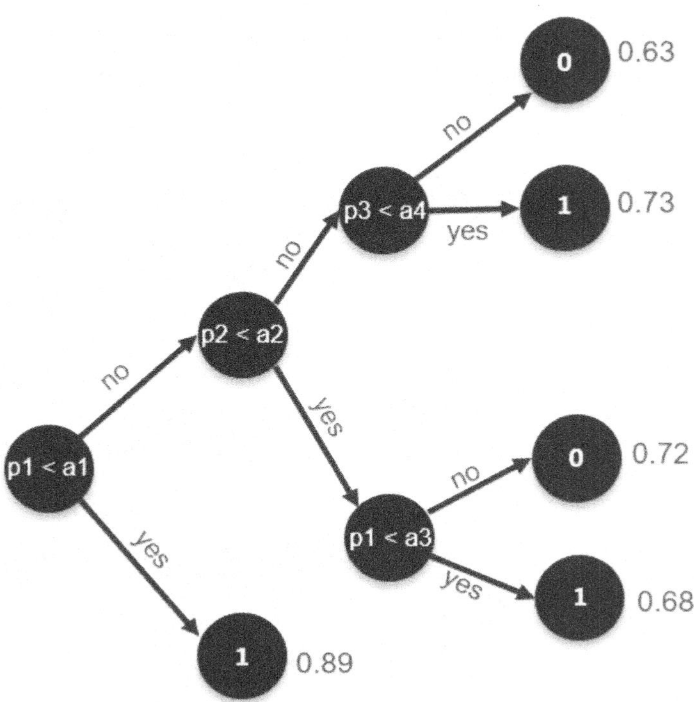

Figure 61. Markov analysis

Markov analysis may also be used by companies to predict the proportion of their accounts receivables that will become bad debts. Certain stock-price and option-price forecasting methods also incorporate Markov analysis. In addition, companies often use it to forecast future brand loyalty of current customers and the outcome of these consumer decisions on a company's market share.

Sentiment Analysis

One area that has not been discussed much yet is *unstructured data*. Think about the amount of user-generated content that is available online in the form of reviews and ratings. Consider all the information available in emails sent to customer-support teams. The ability to harness this unstructured data and turn it into knowledge and wisdom is extremely valuable. One technique that helps with this is sentiment analysis. *Sentiment analysis* takes unstructured data and organizes it into various categories that can be further analyzed to show positive or negative sentiment. This technique commonly uses natural language processing to data mine the unstructured content.

Natural language processing (*NLP*) involves computers reading and understanding spoken and written language.

Let's look at an example. Assume a company has just launched a new product. In addition to the reviews by analysts, the company wants to get sentiment from the user population. Using sentiment analysis, the company can track positive and negative sentiment. Specifically, it can also mine social media posts, reviews on websites, and discussion forum posts to get insights on customers' opinions on its product. Those insights may be used to discover possible issues that need improvement. Over time, the same company can plot the product sentiment on a line chart so that it can notice trends and investigate any positive or negative spikes.

Automating Decisions Using Prescriptive Analytics

Prescriptive analytics is the final and most complex level of analytics. It takes into account the understanding of what has happened from descriptive analytics, why it has happened from diagnostic analytics, a variety of "what-might-happen" predictions from inferential statistics or predictive analytics, and then prescribes the next action to take. This prescription is typically an automated decision. Let's take a look at an example.

Assume a retail store uses descriptive and diagnostic analytics to understand buying patterns and trends around its products. The store can predict that Product A is going to spike in sales during the holiday season. The company realizes it typically does not have a lot of extra Product A inventory but projects that the inventory should be higher during the holiday season. Prescriptive analytics will request a resupply of inventory as soon as the inventory reaches critical mass.

Prescriptive analytics uses advanced tools and technologies and therefore is not for everyone. More details on prescriptive analytics are covered in the Announce phase chapter, where you will learn about announcing and acting on a decision.

Summary and Key Takeaways

- Businesses succeed when they can turn data into wisdom and hindsight into insight to gain competitive advantages. Actionable insights are enablers for growth and innovation and for making better data-informed decisions.
- One critical step in that process of turning data into wisdom is analytics. Relying on descriptive analytics techniques like traditional business-intelligence reports and dashboards helps you look at past events or the current state. Companies need to

leverage that information but then apply advanced analytics to gain insights and to answer questions like why something is happening, what will happen next, and what the optimal outcome should be.

- Understanding the full stack of analytics within a culture that fosters data literacy and data-informed decision-making is required to compete and needs to be thought about when considering any transformation initiatives.

CHAPTER 7

PHASE FOUR – THE APPLY PHASE

"People who learn to read situations from different (theoretical) points of view have an advantage over those committed to a fixed position. For they are better able to recognize the limitations of a given perspective. They can see how situations and problems can be framed and reframed in different ways, allowing new kinds of solutions to emerge."[48]

—Gareth Morgan

Steps Involved in This Phase

7	Review and orient yourself to the data and information so far, apply your personal experiences to it, and create a hypothesis.
8	Challenge the data, and actively look for information to see if you can disprove your hypothesis.
9	Leverage strategies to become aware of and to mitigate bias, and then make a decision.

The Apply phase is the most important phase of the entire process as it is ultimately the point at which a decision is made. However, there are multiple steps that should be followed before this decision is made, and these steps often get overlooked. Many individuals and organizations jump from the Analyze phase to directly making a decision based on the analysis. However, it is during the Apply phase that you want to orient yourself to the data and information obtained so far as they relate to the problem or question being asked. You will want to apply your personal experiences, your intuition, and your mental models to the analysis and form a hypothesis for your decision. You will then want to challenge the data and your assumptions and actively look for information to see if you can disprove your hypothesis. This will require you to be aware of and to mitigate any potential cognitive bias. You will also want to review your hypothesis with a cognitively diverse team and make sure everyone shares their thought process. This involves teammates trying to mitigate groupthink and focusing on how to help each other unlearn outdated mental models. If you cannot review your hypothesis with a cognitively diverse team, you can try reframing and playing devil's advocate with your own thought process. After all these steps, you can then make your decision.

Balancing Data, Experience, and Intuition

While you have used data up until this phase to build a case for your decision, it is important to not forget the human element of decision-making. Experience and intuition are just as valuable as data. Data is really important, but it will never tell you the full story. It will never alone tell you exactly what the right decision should be. You need to balance the data with your experience and intuition (figure 62).

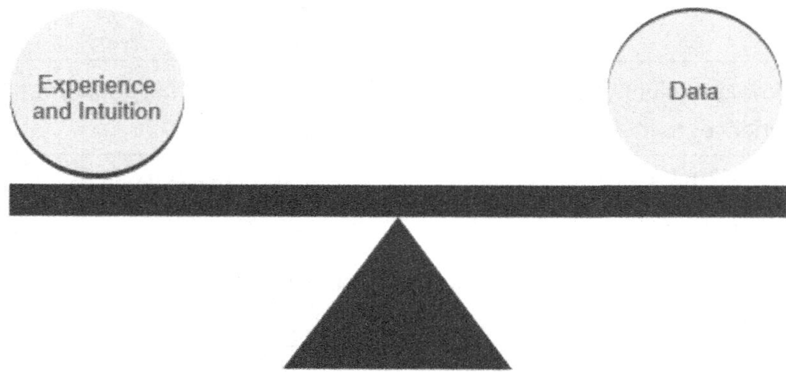

Figure 62. Balancing data with experience and intuition

Here is one example that highlights the importance of leveraging both data and *experience*. A hospital was using data and analytics to review its staff productivity. One such measurement was the average amount of time it took for a hospital room to be cleaned after one patient was discharged and another one could be admitted into that same room. The analysis shows that the average turnaround time was much longer than it should be. Based on its use of diagnostic analytics, the hospital was able to identify some deeper patterns. The delays typically happened on the weekend and occasionally on Wednesdays. However, despite this information, the hospital was still unable to determine root cause. On the surface, it could appear that the staff working weekends were not properly trained, or maybe there was a resource constraint. However, when discussing the problem and what decision to make to improve on it, one of the managers applied her experience to the problem and realized that those times are typically when the local football team plays. Sure enough, the hospital was able to use this experience from a team member along with the data to pinpoint the root cause. In this example, the root cause was that the cleaners were sitting down on the hospital beds to watch the football match and were not cleaning during that time.

Intuition plays a critical role during the Apply phase of the process too. *Intuition*, commonly referred to as a gut feeling, is an unconscious process for making a rapid judgment, decision, or action. We termed these decisions **System 1 decisions** back in "The Science of Decision-Making" chapter. Relying on your intuition has generally received a bad reputation, with many people thinking it is guesswork without the support of information and analysis. However, this is not a true statement. Intuition is the result of substantial processing within the brain, comparing the incoming sensory information and context with stored knowledge and prior experiences. So, should we trust our intuition to make decisions? The more experiences you have with a given domain, the more of a match the brain will make, and the more reliable your intuition will be. However, intuition-based decisions are open to flaws. For example, if you have little or no experience with a given domain, the brain will not be able to find a match, and your intuition will be unreliable. In addition, the brain has a built-in defense and survival mechanism that causes our intuition to try to protect us, even when the current situation is not an exact match to a previous traumatic experience. Despite this, it is not recommended that you ignore your intuition. When it comes to important and strategic decisions, you want to use your intuition as one of the inputs into the decision-making process and balance it with the data, your experiences, and perspectives from others.

Challenging the Data and Your Assumptions

When people make decisions, they are typically constructing mental models of the reality of the situation, including their assumptions, beliefs, experiences, and biases. During this step in the decision-making process, it is absolutely critical to challenge both the data and your assumptions.

CHALLENGING THE DATA

In science, the scientific method is used to explore observations and answer questions. The *scientific method* has traditionally been defined as a cyclical process that includes systematic observation, measurement or assessment, and experimentation that leads to the formulation, testing, and modification of hypotheses. The key value of using the scientific method for data-informed decision-making is that it requires testing the hypothesis with data and actually trying to disprove it instead of looking for data to try to prove it. In many situations, people unconsciously have confirmation bias and look for data to validate their hypothesis or decision rather than to invalidate it.

This practice of challenging the data is where many of the **soft skills** discussed earlier in the book come into play, skills that include systems and enterprise thinking, critical thinking, and active listening. **Systems thinking** is important as it helps us to see the bigger picture and how everything is interrelated. It also helps us to determine root causes. Critical thinking is important as it allows us to challenge the data and to think critically about whether it is really telling us what it appears to be telling us. Active listening is important as it allows us to be open-minded and to hear other perspectives on how to interpret the data.

CHALLENGING YOUR ASSUMPTIONS

When challenging the data, you should also challenge your **assumptions**. These include any of your **mental models** (perceptions on how the world works). You need to orient yourself to your assumptions and mental models by consciously being aware of the ones you are working with. You can do this by following something called a "mental-rehearsal drill." Just like when rehearsing a speech or a play for a sporting event, you go through a rehearsal in your mind of what might happen as a result of your decision. You might think of this rehearsal as trying to play chess with your decisions to determine what might happen two steps down the road. This helps you not only to be aware of your assumptions and mental models but also to develop better on-the-spot thinking by shortening your reaction time. If you have rehearsed decisions in advance and are prepared for actions that may occur as a result, you will be quicker to react if they do, in fact, occur.

Take time during this Apply phase of your data-informed decision-making process to really understand your assumptions and your mental models and to try to contradict your thoughts to poke holes in them. Two people with different mental models can see the same situation very differently. A carpenter, for example, will solve a problem differently than a poet. To overcome this contradiction at the organizational level and to use the different perspectives as an opportunity, you should work to create a culture of continuous learning and knowledge sharing. You should drive collaboration through reflective conversations. You should promote innovation and focus not just inwardly but also externally at trends in the industry. Many times, organizations are so inward focused, they fail to see the external trends that will have a huge impact on their decisions. This is why it is important to take a systems perspective during the Acquire phase.

Google. Let's take a look at a real-life example from Google. Google's goal is to ensure that all its decisions are based on data, analytics, and scientific experimentation. Part of the company culture is to discuss questions, challenge assumptions, and not jump to quick answers at its meetings.

Google created the "People Analytics Department" to help the company make HR decisions using data, including deciding if managers make a difference in their teams' performance. To answer this question, Google looked at performance reviews and employee surveys from the managers' employees. This information was then plotted on a graph, and it was determined that managers were generally perceived as good. Google then went a step further and split the data into the top and bottom quartiles, then ran regression models. These tests showed large differences between the best and worst managers in terms of team productivity, employee happiness, and employee turnover. So, good managers make Google more money and create happier employees, but what makes a good manager at Google?

To assist with answering that question, Google created the "Great Managers Award" to encourage employees to nominate managers they felt made a difference. Employees were required to provide examples of good manager behavior in the nomination application. Google also interviewed managers about their practices.

Using this data, Google established eight behaviors for good managers and uncovered the top-three reasons managers might struggle in their roles. The company then used this data to measure managers against these behaviors, to enact a twice-yearly feedback survey, and to revise its management-training program.[49]

Becoming Aware of and Mitigating Bias and Groupthink

Chapter 3 introduced the topics of bias and **groupthink** and how they can lead decision-makers to make ineffective decisions. In this section, we will learn what situations can trigger bias, how to become aware of bias and groupthink, and how to mitigate bias and groupthink in the decision-making process.

SITUATIONS THAT TRIGGER BIAS

Bias can creep into any decision-making situation. However, there are certain triggers that increase the likelihood of bias being introduced. These include *cognitive overload, ambiguous information, perceived threats, being short on time, emotional overload,* and *overconfidence.*

Cognitive overload. Certain decisions can be categorized as *complex decisions.* Complex decisions are ones for which there are multiple interrelated factors that need to be considered. When trying to analyze and process all these factors, you may hit *cognitive overload.* Cognitive overload is when the volume of data and information you are processing exceeds the capacity of your brain to process it. When this happens, bias is likely to come into play as you will start to make generalizations and only notice specific things like changes, repetition, and information that confirms your thoughts.

Ambiguous information. *Ambiguous information* is information that is missing something relevant to the decision being made. When we see ambiguity, we tend to seek out clarity, even at an unconscious level. This process of trying to seek out clarity for ambiguous information can lead to bias if we make generalizations, look for existing patterns, and rely too much on our current mindset.

Perceived threats. The amygdala is the emotional part of the brain, and it responds to fear. The amygdala has increased activity when the brain is responding to *perceived threats* and is susceptible to biases as a survival mechanism.

Short on time. The process of assimilating all of the information required to make a decision, deriving meaning and insights from it, and ultimately making a decision from it takes a long time. When the decision needs to be made quickly and you are *short on time,* bias will creep into the decision-making process if you make assumptions.

Emotional overload. Research has shown that the process of decision-making depends on specific neurons within the prefrontal cortex in our brains. When we feel an *emotional overload,* including stress, anger, and frustration, those neurons in the prefrontal cortex get disrupted. When this happens, our brains are more reactionary, and they compensate by either limiting the options for a decision or by making quick and premature decisions. Some common causes of emotional overload are found in the popular acronym HALT, which stands for hungry, angry, lonely, and tired.

Overconfidence. When decision-makers are *overconfident* in their belief that they are making a rational and objective decision, they are actually more prone to bias.

If you encounter any of these situations, you should not shut down the decision and do nothing. Some of the situations may be short term, like emotional overload, and can be addressed by leaving the decision and coming back to it another day. Other situations may not be resolved so simply. In these situations, you should use strategies to become aware of the bias that may be present and then use those strategies to mitigate the bias.

MITIGATING BIAS

There are proven strategies and techniques to help you mitigate bias. This practice of trying to *mitigate*, or reduce, bias is sometimes referred to as *debiasing* or *cognitive-forcing strategies*. In these situations, you are becoming aware the bias exists and then working toward limiting its impact on your decisions. The following section highlights some of these strategies that can be used during the Apply phase to help mitigate bias in your decision-making. These strategies can be applicable to multiple levels in an organization: at the individual level, the group level, and the organizational level.

Strategies for Mitigating Bias at the Individual Level

In most cases, the first step to mitigating bias is becoming aware that a bias is impacting you. This will help you with self-awareness. One way to become more aware is by using the Implicit Association Test or similar tests. The *Implicit Association Test* is a set of online tests created by Harvard University.[50] These tests are designed to detect someone's unconscious and implicit stereotypes. In addition, the following section highlights some strategies that can help mitigate bias at the individual level.

STRATEGY 1: SLOW DOWN YOUR THOUGHT PROCESS

When time is not a major factor in the decision, one technique is to slow down and think through the information you are trying to process. This allows you to reflect on your reasoning process and to think through alternative suggestions rather than quickly acting on potentially biased information. You may have been following this process innately without even knowing it. Have you ever told yourself you were going to sleep on a decision and decide the next morning?

STRATEGY 2: SEEK PERSPECTIVES FROM COGNITIVELY DIVERSE INDIVIDUALS

Chapter 2 highlighted the importance of diversity as part of data-informed decision-making. Scott E. Page, author of *The Difference*, highlights that "diversity trumps ability: Diverse groups generally do better than 'high-ability' groups at problem-solving or prediction. These are not political statements; they are mathematical truths."[51]

When looking at diverse perspectives within decision-making, it is important to look at cognitive diversity. **Cognitive diversity** is the inclusion of people who have different styles of problem-solving and can offer unique perspectives because they think differently. In *The Difference*, Page highlights four dimensions of cognitive diversity: diverse perspectives, interpretations, heuristics, and predictive models:[52]

1. **Diverse perspectives.** People have different ways of representing situations and problems. As a result, people also have different solutions to improve those situations or problems.

2. **Diverse interpretations.** People put things into different categories and classifications and have different interpretations of the world. For example, some people may think of me, the author of this book, as a teacher. Others may think of me as a parent, a coach, a data-literacy expert, or something else. These are all different interpretations of who I am.

3. **Diverse heuristics.** As a reminder, **heuristics** are rules-of-thumb, or mental shortcuts, that the brain uses to quickly assess a situation and make a decision. People have their own heuristics, which means they have different ways of generating solutions to problems.

4. **Diverse predictive models.** People have different ways of assessing a situation or problem. Some people may analyze the situation. Others may listen to a story to understand how to act.

STRATEGY 3: LEVERAGE EXISTING TOOLS, MODELS, AND FRAMEWORKS WITHIN THE PROCESS

A variety of tools, models, and frameworks exist to help decision-makers mitigate bias during their decision-making. Chapter 10 will introduce a few of the important ones, such as the following:

- **The Zig-Zag process model for problem-solving.** This process model uses the idea that individuals experience the world using four functions: sensing, intuition, thinking, and feeling. These four functions are used in a specific order to help individuals understand the most efficient and successful way to make a decision.

- **The Ladder of Inference.** This tool, created by organizational psychologist Chris Argyris, helps you avoid incorrect inferences in your decision-making process by using a step-by-step reasoning process.

- **Strategic Foresight.** This business-planning process is focused on preparing for the future by allowing individuals to think differently about situations using a mindset of openness and awareness.

- **Future Search.** This model is useful in team meetings to enable organizations and communities to quickly transform their capability to action.

STRATEGY 4: EXAMINE ALTERNATIVES

Another strategy to avoid bias is to systemically explore multiple alternatives to a question based on the data and analysis provided. For each alternative, identify potential outcomes and explore potential consequences. A good example of this can be seen in the healthcare industry. When a patient visits the doctor, the first step is for the doctor to listen to the patient's symptoms and take some vitals, like temperature and blood pressure. Next, the doctor will review all this information and begin the diagnosis with multiple potential causes of the symptoms. The doctor may then order more tests, like blood work, and will then review the results to see how they relate to all alternatives. Some alternatives will be ruled out, and others will stay in consideration. Had the doctor started with just one possible diagnosis, he or she may not have performed tests and found data that could be relevant to the actual root cause of the symptoms. Similar in business, when decision-makers focus on only one possible decision/answer to a question, the business may ignore vital data and information because the focus is only on what may be relevant to that one specific decision/answer and not on any potential alternatives.

Strategies for Mitigating Bias at the Group Level

When working in a group or team to make a decision, all of the strategies listed for mitigating bias at the individual level are still applicable, but there are additional strategies that should be used to achieve a greater outcome from the data-informed decision-making process. The following section highlights some strategies that can help mitigate bias at the group level.

STRATEGY 1: SET UP INDEPENDENT GROUPS

There should be several independent groups set up to simultaneously work on a specific task or problem, especially when the decision that needs to be made is a strategic one. These groups will facilitate different perspectives. For example, if an organization is working on developing a new product to bring to market, the organization could create two separate independent groups; provide them the same questions, data and information, and expectations; and then ask each of them to work on possible answers to the question. In this example, since both groups are working independently of each other, their ideas are not influenced by anything the other group is thinking about.

STRATEGY 2: APPOINT A CRITICAL EVALUATOR

If there is one person in the group who manages the majority of the other group members, this individual can influence the other group members' decisions, which limits the idea of diverse perspectives. In this case, another group member (one for each independent group) must be appointed as the "critical evaluator," also referred to as the "devil's advocate." This person's responsibility is to critically weigh the value of each team member's viewpoints and possible decisions. This way, each viewpoint can be dissected, and the team can together arrive at the best possible solution. In addition to appointing a critical evaluator, to get an unbiased perspective, team members' opinions ideally should be discussed with a trusted person who is outside the group but still within the organization.

STRATEGY 3: HAVE LEADERS AVOID EXPRESSING THEIR PERSONAL OPINIONS

Another strategy for avoiding bias at the group level is to ensure that the group's leader avoids expressing his or her personal opinions while assigning tasks. According to social psychologist Irving Janis, author of *Victims of Groupthink*, this strategy is designed to reduce the pressure on other members to conform to their leader.[53] Ideally, the leader would even stay away from meetings in which decisions are being discussed, to avoid swaying the members' opinions.

STRATEGY 4: DIALOGUE; DON'T DISCUSS

One common mistake with decision-making is that the decision-maker uses the same approach during the Apply phase as during the Announce phase (when the decision is communicated out to all stakeholders). This is a mistake, for during the Apply phase, when you are gathering perspectives from others to help make the decision, it is important to have an open dialogue. This approach helps teams make decisions and avoid nonproductive conflict. A dialogue starts out with an unbiased and unemotional approach, getting everyone's ideas and input without passing judgment and then comparing ideas to foster discovery and dialogue before moving toward action. *Dialogue* is different than a *discussion*. According to systems scientist and author Peter Senge, with a discussion, people talk about their views and try to get them accepted by the other team members.[54] In a discussion, the emphasis is often on winning. In dialogue, team members suspend any of their own ideas and judgment of others and just listen. Rather than winning, it is about the team gaining more knowledge about the situation and agreeing to do what is right.

When conflict does arise during this process, handle it in a way that it can turn into productive conflict management. You can accomplish this by starting to find commonalities between the two sides. Then, ask each side to explain their thought process, and use that information to compare ideas. Continue to foster this discovery-to-dialogue process as you move toward a decision.

STRATEGY 5: REFRAME

If any of the team's thought process does include a bias, use a technique called *reframing* to help them see different perspectives. *Framing* is a type of heuristic in which people tend to reach decisions based on whether the situation was presented with positive or negative connotations. When the situation is presented in a negative connotation or with a bias, reframing can be used to help the team see the thought process in an alternative way.

As discussed in chapter 3, humans absorb new information by fitting it into a framework of something we already understand. We use **heuristics** and **mental models** to make sense of the world. These filters are based on our experiences, values, assumptions, and cultures, and they influence our decisions. Frames can be used to challenge these filters and can be conveyed and triggered by various communication elements, including the following:

- **Metaphor.** A metaphor can be used to compare an existing problem with another problem. Even if the problems seem dissimilar on the surface, the metaphor can identify some similarities to help reframe. For example, when trying to improve workplace performance or culture, a leader may use a metaphor to frame the conversation by saying that the office is just like a family.

- **Stories.** Stories can be used to frame a topic. For example, if an organization made a poor decision, a leader could tell the stakeholders a story of another organization that had similar challenges but then ultimately went on to succeed.

- **Traditions.** Traditions can be used as a method to frame organizational culture and values. For example, maybe an organization's tradition is to have an all-inclusive lunch every Friday at which each employee comes in and talks about anything other than work topics.

- **Slogans and catchphrases.** Slogans and catchphrases are commonly used to frame a topic in a memorable and familiar way. For example, Kentucky Fried Chicken's slogan "Finger Lickin' Good" and Walt Disney World Resort's slogan "The Happiest Place on Earth" both frame topics in a memorable way.

- **Artifacts.** Artifacts, like traditions, can be used as a method to frame organizational culture and values. For example, to support a culture of inclusion and openness, an organization may decide to have an open floor plan in which leaders share the same cubicles as nonleaders.

- **Contrast.** Contrast is a comparison between two separate thoughts, or a description of what something is not—for example, if someone says, "It could be worse. There are worse situations to be in, such as [insert worse situation]." In this example, you are reframing the current circumstance as better than another. Another example, seen a lot in marketing, would be if an advertisement said, "What if we told you this [item] costs $2,500, but today, we are not going to charge you that? Today, it only costs $1,500."

- **Spin.** Spin is a very common frame in which an individual describes a concept in either a positive or negative connotation. The frame does not change the concept or situation, but it allows the audience to put it in a more positive perspective.

> For example, if a leader is seen as a quiet individual, people may see that as a negative. However, this trait can be framed by providing it with a positive connotation. For example, someone could say, "I know [insert leader name] is quiet. That tells me that they are really thoughtful and reflective in the words they speak."[55]

According to Lee Bolman, coauthor of *How Great Leaders Think: The Art of Reframing,* decision-makers need to see the world they live in through various lenses, but this is something that takes time to learn, and it may require the help of others who can provide different perspectives.[56]

When either discussing possible decisions or communicating a decision out to stakeholders, a variety of techniques can be used for framing the relevant information to help people see a different perspective. These include the following:

- **Values-based framing.** People make decisions based on more than just the facts alone. Values-based frames access people's underlying values to motivate them toward the decision.

- **Financial-benefits framing.** This approach highlights the financial benefits of the decision.

- **Gain framing.** This approach focuses on what users will gain from the decision. This ties into the concept of "what's in it for me?" (discussed in the Announce phase chapter).

- **Loss framing.** A loss frame focuses on what people will lose from either engaging or not engaging in the decision.

Specific to leaders who need to communicate decisions, framing can be used to reflect a given leadership style they need to use for a particular situation. In their book *Primal Leadership: Realizing the Power of Emotional Intelligence*, Dr. Daniel Goleman, Richard Boyatzis, and Annie McKee state that the best leaders act according to one or more of six distinct approaches to leadership: visionary, coaching, affiliative, democratic, pace-setting, and commanding:[57]

1. **Visionary.** Visionary leaders mobilize their teams toward a vision.

2. **Coaching.** Coaching leaders develop employees for the future.
3. **Affiliative.** Affiliative leaders create emotional bonds and harmony with their teams.
4. **Democratic.** Democratic leaders build consensus with their teams through education and participation.
5. **Pace-setting.** Pace-setting leaders expect their teams to be self-directed and to excel.
6. **Commanding.** Commanding leaders demand immediate compliance from their teams.

Their research concluded that the best results happened with leaders who practice more than one style on any given day, depending on their business's needs. Framing can shape a manager's communication to reflect the leadership style the manager needs for a particular situation. For example, a company has just received bad press when a major bug in its software got announced publicly. Regardless of the leader's natural style, his or her next communication should reinforce the company's vision and that everyone is part of the process to improve the software going forward. This communication would be framed as visionary and democratic.

STRATEGY 6: LEVERAGE DOUBLE-LOOP LEARNING

Earlier in the book, we talked about **groupthink** (the tendency to favor choices of mass populations and to strive for consensus at the cost of rational assessments of alternate decisions) and its impact on group and organizational decision-making. Groupthink can occur without any willful intent. However, there are other more-deliberate organizational and political factors that can negatively impact decision-making within groups and organizations. These factors include avoidance of uncertainty, playing politics, competitive games between groups, blind loyalties, personal ideologies, and many more. For example, even after a leader has had many incidents of bad behavior with individuals on his or her team, the organization could choose to look the other way due to blind loyalties to that leader. Or, a leader could make a decision that is influenced by his or her personal ideology, even if that ideology differs from the organization's views. The outcomes of these decisions could include the distortion and manipulation of information, such as the leader reporting only information that aligns to his or her view and the suppression of open dialogue among a team.

Individuals tend to look for data and information that does not question the fundamental vision, strategy, and goals of their organization. When decisions discussed involve potential threats or negative information concerning individuals or organizations, that relevant information tends to be minimized and not shared. One way a group or organization can overcome hiding information is by leveraging **double-loop learning** either during the decision-making process or while assessing the decision. Double-loop learning, first modeled by business theorist Chris Argyris and organizational consultant Donald Schön,[58] is a reflective process in which the decision-making team challenges the assumptions, norms, and objectives for the decision.

Sometimes, feedback from a decision made is that the decision may not have been optimal because the underlying assumptions of the system behind the problem were inaccurate. For example, if an organization is trying to make a strategic decision about whether or not to change go-to-market models based on the organization's mission and strategy, the double-loop learning process would allow the decision-makers to challenge whether their underlying assumptions of the go-to-market models are correct, rather than to just assume they are and make a decision based on them. A real-life example of this is the story of Blockbuster and Netflix.

At one point, Blockbuster was the largest video-rental chain in the world. Around 2000, the company was presented with an opportunity to purchase Netflix. Netflix delivered movies to consumers, just like Blockbuster, but it delivered them via the mail, while Blockbuster delivered them physically from video-rental stores. Blockbuster's decision was to not purchase Netflix.[59] Looking at the decision in the context of the time, one can see why this decision seemed to make sense. Blockbuster believed that customers would not want to wait for their movies to be delivered via mail over a couple days. However, if Blockbuster had used double-loop learning to challenge the assumptions and norms from the current state to the potential future state, the company may have seen the possibility of next-day deliveries and streaming on the horizon.

When organizations reflect on their decisions and how to learn from them, they can either be practicing single-loop learning or double-loop learning. *Single-loop learning* is when the lessons learned are on the actions and decisions taken themselves. *Double-loop learning* goes further to actually question and modify the system and mental model of the underlying assumptions tied to the problem statement. This process helps decision-makers and their organizations think outside the box to improve their understanding of the causes of the problems and the effective way to solve them. It helps organizations learn from their errors and improve the mental models that surrounded their original decisions.

One example of an organization that practices double-loop learning is Southwest Airlines, a low-cost airline based in the United States. While most airlines were struggling at the time (in the 1990s) to make a profit, Southwest challenged the underlying assumptions and norms and thought outside the box. The ongoing assumptions at the time were that flights had to land at major airports and in-flight amenities like food and separate classes of travel were required. Southwest, however, was able to create a low-cost niche market by flying into smaller destinations, which cost less. The airline also did not provide in-flight food service and launched with only a single class of travel. By challenging the norms, Southwest was able to create new opportunities that did not follow traditional rules. What were the results? By the 1990s, Southwest was consistently profitable when many other airlines were losing money and even filing for bankruptcy. By 2011, Southwest had flown the most passengers annually within the United States.[60]

Strategies for Mitigating Bias at the Organizational Level

Organizational culture comprises the values, beliefs, assumptions, and behaviors that are shared by all members of an organization and that contribute to the environment of an organization. The right organizational culture will encourage continuous experimentation with new approaches and will encourage the blend of data and experiences from a cognitively diverse perspective to make data-informed decisions. The following section highlights some strategies that can help mitigate bias at the organizational level.

STRATEGY 1: CREATE AN ORGANIZATION-WIDE DATA AND ANALYTICS STRATEGY

Organizations that have a data and analytics strategy will be less likely to have their decisions tainted with cognitive bias. The data and analytics strategy will put into process the right data definitions, collections, and calculations to ensure that the data is trusted and that individuals are using the right levels of analytics to address the decision they are trying to solve. This helps to prevent organizations from starting with the data first and then trying to model a way to use it.

STRATEGY 2: USE A SYSTEMATIC AND SYSTEMIC PROCESS AND METHODOLOGY (LIKE THE ONE TAUGHT IN THIS BOOK)

Leveraging a systematic and systemic process and methodology, like the one taught in this book, can help organizations to mitigate bias. This book's six-phase, twelve-step process and methodology, for example, requires listening to multiple perspectives from cognitively diverse individuals, continually challenging the data, and having a sound data strategy, which will also help to minimize unintended consequences.

STRATEGY 3: EDUCATE

Organizations should create educational programs that educate their workforce on all aspects of data-informed decision-making. The foundation should start with training on bias in general. Then, there should be training programs to provide everyone with a foundational understanding of data and data literacy along with the soft skills discussed in the "Introduction to Data-Informed Decision-Making" chapter, which include active listening, critical thinking, and communicating with data. Finally, specific programs should be put into place to teach everyone about the organization's data-informed decision-making process, including its data and analytics strategy.

STRATEGY 4: FOSTER A SAFE ENVIRONMENT TO BE CURIOUS, TO CHALLENGE, AND TO FAIL

As discussed throughout this book, employees need to unlearn old mental models and change their mind when presented with convincing data and evidence. To do this, employees need to be curious and to challenge their assumptions. To support this, organizations need to provide a safe environment that supports failing fast, fixing fast, learning fast, and then disseminating what is learned to the rest of the organization.

Making a Decision

Ultimately, the time has come to make your decision. Back in chapter 1, we discussed the fact that one of the biggest challenges to decision-makers is failing to make any decision because they do not feel they have all the information. There may always be some uncertainty. The key is to be explicit about the uncertainty. Individuals and organizations need to weigh what the right level is for them to feel comfortable making a decision. As discussed in chapter 1, Amazon CEO Jeff Bezos told his annual shareholders in 2016 that "most decisions should probably be made with somewhere around 70 percent of the information you wish you had. If you wait for 90 percent, in most cases, you're probably being slow."[61] To help you weigh what the right decision-making level is for you and your organization, you should factor in the classification of the decision, discussed back in the Ask phase chapter—specifically, whether the decision is a programmed or nonprogrammed decision and whether the decision is a Type 1 or Type 2 decision. As a reminder, **programmed decisions** are reoccurring decisions, and **nonprogrammed decisions** are one-off decisions that are not part of a routine. **Type 1 decisions** are irreversible, and **Type 2 decisions** are decisions that you can always revert back from if they end up not being ideal.

When time is of the essence in decision-making, there is a model called the OODA (observe, orient, decide, and act) loop that can help. The OODA loop is discussed in greater detail in the "Tools, Frameworks, and Models" chapter.

Summary and Key Takeaways

- After you acquire your data and analyze it, remember to spend time orienting yourself to it, applying your experiences, intuition, and mental models to form a hypothesis for your decision.
- Challenge the data, and actively look for information to see if you can disprove your hypothesis.
- Be aware of and mitigate any potential cognitive bias.
- Time is of the essence in today's climate. While this doesn't excuse carelessness, it is something that needs to be considered in decision-making.

CHAPTER 8

PHASE FIVE – THE ANNOUNCE PHASE

"Numbers have an important story to tell. They rely on you to give them a clear and convincing voice."[62]

—Stephen Few

Steps Involved in This Phase

10	Announce your decision at the right level to ALL stakeholders (direct, indirect, upstream, and downstream) by leveraging tools like reframing, the Pyramid principle, and the Rule of Three in your storytelling.
11	Provide adequate time for stakeholders to unlearn any outdated mental models and to learn new ones.

You may have just come up with a decision that will save your organization millions of dollars, save countless lives, or do something else just as spectacular. However, if you cannot communicate the right information at the right time in the right way to the right people, your decision may be ignored or ostracized. Your ability to come up with key insights to help with your decision is one skill, but communicating it out is another skill entirely. Good communication of your data-informed decision can help stakeholders to understand, accept, and then act on the decision. Remember our example from chapter 1 with the Challenger space-shuttle explosion? Engineers knew the high probability of an explosion, but they communicated to NASA using a visualization that included only a subset of the data they used to gain their insights. That visualization was misinterpreted by NASA, who deemed that the launch was not at risk. Therefore, the launch happened, and the space shuttle exploded during takeoff.[63]

The "Introduction to Data-Informed Decision-Making" chapter discussed how data-informed decision-making requires both **hard skills** and **soft skills**. This is one reason it is best done as a team sport. This is true during the Announce phase as well. It is during the Announce phase you will communicate your insights and your decision out to all stakeholders. At a high level, there are two components to this: 1) the visuals of the data and insights you will use in your communication and 2) the story you will tell to weave everything together. After the announcements are done, you will then provide adequate time for stakeholders to **unlearn** any outdated mental models that were uncovered as part of the decision-making process.

Defining Your Audience

The first step in the Announce phase is to ensure that you are thinking about all the various stakeholders of the decision. *Stakeholders* are any individuals or groups who are involved in or affected by the decision you are making. This includes stakeholders who are within the organization as well as stakeholders external to the organization, like customers, suppliers, and shareholders. Another classification of stakeholders is whether they are upstream or downstream. *Upstream stakeholders* are individuals who are involved in the implementation of the program or offering the decision has set forth. *Downstream stakeholders* are individuals who will receive, use, or participate in the program or offering the decision has set forth. The downstream stakeholders can be directly or indirectly impacted. *Direct impactees* are typically employees within the program or offering for which the decision was made, while *indirect impactees* are typically external to the organization or group. For example, if an organization is looking to make a decision about whether or not to invest in its internal new-hire onboarding program, it may have the following stakeholders, shown in table 5.

Table 5. Example stakeholders

UPSTREAM STAKEHOLDERS	DOWNSTREAM STAKEHOLDERS
Resources who are responsible for building the onboarding program and its contents	New hires going through the onboarding program (direct)
Any administrators who administer systems that are used by the onboarding program	External customers whom the new hires interact with after onboarding (indirect)
	Managers of employees going through the onboarding program (indirect)
	Colleagues of employees going through the onboarding program (indirect)

Therefore, a good first step in announcing your decision is to make a list of all your decision's stakeholders. Next, it's important to consider how the stakeholders might receive the decision and how you might present it best to the individual or group. Since the way data is presented can impact people's reactions and resulting actions, it is imperative to communicate the decisions and actions in a way that is both understandable and usable to your target stakeholders—and ideally in a way that creates a connection. This is partly because a human's actions and responses to communication are based more on emotional reactions than on rational thought. This means you may potentially need multiple communications.

CULTURAL IMPLICATIONS FOR COMMUNICATION

We talked earlier about how perceptions impact a person's behavior and decisions. A big factor in this is a person's cultural background, or *cultural lens*. This cultural lens is vitally important as you plan your communications. In her book *A Manager's Guide to Virtual Teams*, Yael Zofi discusses two communication challenges related to this cultural lens: differences in perception and differences in interpreting context.[64] We already talked about differences in perceptions back in chapter 3, but let's learn a bit more about the differences in interpreting context.

Differences in Interpreting Context

Late anthropologist Edward Hall highlighted that context determines human behavior, more so than personality. **Context** is defined as the circumstances that form the setting for an event or idea so that event or idea can be fully understood and assessed. According to Hall, "What one pays attention to and what one does not attend to is largely a matter of context."[65] Hall believed that contextual awareness is actually developed through culture. Humans take in and try to process contextual information to help understand what is happening. However, according to Hall, it is our culture that determines to what degree this information is critical for meaning or is to be ignored.

Hall went a step further and created a framework of culture-based communication styles, explaining how people in different countries decode messages based on their cultural expectations.

Cultures can be classified as high context or low context. These cultures are vastly different in terms of what is important to communicate.

High-context cultures put an emphasis on cultural values. These cultures value family and collectivism over individualism. They tend to emphasize visuals over text. Communications within these cultures tend to focus on underlying context, meaning, and tone in the message, and not just the words themselves. Typically, communications are rooted in the past, and changes occur slowly.

Low-context cultures tend to favor individualism over collectivism, and a person's identity tends to come more from his or her individual accomplishments than from the person's family or similar groups. Low-context cultures tend to emphasize text over visuals. These cultures honor privacy, personal space, and individuality. Typically, change happens fast. Communications tend to be explicitly stated so that there's no risk of confusion, and if a message isn't clear enough, it will slow down the process of communication.

While Hall highlighted certain countries and what type of culture they were,[66] as shown in figure 63, it is important to note that every person uses both high-context and low-context communication. Depending on the relationship and circumstance, people will resonate more with literal (low-context) or implied (high-context) meanings. In today's world, it is more likely you will be communicating to a group of stakeholders that includes both high- and low-context cultures. Not tailoring your communication to the type of culture with which you are communicating can lead to misunderstandings, disappointment, and even failures in business. As a result, it is important that people understand and respect different cultures and ensure their communication is cross-cultural.

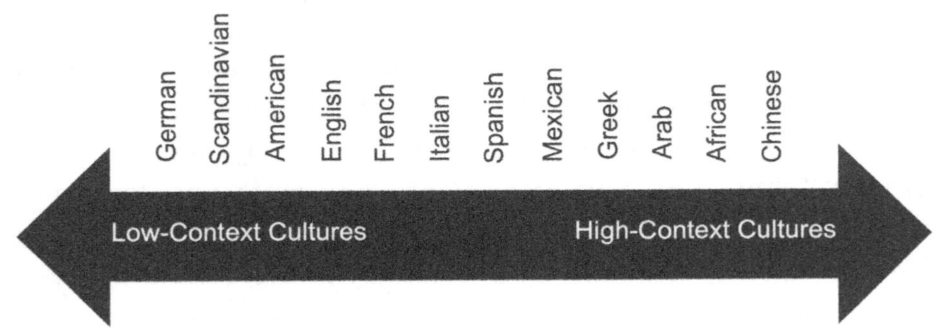

Figure 63. Low-context and high-context cultures

Planning the Story

As you are planning your communications, it is important to ensure that you tie them back to what you know about your audience (from the previous section), including their role and cultural background. For each audience type—upstream and downstream, direct and indirect, high context and low context—you should think about the following questions. In an ideal world, this planning is done proactively and as part of an overall decision-making project plan from the very start.

What is the key decision and insight you want to share with the stakeholders? How does this decision relate to your key strategic objectives? Help the audience see the connections and the relevance of this decision to the long-term picture of the organization.

Have you explained "why"? People need to understand the "why." Too often, decision-makers describe the "what" but never address the "why." Knowing *why* a decision has been made does more than just clarify a reason for the decision; it shows people they are worth your effort and time. It makes them feel valued and helps them take ownership to understand, drive, and accept the decision. As you draft your communication, consider why the stakeholder will be interested.

How will the decision be communicated? The "what" and the "why" of the decision are important but so is "how" the decision will be delivered. The *how* relates to contextual communication. Selecting the best medium for the communication is key. If you are interested in environmental cues and other feedback, delivering the communication in person or in a live videoconference is ideal. Referring back to high- and low-context cultures, generally speaking, high-context cultures prefer oral communications, while low-context cultures prefer written communications.

Who will deliver the communication? Is one executive making the announcement or sending the email to everyone within the organization? Is each individual manager sharing the message with his or her own groups separately? Is there some combination of both? Purposely decide *who* will be communicating. It is important to know to whom you will be communicating and who will be best for communicating to this target audience(s).

What is the feedback loop on the decision communicated? Communication is a two-way process. A complete communication plan makes sure that people not only receive the communication but can also understand it and provide positive and negative feedback on it. To be most successful, you need to create some sort of *feedback mechanism*. This can range from asking all the stakeholders to rate their buy-in from zero to ten to performing interviews and focus groups. One famous decision-making model that promotes a quick feedback loop is the *OODA loop*. This model is covered in more detail in the "Tools, Frameworks, and Models" chapter.

What is the right source to use for the communication? Before you begin crafting the communication, you will want to revisit the list of stakeholders and identify the ideal way to communicate to them. Back in the Acquire phase chapter, we discussed that there are three *sources of insight*: data, theory, and intuition. The amount of data, theory, and intuition you should include in a communication depends on the stakeholder and the stakeholder's background:

- If the stakeholders do not believe they have the right facts regarding the decision, the communication should focus more on data. This will allow the stakeholders to feel more comfortable that they have the right facts.
- If all the data needed is not available and the stakeholders are not too familiar with the problem domain, the communication should focus more on theory, including the assumptions and the logic that led to the conclusions from those assumptions. This will enhance their reasoning about the problem.
- If the stakeholders either do not have a gut feeling on the decision or typically have poor intuition on these types of decisions, your communication should leverage more examples and stories, as these will enhance their judgment on the decision's problem domain.

Crafting the Story

Once all of the planning steps are decided, you can start the process of crafting your communication and story. This part includes having a cognitive strategy to avoid information overload. It also includes presenting and potentially reframing the decision in multiple approaches, including verbal, visual, and mathematical, to account for the fact that different people process information in different ways.

THE VISUALS

Visualizations provide another interesting connection to the importance of understanding the brain. Humans are visual first, verbal second. Visuals are the most effective communication vehicles for evoking emotion and getting people to act. Therefore, you must ensure that you use the right visuals within your communication. One of the biggest mistakes decision-makers make is using the same visuals they created in the Analyze phase during the Announce phase. The visuals decision-makers use to gain insights may not have the right context, or they may contain too-much data for the audience being communicated to in the Announce phase.

The main purpose of using visuals to communicate is to aid in the persuasion of the stakeholder. According to data-visualization guru Stephen Few, data visualization is effective because it shifts the balance between perception and cognition to take fuller advantage of the brain's abilities.[67] Unless physically blind, humans can see (visual perception) with little effort. Thinking and cognition, however, are handled by another part of the brain and are much slower and less efficient. While this book is not going to focus on how the brain interprets visualizations (or how visualizations are impacted for those with various visual impairments, certainly a very important subject), a higher-level background on visualizations will help decision-makers when they are determining how to design visuals to include in their communications. It is worth mentioning that many analytics software products have been designed to take into account accessibility for those with various visual impairments, such as color blindness, for example.

The Three Types of Memory

To better understand what to include in visualizations, we need to understand a little bit about the types of memories in the brain. There are three main types of memories in the brain: sensory, short term/working, and long term:

1. **Sensory memory.** Sensory memory holds a quick flash of everything that our sensory systems—eyes, ears, nose, etc.—take in. This memory lasts at most up to a second.[68] Going back to chapter 3, which discussed the science of decision-making, this is where much of our brain's filtering comes into play as most of this information does not even become part of our conscious awareness. There are different types of sensory memory that tie to the five senses. The one that we will discuss more in this chapter is *iconic memory*. Iconic memory is a type of sensory memory that relates to the mental representations of visual information, commonly called our visual perception.

2. **Short-term/working memory.** Short-term memory, also commonly referred to as working memory, holds onto a few pieces of information at a time, around 5–9 items.[69] It helps you remember a phone number for long enough to dial it or something your coworker says for long enough to write it down. Some information in short-term memory will eventually be stored in long-term memory, especially if we give it our attention, but most of it will fade.

   Short-term memory also helps to control our attention. This is commonly referred to as *concentration*. This memory type helps us keep our tasks in mind for long enough to finish them while filtering out distractions.

3. **Long-term memory.** Long-term memory is what we think of as "permanent storage," and it is where things we memorize or remember are stored.

Related to visualizations, sensory memory's iconic part (iconic memory) and short-term memory are the ones that interact with visualizations, so we will cover these in a bit more detail.

Applying Principles of Perception to Visuals

A major part of properly communicating your story is to help stakeholders see what you want them to see while limiting anything that can distract them. Visualizations can become more effective by leveraging techniques like using *preattentive visual attributes, gestalt principles,* and *chunking,* which help stakeholders to process important information more easily.

USING ICONIC MEMORY AND PREATTENTIVE PROCESSING TO HIGHLIGHT IMPORTANT INFORMATION

Iconic memory, a form of sensory memory, processes and stores visual information automatically, many times unconsciously, and in less than a second. Since this process is automatic and happens unconsciously before we are even paying attention, it is called *preattentive processing*. This process detects certain visual attributes. These visual attributes "pop out" at us without conscious effort. This is quite important information for decision-makers, as they can use it to make important information stand out in their visualizations.

Colin Ware, author of *Information Visualization: Perception for Design*, defined four categories of preattentive visual attributes:[70]

1. **Form.** Form, or the particular way an object appears, includes attributes like length, width, orientation, curvature, size, shape, added marks, enclosure, blur, and spatial grouping. Many of these attributes are already built into visualizations to increase effectiveness. For example, a bar chart will show bars at varying heights and lengths. A scatter plot can show dots with varying sizes and shapes.

2. **Color.** Color includes attributes like hue and intensity. For example, important data points, like outliers, might be a separate color than the rest of the data.

3. **Spatial position.** Spatial position, or the perception of multiple objects in relation to one another, includes 2D positioning, stereoscopic depth, and concave/

convex positioning. For example, the line chart in figure 69 uses 2D positioning to aid in the perception of the sales trends.

4. **Movement.** Movement includes flicker and motion. While movement is good at calling attention to things, it can quickly become distracting to the rest of the information, so it should not be used on dashboards with multiple points of interest. However, if you are designing a visualization with just one focus point, movement can be really powerful.

Using these preattentive attributes catches users' attention before they even realize it.

USING GESTALT PRINCIPLES TO BRING OUT PATTERNS IN VISUALIZATIONS

In addition to the key visual attributes discussed in the previous section, humans also perceive objects as organized patterns. Developed by gestalt psychologists, the gestalt principles, as shown in figure 64, describe how humans interpret and process complex stimuli around them. *Gestalt* is a German word meaning an organized whole that is perceived as more than the sum of its individual parts. A good way to explain gestalt is to look at a sports team that is executing so well that the team (the organized whole) is playing better than the sum of all the individual players' talents (the parts). Whereas preattentive processing relates to perception and what grabs a human's attention and focus, gestalt principles provide a result, in which we see the whole from a collection.

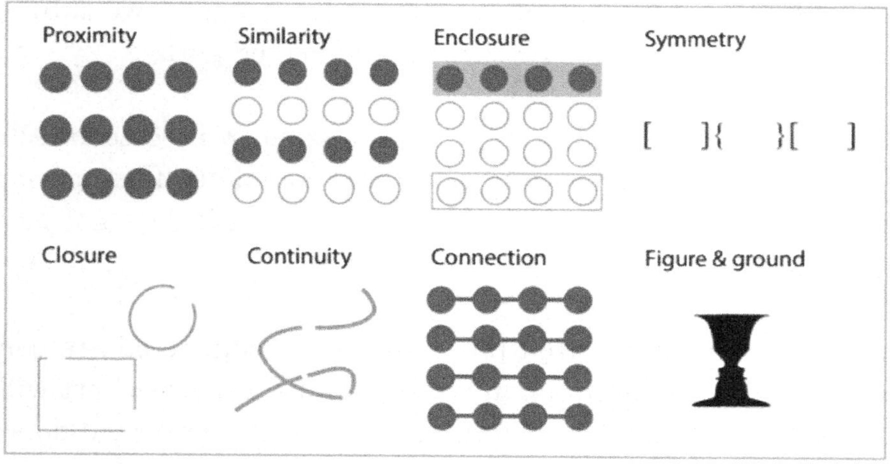

Figure 64. Gestalt principles[71]

Originally, there were six gestalt principles: proximity, similarity, symmetry, closure, continuity, and figure & ground. At least two additional principles were added over time: enclosure and connection. Let's look at each principle in a little more detail.

Proximity. When items are placed in close proximity to each other, the brain assumes that they're in the same group because they're close to one another and apart from other groups. This technique can be used to help users digest the data being visualized. When an element is spaced away from the others, it highlights importance, which will alert the user to focus more attention on that particular part of the data.

Similarity. Gestalt highlights that objects having shared visual properties will be lumped into the same group. In the figure 64 image, the first row and third row use the same color to group them together.

Enclosure. Gestalt highlights that objects that appear enclosed will be set apart and lumped into the same group. In the image in figure 64, the first four dots use a background color, and the last four dots use a border to show those two rows separately.

Symmetry. Gestalt highlights that objects that are symmetrical to each other will be naturally perceived as a group. In the image, we see three pairs of symmetrical brackets rather than six individual brackets.

Closure. Gestalt highlights that objects that seem to be incomplete will be naturally perceived as closed if they are of a familiar shape. In the image, we automatically close the square and circle instead of seeing three disconnected paths.

Continuity. Gestalt highlights that objects that seem to be disconnected or incomplete will be naturally perceived as connected and complete. This principle is similar to closure, but the key for the continuity principle is that it does not have to create a closed object, just a connected one.

Connection. Gestalt highlights that objects that are connected are considered part of the same group. This is why common visualizations of a line chart will connect the dots to form a continuous line. In the image, we view the connected dots as belonging to the same group.

Figure & ground. Gestalt highlights that humans tend to segment visuals into the object that is in focus, called the figure, and the background, called the ground. Looking at the image, we either notice the two faces or the vase. Whichever we notice first becomes the figure and the other the ground.

TIPS FOR USING PREATTENTIVE PROCESSING AND GESTALT PRINCIPLES

Now that you know what preattentive processing and gestalt principles are, below are a few tips on how you can leverage them in building your visuals for your communication. Note that we will not cover every principle in these examples, just the most-common ones:

- Distinguish categorical groups by using similarity, proximity, or enclosure principles. An example of this would be to enclose related items in a different-colored box to distinguish them. In the example shown in figure 65, the eyes are drawn to the vertical bars of interest, shaded with a gray enclosure, which relate to the two largest customer-age bins.

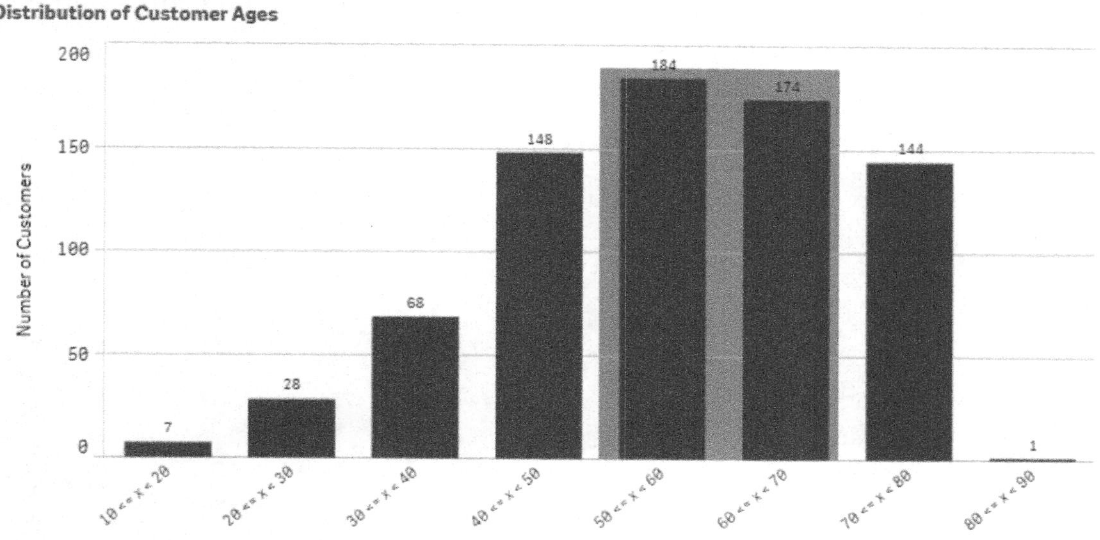

Figure 65. Distinguishing categorical groups using enclosure

- Similarly, if you want to categorize items into groups in a matrix chart, you could color them separately to distinguish them. In figure 66, the dots within each quadrant are a different color.

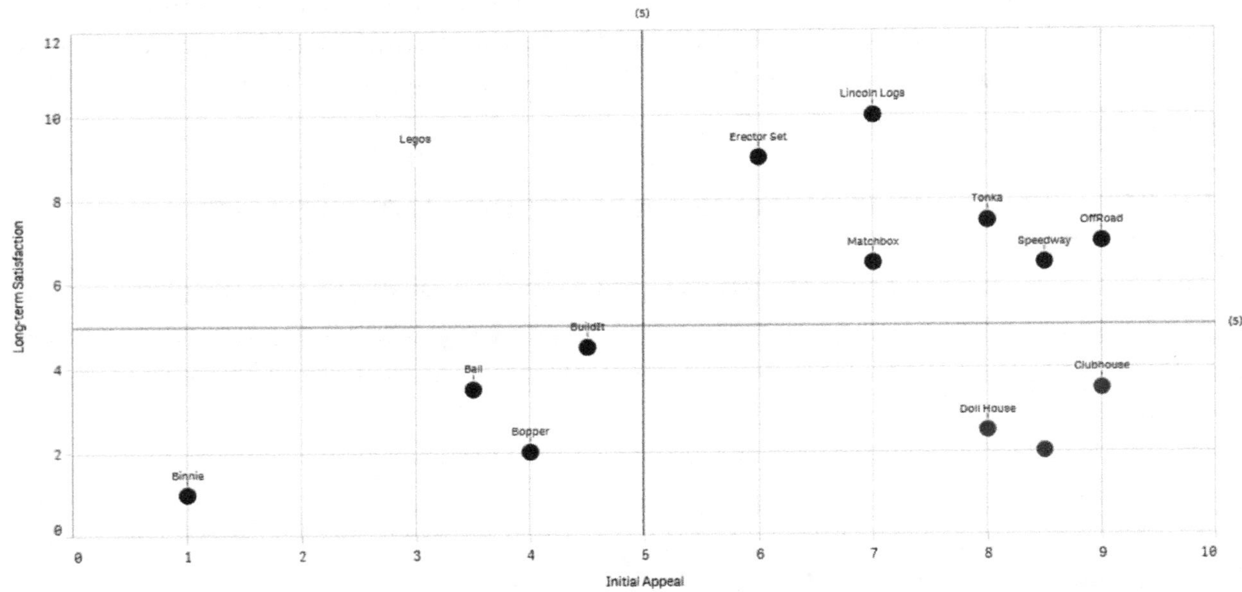

Figure 66. Categorizing items into groups using color

- Use the proximity principle to structure your layout. An example of this could be to overlay the legend directly onto a line chart so that each group's name is next to its line, as shown in figure 67.

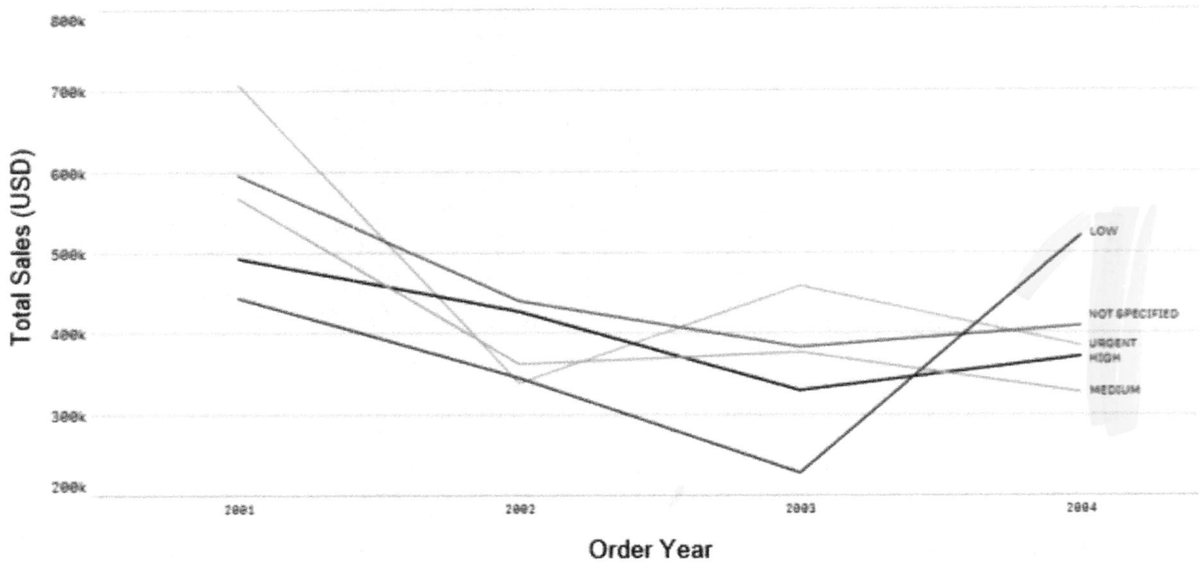

Figure 67. Overlaying the legend onto a chart

- To highlight a group, use color along with the similarity principle. An example of this would be to highlight for discussion the high-performing items in one color and the low-performing items in another color, as shown in figure 68.

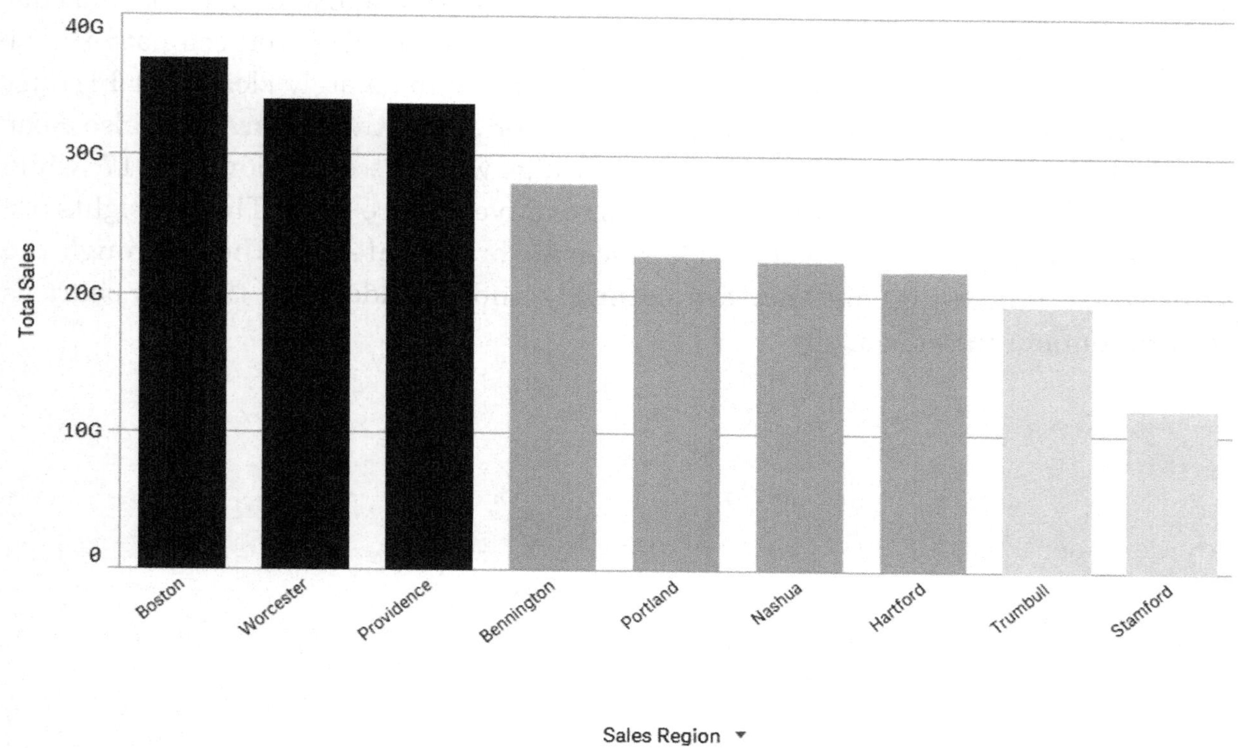

Figure 68. Highlighting groups using the similarity principle and color

SHORT-TERM MEMORY AND CHUNKING

As a reminder, *short-term memory* holds onto a few pieces of information at a time, around 5–9 items, and information stays here for about a minute, according to cognitive psychologist George Miller.[72] Short-term memory is also the memory used when we are working with a visual. The sensory information that is of interest to us is processed in the short-term memory.

Research has shown, however, that the capacity of short-term memory can be increased by using a process called *chunking*. In the chunking process, you group similar items together. Ever wonder why a phone number is typically chunked into smaller numbers?

When information is displayed in the form of visuals that show meaningful patterns, more information can be chunked together. Hence, when we look at a visual, we can process a great deal more information than what we can when we look at the same data in the form of a table.

For example, figure 69 displays two visuals that both show consumer ratings of two separate products, A and B, per year from 2005 to 2019. In the table on the top, can you see any patterns or trends? Probably not. It would take a lot of focus and concentration reading the numbers to find patterns or trends. Can you see patterns or trends with the line chart below the table? Yes. It is immediately clear that Product A has had higher ratings than Product B, except for the last two years. It is also clear that Product A is continuing to have lower ratings with the exception of 2017, while Product B has been increasing its ratings year over year since 2016. These insights are not easily communicated from the table since our brains interpret them through the use of verbal processing, but they are naturally understandable in the line chart as they are communicated visually.

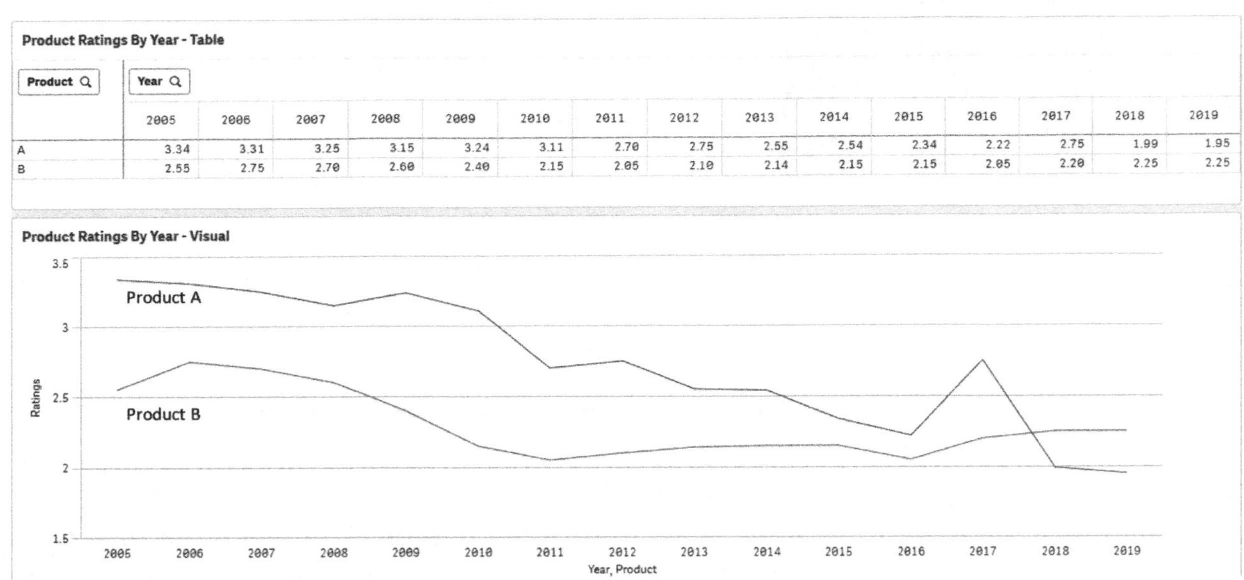

Product Ratings By Year - Table

Product	2005	2006	2007	2008	2009	2010	2011	2012	2013	2014	2015	2016	2017	2018	2019
A	3.34	3.31	3.25	3.15	3.24	3.11	2.70	2.75	2.55	2.54	2.34	2.22	2.75	1.99	1.95
B	2.55	2.75	2.70	2.60	2.40	2.15	2.05	2.10	2.14	2.15	2.15	2.05	2.20	2.25	2.25

Figure 69. Highlighting groups using the similarity principle and color

For a visual to be effective, we need to not provide more data than what our brains can process. The general rule of thumb is to include no more than 5–9 similar items within a visual. It is also important to display the visual on a screen or a single location so that we can see it without having to scroll or bounce back and forth between multiple locations.

THE STORY

In addition to visuals, the story, or narrative, that weaves together the visuals—when done right—will build a connection with the audience that bridges logic and emotion. Just like in earlier phases of the data-informed decision-making process, the brain plays an important role in the Announce phase too. Telling a story that takes the audience on a journey and resonates as well as sticks with them is based in how the brain works.

We won't go into the full chemistry of the brain, but if you are interested, read the study "Empathy toward Strangers Triggers Oxytocin Release and Subsequent Generosity" by neuroeconomist Paul Zak and professor of consumer psychology Dr. Jorge Barraza. In this study, Zak and Barraza explain how brain chemistry is related to storytelling. We learn that personal and emotionally compelling stories engage more of the brain and are better remembered than simply stated data and facts. In fact, they are not only better remembered but also more engaging and persuasive.[73]

So, how do we use this information to tell a story about our decision using data? Data by itself is complex, sometimes ambiguous, and typically void of context. Adding visuals, as described in the previous section, helps, but even visualizations are subject to interpretation. By adding a story, you will connect the data with context, describe how to interpret the data, and build a connection with your audience by taking them on a journey.

The story should follow a model that maximizes the story's impact on the audience. Since the most important question from the audience will be "what's in it for me?", after providing the context of the decision to be made, you should share the "aha" moment, rather than saving it for the end. The aha moment includes the major decision and key insights and why they are important to the audience you are speaking to. Then, you should provide some background information into the current situation and the analytical question(s) that prompted the decision. You can also incorporate visuals that use data from your measurement framework (descriptive analytics that describe KPIs that ultimately tie back to the company's strategic objectives). A major element of communicating to the audience is for you to earn their trust. Ideally, this exists even before you communicate. However, you can build trust during the story as well by showing your work. Doing this will have the added value of showing the audience context. You should highlight the reasons you made the decision and what you expect to happen as a result. The final part of the story should be details about the decision and next steps. Two specific principles that can be used to help craft your story include the *Pyramid principle* and the *Rule of Three.*

The Pyramid Principle

When communicating your story, the audience is unconsciously going to be looking for logical connections and structure between the various things you say. This means it is critically important that your story has a clear structure. This will prevent people from drawing incorrect conclusions, not paying attention, or focusing so hard to understand the structure that they miss other important messages in your story.

One model that provides you with that structure is called the Pyramid principle. The *Pyramid principle*, first created by business consultant Barbara Minto, advocates that ideas should always form a pyramid under a single thought, as shown in figure 70. According to Minto, "The mind automatically sorts information into distinctive pyramidal groupings in order to comprehend it. Any grouping of ideas is easier to comprehend if it arrives presorted into its pyramid. This suggests that every written document should be deliberately structured to form a pyramid of ideas."[74]

The situation. Describe the situation here.

The complication. Describe the complication here.

The question. Describe the question here.

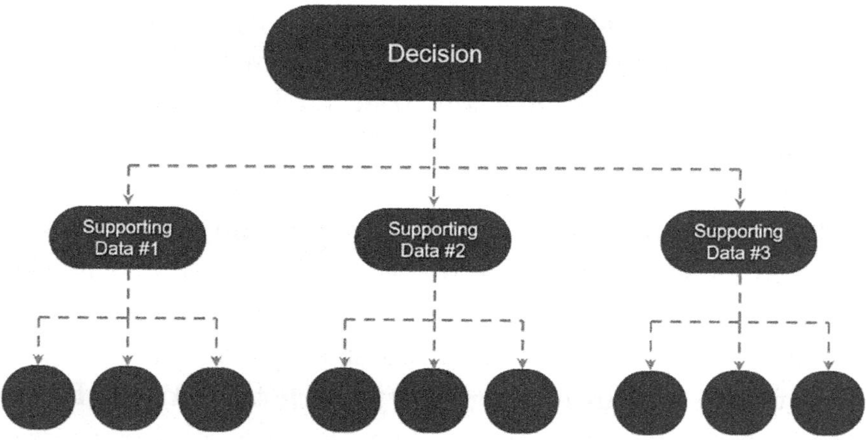

Figure 70. Pyramid principle

When using this model, you begin by communicating the situation, the complication, and the question. The *situation* is a statement about the subject that all the stakeholders will agree to. The *complication* is the complicated event that creates tension in the story. The *question* is the implicit question or decision that needs to be made as a result of the complication.

Next, you share your high-level decision, which answers the question. This model complements what we said earlier about starting with the decision first, instead of saving it until the end. This model gets to the conclusion quicker, allowing everyone to get aligned and have a candid conversation.

Underneath the decision, the next step down is sharing supporting data for the decision. Supporting data can include background information into the current state or key themes supporting the decision. For this level, you should group and summarize the supporting ideas and arguments. Then, for each supporting idea or argument, break it down further into more ideas or arguments that show the data and facts until you have formed a pyramid. Remember, showing the data and facts will help build trust with the audience. Ideas at any level in the pyramid must always be summaries of the ideas grouped below them, and they should always be mutually exclusive from other statements at the same level of the pyramid.

The Pyramid principle is not designed to include the full story and communication. It focuses on the decision itself. Components of the story that come after the decision still need to be added in.

The Rule of Three

The Rule of Three principle ties closely to what we learned about the Pyramid principle. The *Rule of Three principle* ties to the importance of how a story is comprehended more easily when the information for each node of the pyramid is presented in groupings of three (see figure 70). Research has shown that groups of three are often the magic number to make information easy to map, retain, and recall.

When you are communicating your story, there are multiple points at which you have to explain the why, the current state and challenges, what you expect to happen as a result of the decision, and next steps. In each of these places, use the Rule of Three to provide three messages. This will help you prioritize what you want to say and will also keep the communication to a time span that will hold people's attention.

An Example Story

Let's look at an example of a communication that uses both the Pyramid principle and the Rule of Three.

Top Level:

The situation. Our services have high value to our customers, but they incur a lot of costs.

The complication. We would like to increase our profit margin on our services by decreasing our costs by 15 percent.

The question. How can we reduce our costs by $5 million?

The decision (answer to the question). The company can decrease its costs by $5 million by reducing some operational efficiencies.

Second-Level Down:

1. Review outside vendor costs for delivering services, and save $1.5 million.
2. Review the cost to develop the services, and save $3 million.
3. Review internal processes for selling the services, and reduce overlap; save $0.5 million.

Third-Level Down:

1. Review outside vendor costs for delivering services, and save $1.5 million.
    - 1.1. Renegotiate contract with virtual lab provider.
    - 1.2. Review process for augmenting staff with subcontractors.
    - 1.3. Renegotiate contracts with subcontractors to minimize expenses.
2. Review the cost to develop the services, and save $3 million.
    - 2.1. Migrate materials delivered as part of service from printed to online.
    - 2.2. Streamline our development process and cadence.
    - 2.3. Renegotiate contracts with vendors used to develop the services.
3. Review internal processes for selling the services, and reduce overlap; save $0.5 million.
    - 3.1. Outsource selling of services back to another team to reduce overlap.
    - 3.2. Provide an e-commerce engine to be able to sell at scale.
    - 3.3. Provide an easy-to-use bundle of services that can be attached at the point of sale.

You do not need to use the visual element of the Pyramid principle in the communication itself. The visual is more to help you gather your thoughts and to ensure that you are following the principle. In the actual communication, you can use tools like Microsoft PowerPoint to deliver the message.

When creating your story for your communication, not all aspects need to include just data visualizations. Sometimes, the communication of "why" can be done with other types of visuals, such as infographics. Whereas a *data visualization* focuses on visualizing quantifiable data and information, an *infographic* focuses on communicating a plot. Figure 71 is an example visual created when an organization made the decision to move its training manuals from print to digital. The visual was used as part of the communication to course instructors and developers.

Figure 71. Infographic

Acting on the Decision

After the decision has been announced, it is now time to act on the decision. Much of this process, especially for **Type 1 decisions** (irreversible decisions), needs to be coupled with a change management plan. A *change management plan* encompasses the process, tools, and techniques that are used to manage the human side of a change. A change management plan includes how to prepare, enable, and support stakeholders to successfully adopt the change. This book does not cover change management in an exhaustive fashion. However, we do focus on one very specific component that needs to be included in the change management plan. That component is **unlearning**.

Unlearning is not about forgetting a skill; rather, it is about the ability to choose an alternative and more-current mental model. When we learn, we add new skills or knowledge to what we already know. When we unlearn, we step outside a mental model in order to choose a different one or to make updates to existing ones to better guide our decisions. Sounds simple, right? Not really. Remember the story of engineer Destin Sandlin from chapter 3, the man who attempted to ride a backwards bike? It took Sandlin over eight months of riding the backwards bike five minutes each day before he was able to ride it without falling off.[75] This example highlights that when change happens, some mental models that were accurate before the change will now be obsolete. In those scenarios, we have to unlearn the old mental models before we can learn the new way forward. The example also highlights that unlearning an older mental model—even when the person is aware it needs to be done—takes time.

HOW DO WE UNLEARN?

So the question is, *How do we unlearn*? Well, there are three steps. The first is becoming aware and accepting that the model currently being used is no longer working. This is, in fact, the hardest step as many mental models are unconscious. Next, you need to learn a new model independently from comparing it to the old model. When adults learn, they typically start by applying new information to what they already know. However, during unlearning, you need to consciously separate what you already know. Finally, you need to apply that model enough times that it becomes part of your new way of thinking. This is why Destin Sandlin took over eight months to ride a bike backwards. In the beginning, every attempt he made was still leveraging the old model. After lots of practice, however, Sandlin was finally able to ride the bike backwards without having his brain compare it to riding a bike "normally."

Unlearning is a critical step when any of your mental models are outdated due to the changing and evolving times. This scenario can also include when you are doing the same job but at a different company. Even within the same industry, companies will have different structures and practices in place and different organizational cultures. You will need to unlearn in this scenario as well. Just because something worked at one company does not mean it will work at the new one. Leon C. Megginson, professor of management, inferred from Charles Darwin's book *The Origin of Species* that "it is not the most intellectual of the species that survives; it is not the strongest that survives; but the species that survives is the one that is able best to adapt and adjust to the changing environment in which it finds itself."[76]

AUTOMATING DECISIONS AND ACTIONS USING PRESCRIPTIVE ANALYTICS

Prescriptive analytics were introduced back in the Analyze phase chapter along with the other levels of analytics (descriptive, diagnostic, inferential, and predictive). As a reminder, prescriptive analytics leverages insights from the previous levels of analytics to make a decision and take action. Prescriptive analytics fits into this Announce phase of the data-informed decision-making process because prescriptive analytics works not only to automate decisions but also to act on those decisions in real time.

Prescriptive analytics is not applicable to every single decision point, but this analytics type is useful when the decision is reoccurring (a Type 2 decision) and when it could and should be made as quickly as possible, even instantaneously.

Since prescriptive analytics requires almost-instantaneous action, the analysis and resulting decision need to be automated. As a result, prescriptive analytics requires **artificial intelligence**, including **machine learning**.

Prescriptive Analytics Terminology

Before we go any further into prescriptive analytics, let's look at some related terminology.

Artificial intelligence. Artificial intelligence is any program that can sense, reason, act, and adapt. The ultimate goal of artificial intelligence is for a piece of software to help in the decision-making process by thinking like a human can.

Algorithm. An algorithm is a set of instructions that get executed when triggered. An algorithm can be thought of as a recipe of step-by-step tasks to be completed.

Machine learning. Machine learning is a subset of artificial intelligence. It is any algorithm whose performance improves over time as it is exposed to more and more data. The goal of machine learning is for the algorithm to continue to learn and improve its decision-making without any alteration.

Big data. Big data is a term that describes large volumes of data that are analyzed in order to make decisions. Big data is said to have higher velocity, which means the data is more quickly received, analyzed, and then acted upon. The data is also said to have lots of variety, which means it comes in many forms, including structured data, such as from spreadsheets and databases, and unstructured data, such as from social media posts, images, and video files.

Machine Learning's Value in Business

Speed is a critical element of certain business decisions. Through the use of **artificial intelligence**—namely, **machine learning** (an **algorithm** that can improve itself over time)—prescriptive analytics can automate the decision and the action taken as a result of the decision so that they happen quickly.

It is not expected that everyone reading this book will be able to perform prescriptive analytics, but it is expected that everyone understands its potential capabilities, especially when used for reoccurring decisions that need to be made quickly.

Let's take a look at a simplified process for machine learning. The first step is determining what situation you are trying to decide on or predict and then choosing a machine-learning algorithm to make the decision. For example, assume a bank wants to decide whether or not it should provide a loan to loan applicants. The algorithm chosen to help with this decision is a logistic regression algorithm (which is used to analyze multiple variables and determine whether the bank should provide the loan). This algorithm will try to predict if a loan applicant would default on his or her loan.

The second step in machine learning is to acquire the data. In our bank example, the bank would acquire all the historical data it has on the people who did receive a loan and whether or not they defaulted.

The next step is to run the algorithm using the data. In our example, the bank will then run the logistic regression using the data to determine the variables from the data that best predict whether the loan will default. When the bank does that, it will then have a model it can use with future loan applicants. Using machine learning, the bank's algorithm will continuously try to evaluate and improve this model even after it is in production. See figure 55 in chapter 6 for a visual of this example.

Examples of Prescriptive Analytics in Action

Let's look at a few examples of prescriptive analytics in action.

Prescriptive analytics can be of benefit not only in business but also in helping the world. Countries are now able to use prescriptive analytics to save lives in the event of deadly natural disasters, like earthquakes, tsunamis, and hurricanes. They can use predictive analytics to predict the natural disaster, including its location or path, strength, and even timing. They can then use this information to make decisions about how to prevent the loss of life and to automate the actions that need to be taken as a result of each decision (prescriptive analytics). When the prescriptive model triggers a notification saying that a natural disaster is imminent, the decision of what the local government and emergency response teams should do is already made. With natural disasters, advanced warning is key, and speed is critical. Having these prescriptive models ready to prescribe steps to take instantly is extremely valuable and important.

In business, one of the key reasons for prescriptive analytics is to solve optimization-based decisions, like supply chain optimization and inventory optimization. Optimization, as it relates to prescriptive analytics, combines mathematical algorithms to find the best answer to a specific question, which either maximizes or minimizes a metric. For example, retail companies could use prescriptive analytics to maximize the profitability of their products, or they could decide on a strategy for what products to physically store in their shops with the goal of minimizing expenses.

Bias in Prescriptive Analytics

The potential of prescriptive analytics and artificial intelligence to reshape the world we live in today is massive. However, this potential does come at a cost. Like the human brain, prescriptive analytics and artificial intelligence are open to having cognitive bias. Decision-makers need to be aware that this bias can exist and take steps to mitigate it. Otherwise, we may see more harm than good coming from artificial intelligence.

However, this bias doesn't originate from within artificial-intelligence algorithms. It originates from people. People are prone to various cognitive and unconscious biases. Those biases can be passed into the artificial-intelligence algorithms at various steps during the process. In many cases, this has a network effect, and the bias becomes amplified. The result is a systematic error in the decisions or predictions of the algorithm. This is called *algorithmic bias*. Let's take a look at examples of bias in each step.

Human bias, such as a sampling bias, often makes its way into the acquiring-data stage. *Sampling bias* occurs when the data used to train a model does not accurately represent the environment that the model will operate in. There is virtually no situation in which an algorithm can be trained on the entire spectrum of data it could interact with. Nevertheless, there's a science to choosing a subset of that spectrum that is large enough and representative enough to mitigate sampling bias. Imagine you are building models to train an autonomous car that you would like to be operable at any time day or night, but the only data provided is during the daytime with sunlight. Do you think the car would work well autonomously in the dark?

Another common human bias encountered in machine learning is when the data acquired includes a prejudice. For example, if an internal recruiting tool was created to select ideal candidates and it used historical hiring decisions that favored men over women, the model would learn to do the same. Not only would that continue the pattern of prejudice, it would also amplify that problem.

It is also possible for human bias to be introduced during the data-preparation stage. This could be related to which attributes of the data you consider for the specified model. Choosing which attributes to consider, or ignore, can significantly influence a model's accuracy in predictions. But it is hard to assess if this will have an impact on the model's bias or fairness. For instance, it is illegal to deny someone employment based on their gender, race, or similar attributes. But what if the machine-learning model does just that? Is this legal or ethical?

When human bias is introduced in a model, whether from the data-acquisition or preparation stage, it can become amplified as the algorithms evolve. Machine-learning models are not static. They learn and change over time. Initially, a model might make decisions using only a relatively simple set of calculations. However, especially with deep-learning models, which are a subset of machine learning, as the system gains experience, it can broaden the amount and variety of data it uses as input and subject those data to increasingly sophisticated processing. This means that a model can end up being much more complex than it was when initially deployed. These changes are not due to human intervention but rather to automatic modifications made by the machine to its own behavior. In many cases, this evolution can introduce bias or prejudice or socially unacceptable and even illegal decisions.

Summary and Key Takeaways

- Be proactive and value-focused, and have a communication plan.
- Ensure that you communicate the right message at the right level to all stakeholders, focusing on the "why" and the "what's in it for me" questions.
- Ensure that the communication includes visuals and a story that aid in the understanding of the message, and leave out any irrelevant information.
- Ensure that you take into account cultural factors while crafting your communication.
- After the decision has been announced, ensure that you have a solid change management plan, especially for Type 1 decisions.
- Ensure that you provide adequate time for stakeholders to unlearn any outdated mental models and to learn new ones.

CHAPTER 9

PHASE SIX – THE ASSESS PHASE

"I have not failed. I've just found 10,000 ways that won't work."[77]
—Thomas Edison

Steps Involved in This Phase

12	Set up a review mechanism to monitor the impacts of the decision after it is made and acted upon. Leverage that review mechanism, and fail/fix/learn fast, making improvements to data, measurement frameworks, accountability, decisions, and anything else relevant.

The final phase of the data-informed decision-making process is the Assess phase. There are two parts to this phase. You should monitor the outcome and impact of your decision to assess if it was effective, and you should also assess the process used to make the decision by doing a **metaevaluation**, considering opportunities for improvement within each phase. Performing an assessment could require you to go back and adjust some of the frameworks you applied in previous phases so that future decisions will be more effective.

Monitoring and Assessing the Outcome

Once you execute your decision, it is important to assess the outcome and then adjust accordingly, adding what you learn to your mental toolbox to aid you in your decision-making in the future. Organizations that can course correct their less-than-optimal decisions by failing fast, fixing fast, and then learning from their mistakes are the ones that will succeed in today's business climate. This is exactly what Jeff Bezos was referring to in his shareholder report from 2016[78] that we discussed in the Apply phase chapter. The fail/fix/learn-fast mindset is at the heart of an organization that fosters continuous learning and innovation.

Keep in mind that some decisions, especially when you're dealing with complex systems and scenarios, may have a built-in delay in which the situation actually gets worse before it gets better. Ignoring or underestimating this delay can cause you to prematurely assess the decision and course correct when you don't need to. For example, assume an organization makes a decision to change a process to streamline incoming orders. The reason for doing so was the cumbersome order process, which had too many places for failure. If errors increase immediately after launching the new process, this could be due to the normal learning curve of learning a new process.

Performing a Metaevaluation of the Decision

Decisions bring about changes in systems, processes, and people. Therefore, it is important to monitor not only the outcomes of your decision but also the processes used in making the decision. This **metaevaluation** is especially important with strategic decisions. (As a reminder, **strategic decisions** include policies and complex decisions that have a major impact on a business.) The metaevaluation of a decision is similar in nature to what the military uses to learn from choices made in battles or what first responders use to learn from choices made during crisis. In those situations, this metaevaluation is called an after-action review.

When performing a metaevaluation of a decision, the following four questions should be the focal areas:

1. What was expected to happen?
2. What actually occurred?
3. What went well, and why?
4. What can be improved, and how?

Codifying the Decisions

When decisions are made, whether they work as designed or not, it is important to document the thought process that went into them. This is especially important when decisions are made using intuition. One tried-and-true method for organizations to develop organizational knowledge is to take the tacit knowledge that exists within the senior staff who have more experience. It is near impossible to teach intuition using formal learning. However, if senior staff make intuition-based decisions, the organization should ask them to document their thought process. This will help others to learn from their decisions and understand their rationale.

One strategy that can be used during the Assess phase is to ensure a mentoring and apprenticeship approach is in place within groups, pairing senior and junior employees together. Another common strategy is to require decision-makers to think out loud and to show their work. This practice is used a lot in elementary schools to ensure that students get the right answer using the right process. If students do not get the right answer and do not show their work, there is no way the teacher can find out where their logic failed or where they made a miscalculation. This practice is similar with business decisions. No one will learn if you are not explaining why you came to a decision. A final strategy that can be used during the Assess phase is to codify all the knowledge from decisions in a decision-making journal, thereby making the knowledge available to learn from for future decision-making.

DECISION-MAKING JOURNALS

A *decision-making journal* can be anything from a notebook to a digital document. Of course, at an organizational level, it makes sense to store this content in a digital format and to make it centrally located. The decision-making journal should document all aspects of your decision, including how you got there, what alternatives were discussed but not acted on, and details around the assessment of the decision since it was acted on. At a minimum, a decision-making journal should include the following sections:

- **The problem statement or situation.** This includes the business questions and analytical questions from the Ask phase.
- **Data and information relevant to the situation.** This includes anything existing in a measurement framework or similar.
- **Analysis.** This includes any analysis that was performed on the data and any interpretation of the results.
- **Possible decisions.** Include any decisions that were considered but not chosen and why they were not chosen.
- **The actual decision.** Include the actual decision made along with the expected results; this means what you expected to happen and the reasoning behind why you expected it to happen. Also include information on any assumptions made.

- **The communications.** Include any communications that were made to each stakeholder group.

- **Assessment of the decision after it went live.** This assessment should include what has gone well, what could be improved on, what assumptions turned out to be incorrect, and what mental models turned out to be outdated.

As you document each section, be sure to include enough context so that others can read the journal and understand what is being said. Go beyond the brief and obvious insights.

Summary and Key Takeaways

- Set up a review mechanism to monitor the impacts of the decision made.
- It is ok to fail, but make sure that you fail, fix, and learn fast.
- Sometimes, the right decision will make a situation worse before it gets better.
- Perform a metaevaluation on your decision to find areas of improvement for the future.

CHAPTER 10

TOOLS, FRAMEWORKS, AND MODELS

Within the data-informed decision-making process and methodology, there are countless tools, frameworks, and models available to help guide you. This chapter provides an introduction to some of the important ones. Chapter 12 will show these tools, frameworks, and models in action by people and businesses using the six-phase, twelve-step process and methodology.

TOOL, FRAMEWORK, OR MODEL	PHASES USED IN
Logic Model	Ask, Analyze, Assess
OODA Loop	Acquire, Apply, Assess
Behavior Engineering Model (BEM)	Acquire, Analyze
Vroom-Yetton-Jago Model	Apply
Pugh Matrix	Apply
Force Field Analysis	Acquire, Apply, Announce
Zig-Zag Process Model for Problem-Solving	Apply
Ladder of Inference	Apply
Strategic Foresight	Apply
Future Search	Apply
Theory of Constraints	Apply
Competing Values Framework	Apply

LOGIC MODEL

Phases Used In: Ask, Analyze, Assess

A *logic model*, or *program logic model*, is a tool used for assessing the impact achieved by an organization's application of resources to one of its programs. The logic model can also be used to describe how an organization works, including the theory of how it *should* work. A logic model typically depicts the inputs (or resources); activities (or processes, strategies, or methods); outputs; outcomes; and impacts associated with an organization and its programs. The model helps to link outcomes and impacts, both short and long term, with program activities/processes and the theoretical assumptions/principles of the program, such as financial assumptions. A logic model is especially valuable when trying to set up a measurement framework as it will help you to determine the key inputs and outputs that could be leading and lagging indicators. To refresh your memory, **leading indicators** can be thought of as drivers, and **lagging indicators** can be thought of as outcomes.

Sometimes, logic models are referred to as action plans. However, action plans are guides for running a specific project or program, and they include tasks and timelines for implementation. While action plans are absolutely useful for decision-making, a logic model illustrates the presumed effects in terms of what should happen as an outcome from the program. If an outcome is behind its target, the logic model helps the decision-maker to better see the outcome's connection to activities/processes to potentially understand why the outcome is behind. It is for this reason that logic models can also be helpful during the Assess phase.

The following are the main aspects of a logic model.

Inputs (or resources). Inputs, also called resources, are the materials that an organization or program takes in and then processes to produce the results desired by the organization or program. Types of inputs are people, people's ideas, people's time, money, equipment, facilities, supplies, etc. Inputs can also be major forces that influence the organization or program—for example, if the program has to adhere to external standards or certifications.

Activities (or processes, strategies, or methods). Activities, also called processes, strategies, or methods, are used by an organization or program to manipulate and arrange items to produce the results desired by the organization or program. Activities can range from putting a piece of paper on a desk to manufacturing a space shuttle. Logic models, however, are usually only concerned with the major recurring activities associated with producing the results desired by the organization or program.

Outputs. Outputs are usually the tangible results of the major activities in the organization or program. They are usually accounted for by their number. Outputs are frequently misunderstood to indicate the success of an organization or program. However, if the outputs aren't directly associated with achieving the benefits desired for the intended recipients, then the outputs are poor indicators of the actual success of the organization or program.

Outcomes and impacts. Outcomes and impacts are the impacts on those people whom the organization wanted to benefit with its program. Outcomes and impacts are usually specified in terms of:

- learning, including enhancements to knowledge, understanding, perceptions, attitudes, and behaviors
- skills (behaviors to accomplish results or capabilities)
- conditions (increased security, stability, pride, etc.)

Outcomes are often split into two categories: short term (0–3 months) and intermediate (12 months). Impacts are typically 1–2 years. Some logic models will define impacts as long-term outcomes.

> **Note:** For those of you familiar with Six Sigma, there is a tool called a SIPOC (suppliers, inputs, process, outputs, and customers), which is similar to a logic model. While both look at various inputs and outputs, the SIPOC is focused from the perspective of a given process, whereas a logic model can be focused at a higher level on a program.

Example of a Logic Model

Table 6 is an example of a logic model for a software organization's customer-onboarding program. The objective of this program is to ensure that users of the software are able to properly make use of it to obtain value within the first thirty days of purchase.

Table 6. Example logic model

INPUTS/RESOURCES	ACTIVITIES	OUTPUTS	OUTCOMES	IMPACTS
What resources should be used?	**What activities should be performed?**	**What assets/info should be created/used to support the intended outcomes?**	**What changes should be made in the next 3 months (short term) or 12 months (intermediate)?**	**What changes are expected in 1–2 years due to the outcomes?**
People Subject matter experts Instructional designers Interaction designers Technical writers Web developers IT system administrators Data analysts **Technology** Amazon Web Services cloud server Customer sign-on identity protocol Surveys Search appliance integration with salesforce.com Logs and reports	Design and develop awareness videos that highlight outcome-based solutions using the product Design and develop learning modules based on user roles Identify and document common links (like system requirements) based on user role Implement user experience to support personalized and adaptive content Implement Google-like search Implement prescriptive journeys for new customers based on their user role and buyer journey Implement analytics for every interaction on the portal Implement basic survey/feedback	# of new users with an organization's sign-on identity protocol account # of posts on organization's discussion board by new users # of learning modules consumed by new users # of searches in the portal by new users Weekly analysis and reports on feedback, key search terms, and most-used assets	**Short term** New customers are able to comprehend the value they will get with the product's solution New customers build their first application with the product New customers understand the product's ecosystem and how, when, and why to do the following: - where to go when they have a question about the product or its use - where to go when they have a system outage **Intermediate** New customers share insights from their solutions to other stakeholders New customers (consumers) consume and gain insights from solutions built for them New customers promote their solutions to internal users New customers maintain their product environment	Organization has an increased loyalty in customers (as evidenced by an increase in the customer-engagement survey from 20 to 25 percent this year) Organization increases its renewal rates to achieve or exceed a 95 percent renewal rate Organization increases retention from 87 percent to 90 percent

With this logic model completed, you now have very specific measurements that you would like to track in your measurement framework that relate to the organization's strategic needs. In this example, it would be measures from the outputs and outcomes as leading indicators and measures from the impact category as lagging indicators. Your dashboard should include details about not only what the current values are for those measurements but also what the target values should be. For example, one of the measurements in this example is the number of new users who are using the organization's single sign-on to log into their community and learning pages—you will want to track that number and compare it to the target. When the number is below the target, that is a leading indicator that something is wrong. Decision-making is an iterative, recursive process, so the insight gained here will most likely cause you to go back to the Ask phase and ask appropriate questions to determine why that number is below target. A blank logic-model template is available in this book's "Templates and Job Aides" chapter.

OODA LOOP

Phases Used In: Acquire, Apply, Assess

The *OODA loop* is a decision-making model that emphasizes the critical aspect of time in decision-making. This model could be used as part of the Apply phase when trying to make a decision. The OODA loop, as shown in figure 72, is an iterative model for decision-making consisting of four phases: *Observe, Orient, Decide,* and *Act* (OODA). It is a loop whereby the outcomes of actions may be observed and influence subsequent decision-making. In particular, poor decisions may be cancelled or updated as can decisions that are rendered inappropriate by a changing environment. As one accelerates this process, the effect of poor decisions is minimized, and the ability to adapt is maximized.

The OODA loop was created by US Air Force Colonel John Boyd to explain how to direct efforts to survive and defeat adversaries, specifically for fighter pilots during the Korean War. But now, the theory has been broadly applied for use in not only the military but also in commercial and learning processes.

Colonel Boyd observed that speed through the loop was more important to success than the quality of individual decisions. Time is the dominant parameter. The pilot who goes through the OODA cycle in the shortest time prevails because the pilot's opponent is caught responding to situations that have already changed.[79] Boyd's observation is just as critical in business as in combat. Companies gain significant advantages when they make decisions faster and more accurately than their competitors.

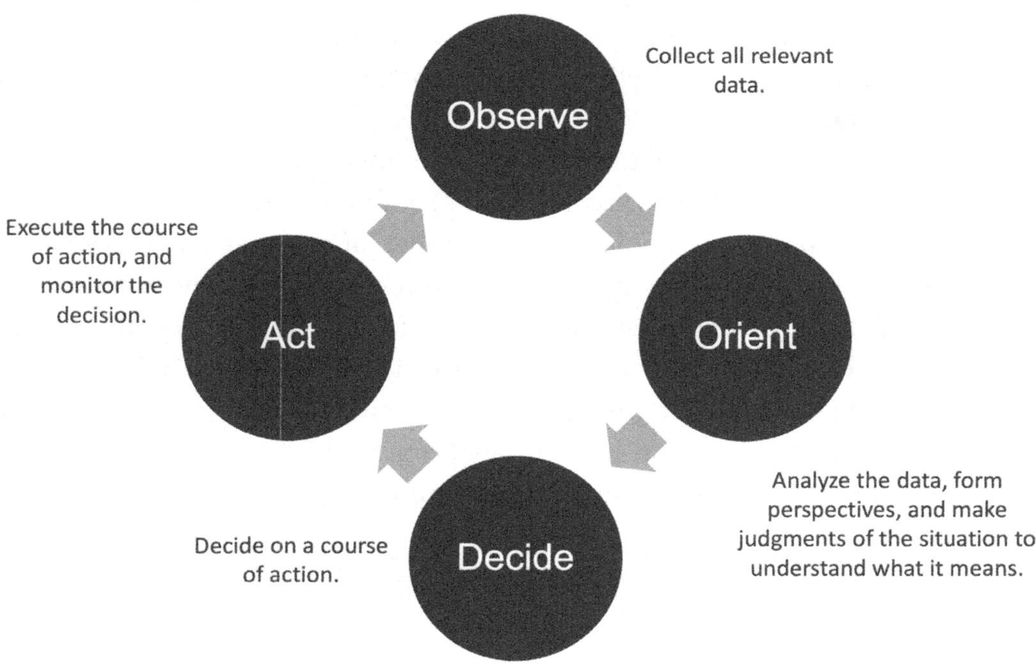

Figure 72. OODA loop

The four phases of the OODA loop are as follows:

1. **Observe.** The *Observe* phase of the OODA loop includes the collection of all relevant data. This data collection relates to the concepts discussed as part of the Acquire phase. It is important that the observation/data collection include not only what is directly visible within the organization but also anything external that is potentially related to the situation. For example, if an organization is seeing a decrease in market share, it is important for the organization to observe external factors such as the economy, the supply chain, and what its competitors are doing.

2. **Orient.** The *Orient* phase requires you to analyze the data, form perspectives, and make judgments of the situation to understand what it means. This includes applying your previous experiences. You then analyze and synthesize all of this with your observations. The goal here is to not just confirm what you already know. It is actually the opposite. The goal is to find mismatches and errors in your previous thoughts. This is where speed comes into play. For example, if an individual is about to make a decision using the OODA loop, it is at the Orient

phase that the individual should become aware of any unconscious bias and challenge his or her assumptions and mental models.

3. **Decide.** The *Decide* phase requires you to decide on a course of action.

4. **Act.** The *Act* phase requires you to execute the course of action and monitor the decision. After this phase, the OODA loop starts all over again.

Let's take a look at a basic example of the OODA loop in action.

Imagine you are driving your car on the road. You *observe* that the car in front of you has its brake lights on. You then *orient* to your surroundings. How fast are you going? How fast is the car in front of you slowing down? Are there any cars in the driving lanes to the left or right? You try to think about any assumptions you are making about the situation from past experiences. Then, you *decide* what to do, and you *act* on that decision. Based on your action, the process starts over as you observe what happened as a result of your action. For example, if during the Orient phase, you determined it would not be feasible to stop in time and so decided to veer to the left as you did not see a car there, you now start observing if the car behind you stopped or if other cars moved and are now a danger to you. While this is a simple example and not related to business, it highlights the importance of speed throughout the OODA loop.

The organization that completes the OODA-loop cycle in the shortest period of time wins by compelling the opposition to react to a situation that has already changed. In short, we must think and act faster than our opponents in order to survive and succeed.

Klaus Schwab, chairman of the World Economic Forum, coined the term "fourth industrial revolution" (a term defined at the start of chapter 1). According to Schwab, "In the new world, big fish do not eat small fish, but fast fish eat small fish."[80] In this, the era of the fourth industrial revolution, it is said that companies that make decisions and act faster than their competitors are competitive.

Let's take a look at some examples of the OODA loop used in business.

Honda countered Yamaha's initiative to build a new grandiose factory and to take the title of "World's Largest Motorcycle Manufacturer" away from Honda not by building an even-larger factory but by a smart maneuver of introducing 113 new models to Yamaha's 37. Honda neither waited to see what Yamaha was going to do nor copied Yamaha's strategy. Instead, the company processed a faster OODA cycle to seize the initiative of shaping the marketplace, with decisive effect. At the end of eighteen months, Yamaha publicly acknowledged defeat.[81]

Similarly, Amazon bases its success not on a reactionary approach of detecting market trends but by a fast OODA loop to create such trends in the first place. Amazon CEO Jeff Bezos stressed the importance of quick decision-making in a letter to his annual shareholders in 2016 (that was mentioned earlier in this book):

> Most decisions should probably be made with somewhere around 70 percent of the information you wish you had. If you wait for 90 percent, in most cases, you're probably being slow. Plus, either way, you need to be good at quickly recognizing and correcting bad decisions. If you're good at course correcting, being wrong may be less costly than you think, whereas being slow is going to be expensive for sure.[82]

BEHAVIOR ENGINEERING MODEL (BEM)

Phases Used In: Acquire, Analyze

There are times when an organization needs to make decisions regarding problems that are considered performance problems. Examples could be sales teams that are not achieving their targets, technicians who are not achieving their quality-standards targets, or customer-support employees who are not hitting their target for closing customer-support cases. While the quick reflex is to think that these problems are due to lack of training, research has shown that 75–85 percent of the performance issues in an organization are caused by something in the work environment.[83] Therefore, a cause-analysis model called the *Behavior Engineering Model (BEM)* was created to help identify what factors are negatively impacting performance in these types of problems. The model was originally created by psychologist Thomas Gilbert and then later updated by independent performance consultant Roger Chevalier. The Behavior Engineering Model states that there are six components of behavior that can be manipulated to change performance. These six components fall into two separate categories: components that relate to individuals and components that relate to the environment. The six components are information, resources, incentives, motives, capacity, and knowledge and skills.[84] Figure 73 shows the components visually laid out with specific details about each.

*Environment	Information	Resources	Incentives
	• Roles and performance expectations are clearly defined; employees are given relevant and frequent feedback about the adequacy of performance. • Clear and relevant guides are used to describe the work process. • The performance management system guides employee performance and development.	• Materials, tools, and time needed to do the job are present. • Processes and procedures are clearly defined and enhance individual performance if followed. • Overall physical and psychological work environment contributes to improved performance; work conditions are safe, clean, organized, and conducive to performance.	• Financial and non-financial incentives are present; measurement and reward systems reinforce positive performance. • Jobs are enriched to allow for fulfillment of employee needs. • Overall work environment is positive, where employees believe they have an opportunity to succeed; career development opportunities are present.
Individual	**Knowledge/Skills**	**Capacity**	**Motives**
	• Employees have the necessary knowledge, experience, and skills to do the desired behaviors. • Employees with the necessary knowledge, experience, and skills are properly placed to use and share what they know. • Employees are cross-trained to understand each other's roles.	• Employees have the capacity to learn and do what is needed to perform successfully. • Employees are recruited and selected to match the realities of the work situation. • Employees are free of emotional limitations that would interfere with their performance.	• Motives of employees are aligned with the work and the work environment. • Employees desire to perform the required jobs. • Employees are recruited and selected to match the realities of the work situation.

*We have adapted the BEM to provide a more efficient method for troubleshooting performance and for discovering the most important opportunities for improving individual performance. Like the original model, the updated model shown here serves as a diagnostic tool for troubleshooting performance problems. It is important to remember that cause analysis does not direct us to the best solutions for correcting the problem, but rather provides a framework for discovering underlying causes.

Figure 73. Behavior Engineering Model[85]

You should work through each condition from left to right and then top to bottom (information > resources > incentives > knowledge/skills > capacity > motives) and fill out the table cell with details based on data you captured. After completing the table, you will then analyze which components can be improved upon. Generally, performance problems are not due to any one reason, but many.

To see an example of the BEM in action, read the fifth example in the "Example Use Cases and Case Studies" chapter. A blank BEM template can also be found in the "Templates and Job Aides" chapter.

VROOM-YETTON-JAGO MODEL

Phases Used In: Apply

When trying to make a data-informed decision, sometimes it is hard for decision-makers to decide how to make the decision itself. Should they make the decision alone (autocratic), should they consult other people (consultative), or should they work with other people to reach a consensus on the decision (collaborative)? To help understand when to include a group in your decision process, a model called the Vroom-Yetton-Jago model was created. The *Vroom-Yetton-Jago model* is used to determine not only whether to make a decision alone or with a group but also to what extent the group should be involved. While this model can be used with every decision type, Type 2 decisions (decisions that can be reverted back from) ideally should always have some level of group involvement. Therefore, this model is most useful when looking to make Type 1 decisions (irreversible decisions).

The Vroom-Yetton-Jago model highlights that the decisions we make are affected by three main factors that work together: quality, the potential for collaboration, and the amount of time available.

1. **Quality.** This factor is concerned with the distinct characteristics of the decision and how important it is to make the best choice. It also considers the future consequences of the decision. The higher the quality of the decision, the more time and team members should be involved in the decision-making process.

2. **Collaboration.** Is this a one-person decision that an individual or manager can make without consulting the team, or does it require a collaboration and consultation from the team involved in the project? Adding team members to the

decision-making process increases the quality of the output but also the time required to reach a decision.

3. **Time.** What is the time limit for making the decision? The more time available to make a decision, the better the quality of the decision, and more team members can be consulted.

The Vroom-Yetton-Jago model uses a series of seven sequential questions to determine which decision process to use:[86]

1. Is the quality of the decision important?
2. Is team commitment important for the decision?
3. Do you have enough information to make the decision on your own?
4. Is the problem well structured?
5. Would the team support your decision if you made it alone?
6. Does the team share the organization's goals?
7. Is there likely to be conflict amongst the team over the decision?

The Vroom-Yetton-Jago model places these questions within a decision tree, as shown in figure 74.

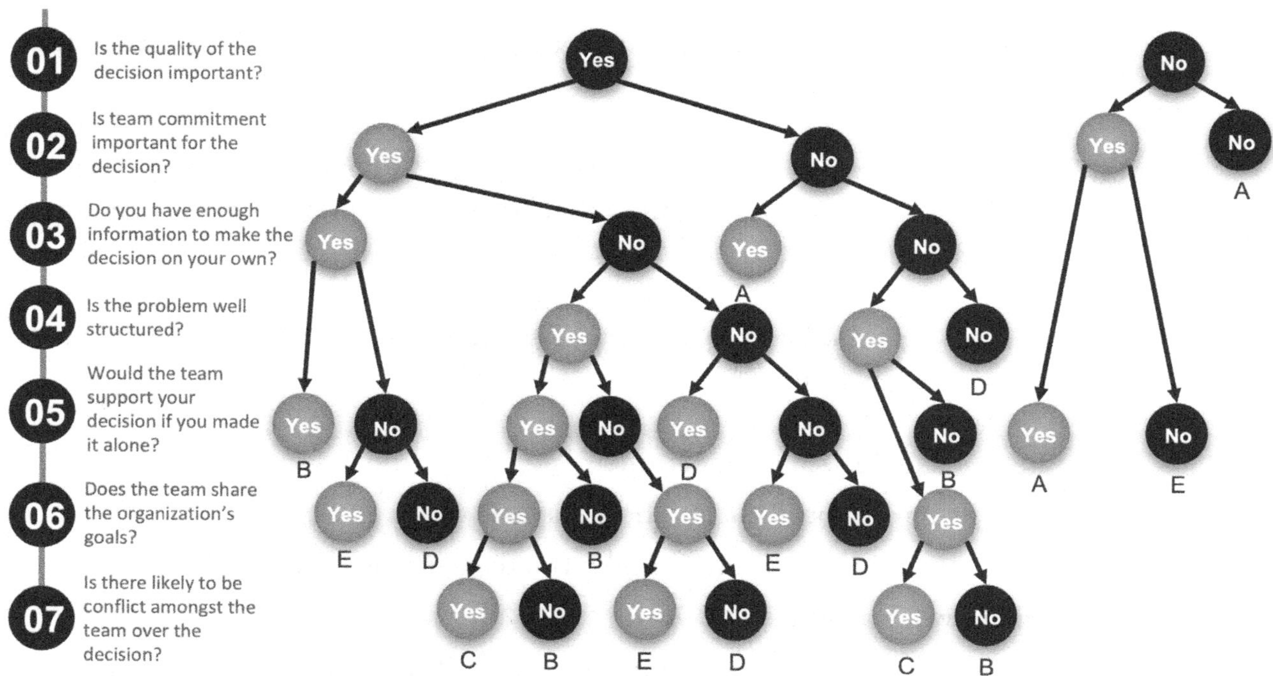

Figure 74. Vroom-Yetton-Jago model[87]

There are five possible outcomes related to how a decision should be made and who is involved:

A. The manager alone makes the decision.

B. The manager elicits information from team members but makes the decision alone. Team members may or may not be informed about the situation.

C. The manager shares the situation with team members individually and asks for information and evaluation. Team members do not meet as a group, and the manager alone makes the decision.

D. The manager and team members meet as a group and discuss the situation, gathering ideas and suggestions, but the manager alone makes the decision.

E. The manager and team members meet as a group to discuss the situation. The group defines alternatives and together makes a consensus decision. The manager acts more as a facilitator in this process and allows the group to agree on the final choice.

PUGH MATRIX

Phases Used In: Apply

When making data-informed decisions, it is important to not just have one possible decision but multiple alternative decisions. Developed by design professor Stuart Pugh, the Pugh matrix, sometimes called a decision matrix, is a method used to make the best data-informed decision once a number of alternate solutions have been generated. Let's take a look at the steps involved in using the Pugh matrix and then at some specific examples and visuals to help us understand its use a little better. The Pugh matrix steps are as follows:

1. **List the criteria that will be used for evaluation.** Although the possible criteria could be many, the Pugh matrix suggests using at least three criteria: technological impact, cost impact, and organizational acceptance. Of course, those criteria are not applicable to all decisions, so other criteria should be used in those cases. For example, if the decision is where to open up a new retail location, the criteria could be cost of facilities, potential market share, and potential employee pool.

2. **Weigh the importance of each criterion.** Various weighting strategies can be used. The higher the weight, the more important the criterion. For example, for three levels of importance, 3 is of most importance, 2 is of middle importance, and 1 is of lowest importance.

3. **Set the baseline.** This is typically the current-state solution. The scores for each criterion for the current solution should be 0 as the baseline. If your decision does not have a current solution or if there is no option to keep the current solution, then you can skip using a baseline.

4. **List all the alternative solutions.** This will create a matrix with the criteria on the vertical axis and the solutions on the horizontal axis.

5. **Score for each alternative decision.** There are different variations on how to score the Pugh matrix. Some will use 1, -1, or 0 to score against the baseline:

    - "1" means a particular solution scores better on a particular criterion as compared to the baseline.

- "-1" means a particular solution doesn't score better on a particular criterion as compared to the baseline.
- "0" means a particular solution scores the same on a particular criterion as compared to the baseline.

With this model, there is no scale to the positives or negatives to compare if the particular criterion is somewhat positive or negative compared to very positive or negative compared to the baseline. This is where the human element of decision-making comes into play. Alternatively, you can adjust the scoring to rank solutions using a five-point scale (+2, +1, 0, -1, and -2) to further differentiate them.

6. **Finally, total the scores for each particular criterion.** If any solution has a score greater than 0—greater than the baseline—it is considered for selection. If all the scores are less than 0, then the baseline current solution is kept. If a weighting is used, the scores are multiplied by the weighting.

Let's take a look at an example using the Pugh matrix for a personal decision. Perhaps you are trying to decide which car you should buy. You have three possible cars you would like to decide between. The criteria could be the cost to purchase the car, the fuel economy, the visual appeal, the safety, and the performance. In this case, there is not a decision to stay with the current baseline. You have to buy a new car, so you can leave the baseline out. Also, in this case, you want to compare criteria so that you can rank each criterion from 1 to 3, since there are three car choices.

Table 7 is what the completed Pugh matrix could look like for this example. The highest score equals the best decision, meaning, for example, that a score of 3 for the cost-to-purchase criterion is better than a score of 1, meaning the cost is cheaper to purchase.

Table 7. Example basic Pugh matrix

CRITERIA	CAR 1	CAR 2	CAR 3
Cost to purchase	3	1	2
Fuel economy	3	2	1
Visual appeal	2	3	1
Safety	1	2	3
Performance	2	1	3
TOTAL	**11**	**9**	**10**

In this example, Car 1 has the highest score total, so it would be the recommended car to buy. However, this example assumes that all criteria are factored equally. In reality, that may not be the case. Someone may value visual appeal as the top criterion, whereas someone else may value performance and another cost to purchase. Let's see the Pugh matrix filled out in table 8 with an example weighting in which safety is the most important criterion, and cost to purchase is the least important criterion.

Table 8. Example Pugh matrix with weighting

CRITERIA	WEIGHTING	CAR 1		CAR 2		CAR 3	
		SCORE	TOTAL	SCORE	TOTAL	SCORE	TOTAL
Cost to purchase	1	3	3	1	1	2	2
Fuel economy	3	3	9	2	6	1	3
Visual appeal	2	2	4	3	6	1	2
Safety	5	1	5	2	10	3	15
Performance	4	2	8	1	4	3	12
TOTAL			**29**		**27**		**34**

You can see that with the weighting added, the decision changes to now recommend purchasing Car 3.

Now let's look at one final example shown in table 9 that uses a positive and negative scoring system compared to a baseline. In this case, we will use the same example of purchasing a car, but we will compare each criterion to the baseline (the current car owned). When the totals are added up for each of the three car options, the car with the highest total greater than 0 would be the recommended car to purchase.

Table 9. Example Pugh matrix with positive and negative scoring

CRITERIA	BASELINE	CAR 1	CAR 2	CAR 3
Cost to purchase	0	-1	-1	-1
Fuel economy	0	1	0	-1
Visual appeal	0	1	1	-1
Safety	0	-1	1	1
Performance	0	1	1	1
TOTAL	0	**1**	**2**	**-1**

In this example, both Cars 1 and 2 score higher than the baseline, whereas Car 3 scores lower than the baseline. Car 2 has a higher score than Car 1, so the decision would be to purchase Car 2. We could apply a weighting to this example too to see how that impacts the results. You can see through all these examples the flexibility of the Pugh matrix and how you can adjust various aspects of the matrix to suit your needs.

FORCE FIELD ANALYSIS

Phases Used In: Acquire, Apply, Announce

Another tool to help decision-makers rank possible decisions is a Force Field Analysis. A *Force Field Analysis*, developed by psychologist Kurt Lewin, analyzes forces for and against a decision or change. This concept relates back to **systems thinking**, which we learned about in the Acquire phase chapter. Any given situation is maintained by an equilibrium between forces that drive change and others that resist change. For change to happen, the driving forces must be strengthened, or the resisting forces must be weakened.

We start the process of using this tool by brainstorming and thinking systemically about what those forces are—both driving forces that force us to a new desired state and restraining forces that keep us where we are. This is where systems thinking comes into play, as attempting to increase driving forces often causes the pressure of restraining forces to increase. Therefore, the Force Field Analysis tool puts emphasis on understanding the restraining forces against a decision and working to decrease or eliminate them. Examples of restraining forces include things like fear of change and lack of motivation or incentives. Examples of driving forces include things like increased efficiency and executive mandates.

To perform a Force Field Analysis, follow these steps:

1. Describe your potential decision.
2. List all forces for change, and separately list all forces against.
3. Assign a score to each force, from 1 (weak) to 4 or 5 (strong). Driving forces are positive values, and restraining forces are negative values.

The score for each force can then be visualized in a table, as shown in table 10.

Table 10. Force Field Analysis

FORCES	+4	+3	+2	+1	0	-1	-2	-3	-4
Driving force #1									
Driving force #2									
Driving force #3									
Restraining force #1									
Restraining force #2									
Restraining force #3									
TOTAL									

If your driving-forces score is lower than your restraining-forces score, there is a good chance the decision will not work or stick. You should then focus on what you can do to decrease or eliminate the restraining forces.

A Force Field Analysis is commonly done via group discussions. Groups can brainstorm various ideas about what elements are driving a change and what elements are restraining it. Group members can list each element on a sticky note, sort the elements into major categories, and then list those categories on the Force Field Analysis diagram.

For example, assume we are trying to make a decision as to whether we should change up our employee-onboarding program, and we need to assess the likelihood of success for a given proposal. Our team brainstormed and came up with four driving forces that will help drive the proposed change and one restraining force that will work against the proposed change. Each force was then ranked.

Table 11 is an example of that Force Field Analysis, which can be visually depicted using Excel or just a table on a whiteboard.

Table 11. Example Force Field Analysis for changing an employee-onboarding program

FORCES	+4	+3	+2	+1	0	-1	-2	-3	-4
Improved learning outcomes for the new hires									
Onboarding-program administrators have reference points for learner progress									
Allows new learners to practice their skills in a "safe" setting (no detrimental consequences for error)									
New learners receive the feedback needed to synthesize and retain information being presented									
Considerable increase in onboarding-program expenses (e.g., time, financial cost, program-administrator workload, and time employees spend just onboarding)									
TOTAL	**+13**					**-4**			

The driving forces add up to +13, and the restraining forces add up to -4. This makes the final number +9. This means that this particular decision to change the employee-onboarding program has a high likelihood of succeeding.

A Force Field Analysis is also a good tool to announce a decision to your stakeholders and to explain what is being done to achieve the desired state.

ZIG-ZAG PROCESS MODEL FOR PROBLEM-SOLVING

Phases Used In: Apply

We discussed the importance of cognitive diversity during the decision-making process back in the Apply phase chapter. As a reminder, **cognitive diversity** is the inclusion of people who have different styles of problem-solving and can offer unique perspectives because they think differently. One decision-making model that takes into account cognitive diversity is called the *Zig-Zag process model*, as shown in figure 75.

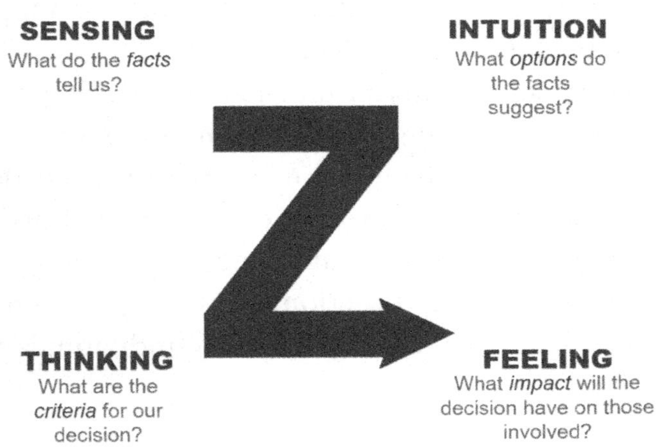

Figure 75. Zig-Zag process model for problem-solving

The Zig-Zag process model harnesses the power of the *Myers-Briggs Type Indicator (MBTI)*. The MBTI is a self-report questionnaire that people fill out to determine their psychological preferences in how they see the world and make judgments and decisions. The MBTI was created by Katharine Cook Briggs and her daughter Isabel Briggs Myers and is based on a theory from psychiatrist Carl Jung that people experience the world using four functions: thinking, feeling, sensing, and perceiving. Jung also believed there are two main character types: introversion and extroversion (Jung spelled it extraversion). This theory led to the MBTI questionnaire that will inform people where they are in relation to those functions:[88]

1. Are they introverted (I) or extroverted (E)?
2. Do they focus on information that is taken in (sensing – S), or do they prefer to interpret and add meaning (intuition – N)?
3. Do they prefer to look at logic and consistency (thinking – T) or at people and the circumstance (feeling – F) before making a judgment or decision?
4. Do they prefer to get things decided and resolved (judging – J) or to stay open to new information and options (perceiving – P)?

A person's MBTI type is the individual's personality traits specific to those four questions. The Zig-Zag process model leverages an individual's MBTI type for sensing/intuition and for thinking/feeling to systematically make well-rounded decisions within a group. The group must identify individuals within the group who have the MBTI types of sensing, intuition, thinking, and feeling.

The Zig-Zag process model is ordered into four steps. Steps 1 and 2 help acquire the necessary information about the given problem, and steps 3 and 4 help focus the information into what is relevant to be able to make a good decision. Groups that have a decision to make would walk through each step outlined below to ultimately come up with a decision. For each step, individuals within the group who fall into that specific MBTI type would work on that section. For example, step 1 is Sensing, and the process within that step should be accomplished by individuals who have sensing in their MBTI type.

Step 1: Sensing

The Sensing step is used to gather concrete data points and information about the current state. You can do this by asking a series of questions:

- Have you been in a situation similar to this before?
- If not, who has been through it successfully?
- If so, how did the process go previously, and what can you keep the same and change?
- What position are you currently in, and how does that factor into the decision?
- What are your current strengths and weaknesses, and how do they relate to the decision?
- What are the outside factors and details that play a part in this situation at the current time?

Step 2: Intuition

The Intuition step will then try to connect that information at a big-picture level to try to come up with some possible options. You can do this by asking a series of questions:

- While trying to think outside the box and to avoid using a filter to eliminate any ideas, what are all of the possibilities for the decision, even those that seem unreasonable?
- What connections do the possibilities have to each other and to different parts of you? Do they have a common theme or all relate to certain values you hold? Do they lean in any particular direction?

- What have you overlooked in previous decisions? Do you tend to avoid certain areas out of fear or for other reasons?
- How will the possible decisions impact the future and growth of the group or organization?

Step 3: Thinking

The Thinking step will then examine the options and information and objectively look at how they relate to the decision to be made. You can do this by asking a series of questions:

- If an acquaintance were trying to make this decision and you were looking at the information as an outsider, what would you advise the acquaintance to do, or what would you think that person should do?
- What are the pros and cons of deciding in each way? Which side has the most pros, and which has the most cons?
- If one of your preconceived notions about the decision is proven wrong, are you open to changing the decision accordingly?
- If you place more weight on logical data than on relationships, which decision makes the most sense? Is this enough to sway your decision in a particular direction?

Step 4: Feeling

The final step, Feeling, is when each option for the decision is examined to understand how each impacts the stakeholders and how those impacts align with the decision-makers' values. You can do this by asking a series of questions:

- What is most important to you? Maybe your pro/con lists have equal numbers, but do some pros and cons outweigh others?
- How do the possible outcomes fit into your values and life?
- How do you feel about each possible outcome, and how do you believe you would feel about each after the fact? Sad? Nervous? Happy? Does anything "click"?
- How would each possibility impact people close to you?[89]

LADDER OF INFERENCE

Phases Used In: Apply

One tool that can be used during the Apply phase to try to identify and mitigate bias is the Ladder of Inference. The tool, created by organizational psychologist Chris Argyris, helps you avoid incorrect inferences in your decision-making process by using a step-by-step reasoning process.

The *Ladder of Inference*, as shown in figure 76, describes the thinking process that we go through, typically without even realizing it, to go from data or information to a decision or an action.

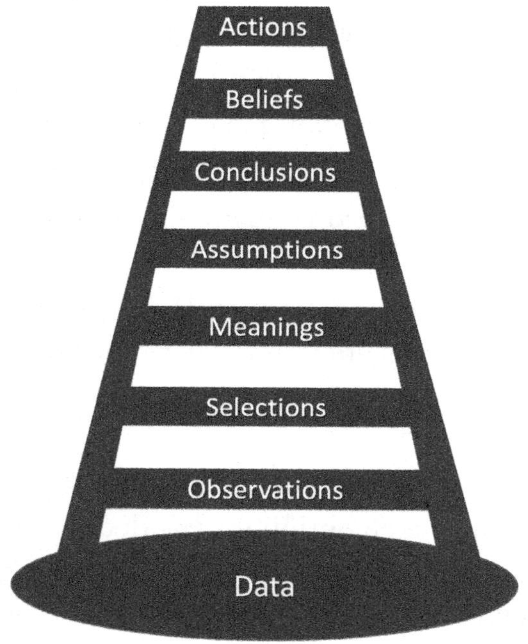

Figure 76. Ladder of Inference

1. At the base of the ladder is all the possible *data* for a given situation.
2. Individuals then see a subset of the data based on their *observation* of the situation.
3. From there, individuals *select* a subset of that data that they feel is relevant, and they discard any data that they feel is irrelevant.
4. Individuals then interpret the remaining data to add *meaning* to it.

5. Individuals then make *assumptions* about the remaining data.
6. Individuals then draw *conclusions* based on their assumptions and on what is good for them and their friends and family.
7. Individuals then adopt *beliefs* based on their conclusions.
8. Finally, individuals *act* on their beliefs as if they are proven facts.

The Ladder of Inference process often occurs unconsciously and in less than a second in the human brain. It happens imperceptibly fast. All the convictions that someone forms influence the next time a situation is perceived. Therefore, the process continues to repeat itself. All of the conclusions reinforce the prior beliefs, which in turn influence the selection of facts. This can lead a person to ignore certain facts altogether and to jump to conclusions. The Ladder of Inference teaches you to take a few steps back in the reasoning process, allowing you to remain objective and to not immediately jump to conclusions.

Through the awareness and use of the Ladder of Inference, you can teach yourself to look at data without bias and to not judge too soon. This tool is a way to use your own convictions and experiences in a positive manner. The Ladder of Inference can be used in every stage of the thought process. Anyone can apply this tool themselves by asking the following questions:

- Am I drawing the right conclusion?
- Why did I assume this?
- Is my conclusion based on facts?
- Why do I think this is the right thing to do?
- Can I do this in a different way?

It is also useful to identify the level of the ladder you are currently on. Sometimes, it is smart to go back to a lower step. By asking yourself what you are thinking and why at each step, you will be able to analyze each step and no longer jump to premature conclusions.

STRATEGIC FORESIGHT

Phases Used In: Apply

You learned that it is difficult during the Apply phase to be aware of **mental models** (how you see the world) that may be outdated. These outdated mental models can bias your decisions. One process that helps you think in innovative ways instead of using linear models that are based on your biases is Strategic Foresight. *Strategic Foresight* is a process that allows you to think differently about things and to be curious and open. It is commonly used as a business-planning process that focuses on preparing for the future, but its tenets can be used to leverage a mindset of openness and awareness as well. Therefore, Strategic Foresight is beneficial to leverage not only when making strategic decisions but also when making decisions under the uncertainty of the future.

One of the most common tools to use as part of Strategic Foresight is the STEEP analysis. The *STEEP analysis* helps you to analyze external environments and how they will impact your organization's strategic plan. The tool has five elements:

1. **Social.** The social element takes into account the social environment including demographics, lifestyle, religion, age, and education.
2. **Technological.** The technological element takes into account technological advances.
3. **Economic.** The economic element takes into account consumers' abilities to obtain products or services given the economic conditions.
4. **Environmental.** The environmental element takes into account any environmental elements, if applicable, like water, wind, energy, pollution, and climate change.
5. **Political.** The political element takes into account the political and legal environment and conditions of the countries and locations you are working or selling in.

Another common tool used for Strategic Foresight is *Visioning*. In his book *Futuring*, Edward Cornish breaks down Visioning into eight tasks. Here they are in his own words:

1. Review the organization's common history to create a shared appreciation.

2. Identify what's working and what's not. Brainstorm and list "prouds" and "sorries."
3. Identify underlying values and beliefs, and discuss which ones to keep and which to abandon.
4. Identify relevant events, developments, and trends that may have an impact on moving to a preferred future.
5. Create a preferred future vision that is clear, detailed, and commonly understood. All participants, or at least a critical mass, should feel a sense of investment or ownership in the vision.
6. Translate future visions into action goals.
7. Plan for action: Build in specific planned steps with accountabilities identified.
8. Create a structure for implementing the plan, with midcourse corrections, celebrations, and publicizing of successes.[90]

FUTURE SEARCH

Phases Used In: Apply

Future Search is a model for team meetings to enable organizations and communities to quickly transform their capability to action. The Future Search meeting has five phases and ideally requires two-and-a-half days. The goal of these meetings is to leave with an action plan for the future of some topic. The Future Search concept requires having a diverse group get together to look at their past, present, and future. In doing so, they are trying to discover common ground and then make an action plan on how to collectively go forward. What is unique about this meeting approach is that every single person in the meeting works on the same exact tasks until the action-planning time. This helps to create a shared and collective vision of the needed values and goals. While not every decision requires a Future Search type of meeting, the core principles of this particular meeting model are transferrable to any type of meeting in which a **strategic decision** needs to be made. Examples of strategic decisions include changing business models, go-to-market approaches, products and services that you take to market, or even organizational culture. There are four key principles to Future Search:

1. **Principle 1: Get the whole system in the meeting.** This requires getting a cross section of stakeholders into the meeting so that you have the skills, know-

ledge, and authority to think and act systemically. These stakeholders include the following types: *upstream* (individuals who are involved in the implementation of the program or offering the decision has set forth), *downstream* (individuals who receive, use, or participate in the program or offering the decision has set forth), *direct* (employees within the program or offering the decision is made for), and *indirect* (individuals who are typically external to the organization or group).

2. **Principle 2: Explore and understand the entire system before trying to fix any part of it.** Understanding the organization's system and taking a systems perspective to making decisions will improve the outcomes. Many times, decisions are made without understanding their impacts on the rest of the system. For example, a decision might be made to increase marketing spend within a software company, but how this would impact the capacity of the sales employees is not considered. These unintended consequences can be avoided if the system is understood by all participants before discussing actions.

3. **Principle 3: Focus on the desired future and common ground.** Many meetings end up being confrontational. Then, the participants spend valuable time trying to resolve those conflicts. When engaging in a Future Search meeting, conflicts are just information and symptoms that are used to help understand the system. They are not acted upon, and time is instead spent on discussing common ground and what participants are willing to do moving forward.

4. **Principle 4: Small groups self-manage and take responsibility for action.** This allows all participants to feel as if they are a part of the process and committed to the outcomes.[91]

Think about any decisions you have made as part of a group. Have you broken any of these principles?

THEORY OF CONSTRAINTS

Phases Used In: Apply

It is a common scenario for companies to come up with multiple aspects of a system that are causing potential problems. The next step is to make a decision on which cause should be improved first. The Theory of Constraints, introduced by business-management guru Eliyahu M. Goldratt in his book *The Goal*, is a model used to help determine which problem aspect to prioritize improving first. The theory teaches us that there are many things we can and must do to a system to increase its efficiency before adding any resources.

Think of a process that has a bottleneck (a halt in progress). If you try to improve any other parts of that process that do not improve the bottleneck, you will not achieve a greater output. In fact, you will only make the problems worse. According to the Theory of Constraints, at any time, just one of a system's inputs is constraining its other inputs from achieving a greater total output. The decision on how to increase a system's output is then to iteratively identify and address the current constraint.

To understand what constraint to prioritize, think about three characteristics of your system:

1. **Throughput.** Throughput is the rate at which the system creates money via sales.
2. **Operational expense.** Operational expense is all the money spent to turn inventory into throughput.
3. **Inventory.** Inventory is all the money invested into things to sell.

The Theory of Constraints describes that the goal is to maximize throughput while decreasing operational expense and inventory. According to Goldratt, there are five steps to follow to increase the throughput: identify, exploit, subordinate, elevate, and repeat:

1. **Identify.** *Identify* the constraint. This would be the current bottleneck.
2. **Exploit.** *Exploit* the constraint. This means we are trying to optimize everything we can from that component to increase its productivity and output.
3. **Subordinate.** *Subordinate* everything else to the constraint. In order to maximize and optimize the current constraint, we need to have all components of the system that are not the constraint supporting the constraint.
4. **Elevate.** *Elevate* the constraint. If the first three steps did not eliminate the current constraint, we need to elevate the constraint by providing additional resources to help resolve it. If this step is needed, major changes to the existing system are considered.

5. **Repeat.** *Repeat* the process for the next constraint. However, if the above four steps did not eliminate the current constraint, repeat them.[92]

Now, let's look at an example of the Theory of Constraints in action—in this case, to make iterative improvements to a company that creates and sells a specialized line of sports furniture. The company's distribution is through ten retail stores. It makes $5 million in sales annually. The company's leadership team has requested the desire to grow their sales to $8 million next year. One of their requirements is that they do not want the solution to involve adding more retail stores.

The team brainstormed possible levers they could execute to increase sales. They thought about the problem systemically, and they leveraged the Theory of Constraints model:

1. To begin, the team *identified* the first constraint: there is not enough foot traffic at their stores.
2. Next, the team tried to *exploit* the constraint and *subordinate* everything else. The decision made was to put all their available resources into marketing.
3. The team then tried to *elevate* the constraint. They realized that the amount of traffic on their website was not ideal and that it led to less-than-ideal traffic in their stores; therefore, they decided to bring in a consultant to help with search engine optimization and internet advertising. This resulted in a steady increase in traffic to the site, but the measurement framework highlighted that sales had not changed.
4. After further dialogue, the team *identified* that the constraint to achieving the leadership team's goal was lack of customers. Therefore, they *repeated* the process with the identification of this new constraint.
5. They then tried to *exploit* this new constraint and *subordinate* everything else. The decision was made to update the marketing and positioning on their site and to add a monthly sales promotion. As a result, the sales orders started to increase. However, the constraint now became fulfillment as major delays in shipping the orders appeared. Therefore, they *repeated* the process with the identification of this new constraint.
6. They next tried to *exploit* this new constraint and *subordinate* everything else. The company decided to add more resources into its fulfillment department. As a result, the fulfillment increased and was able to meet the current demands.

7. As the sales increased, the next constraint *identified* was production. The company offered many customizations of its product, which required a lot of time to switch between styles on the production line. Leveraging diagnostic analytics, the company saw a common mental model in action: the 80-20 rule. Three of the customizations accounted for nearly 80 percent of the sales. As a result, the company decided to stop selling anything but those three styles.
8. While some sales dropped in the beginning as a result of the company shrinking its product portfolio, the system and throughput were maximized, and over time, the company achieved its growth in sales originally requested by the leadership team.

This example demonstrates the iterative nature of the Theory of Constraints process, which uses data and human experience to make decisions driving toward an ultimate objective—which in this company's case was to increase sales revenue, which the company successfully achieved.

ASSESSING ORGANIZATIONAL CULTURE: COMPETING VALUES FRAMEWORK

Phases Used In: Apply

When making decisions, companies need to take into account the company's **organizational culture** in order to ensure success. The right decision to the same problem may be different at one organization compared to another, due to the culture. To help decision-makers understand their organizational culture and how it will impact decisions, business professor Robert E. Quinn and political science professor John Rohrbaugh created the *Competing Values Framework*. This model can be used to help organizations assess whether their current culture is compatible with a company-wide strategic decision that involves change. Also, understanding their organizational culture will help decision-makers understand what they need to do to ultimately reach a decision.

Organizational leaders regularly confront issues such as how to be innovative, how to organize and deploy resources, and how to collectively grow and change as a system. Leaders must determine how to confront these and other issues while recognizing that "effectively" doing so within the scope of an organizational culture requires an awareness of the everyday tensions that exist within their organizations.

The Competing Values Framework model focuses on two dimensions that have been proven important in relation to organizational culture and an organization's effectiveness in making and executing decisions. The first dimension is the organization's focus. On one end of the spectrum is an internal and individual focus. On the other end is an external and organizational focus. The second dimension is the organization's structure and risk tolerance. On one end of this spectrum are flexibility and discretion. On the other end are stability and control.

Mapped onto a chart, those two dimensions make four quadrants, which each represent a distinct set of organizational and individual factors, as shown in figure 77.

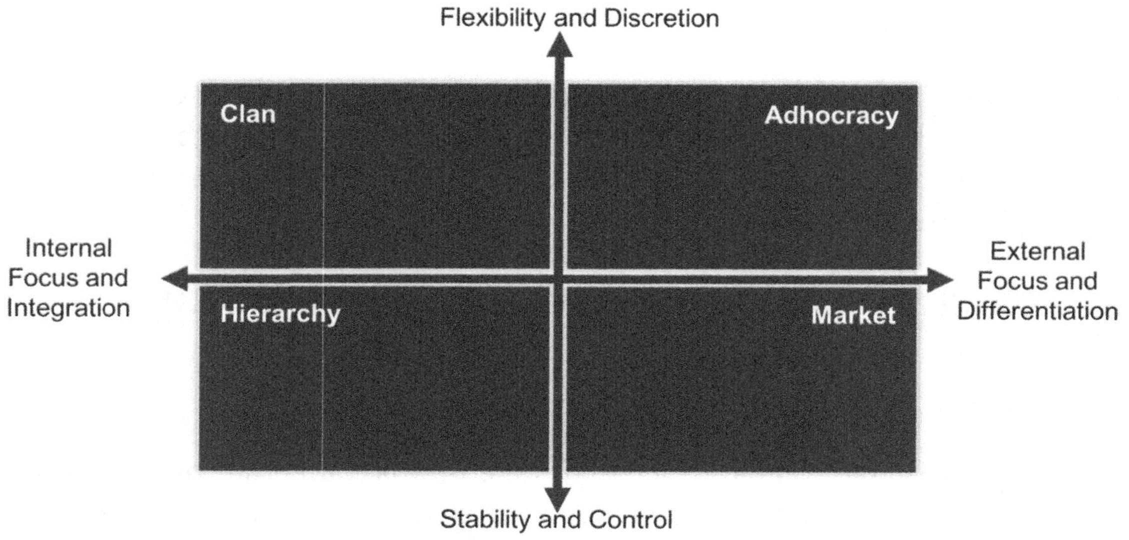

Figure 77. Factors of organizational culture

Clan. Clans put emphasis on internal focus and flexibility and discretion. Clans focus on the relationships between people, connected to flexible processes that care for employees. These organizations are very collaborative and typically require consensus in all things, especially decision-making. When working within a clan, it can feel like things never move forward because everyone wants to have a say in the work being done. It is typical in clans for individuals to get frustrated and push back on decisions if they were not involved.

When making decisions within a clan, the most important thing to do is to bring people along for the ride. Find ways to show teammates how their ideas are helping to shape the team's or organization's vision, and make use of informal one-on-one feedback sessions with people who might need a bit more help getting on board. Regular sharing sessions throughout the process are also helpful. This helps team members to see the process in action and prevents them from feeling like they were not part of the decision-making process at all.

Adhocracy. Adhocracies put emphasis on external focus and flexibility and discretion. Adhocracies focus on creativity—namely, creating new and innovative things. Adhocracy organizations are characterized by an ability to change and be adaptable when new opportunities are created. Leaders within the adhocracy are innovators who experiment and innovate. Flexibility and individualism are important drivers within an adhocracy. While this can be a great thing, it can also lead to feelings of chaos. Adhocracies tend to resist formal processes. When making decisions within an adhocracy, you will need to find ways to add some process without actually calling it a process.

Market. Markets put emphasis on external focus and stability and control. Markets focus on competition and productivity. The external focus of the organization is on relationships. There is a high need for control and stability. Typically, market cultures love numbers. If there's a metric they can point to that tells them they've succeeded, they will follow that metric closely and focus their attention primarily on moving it in the right direction. Market organizational cultures require data for their decisions—but only quantitative data. They tend to not take qualitative data too seriously. When making decisions within a market, don't just focus on descriptive analytics. Also include diagnostic analytics to help identify any anomalies, trends, or hidden relationships that can help explain why the descriptive numbers are what they are.

Hierarchy. Hierarchies put emphasis on internal focus and stability and control. Hierarchies focus on control and top-down leadership. This means that decisions within these cultures require buy-in from senior leadership; executive sponsorship is key. The challenge within a hierarchy is being able to engage with and to cultivate relationships with executive sponsors without having the team become victims of groupthink or blind followers of executive sponsors' opinions.[93]

It is important to note that while your organization as a whole might be one style, the specific groups you work within can be drastically different.

How Do I Assess My Organization's Culture?

Professor Robert E. Quinn along with Professor Kim Cameron developed the *Organizational Culture Assessment Instrument (OCAI)* for measuring the culture of an organization. The OCAI is based on the Competing Values Framework.[94] The tool surveys employees who are asked to score six aspects of their organization's culture: dominant characteristics, organizational leadership, management of employees, organization glue, strategic emphases, and criteria of success. For each aspect, respondents are provided four statements about their organization and are asked to score the statements from most true to least true. The output of the survey is a profile of the organization's current culture as well as the preferred culture the organization should have in the future.

Now that we have been introduced to many important tools, frameworks, and models that can help us make better data-informed decisions, the next chapter will provide some blank templates you can use within your own organization. However, you may want to skip over that chapter for now and move onto the one after it, in which we'll showcase a few examples of these tools, frameworks, and models in action within real situations, both personal and business related.

CHAPTER 11

TEMPLATES AND JOB AIDES

6-Phase Data-Informed Decision-Making Process

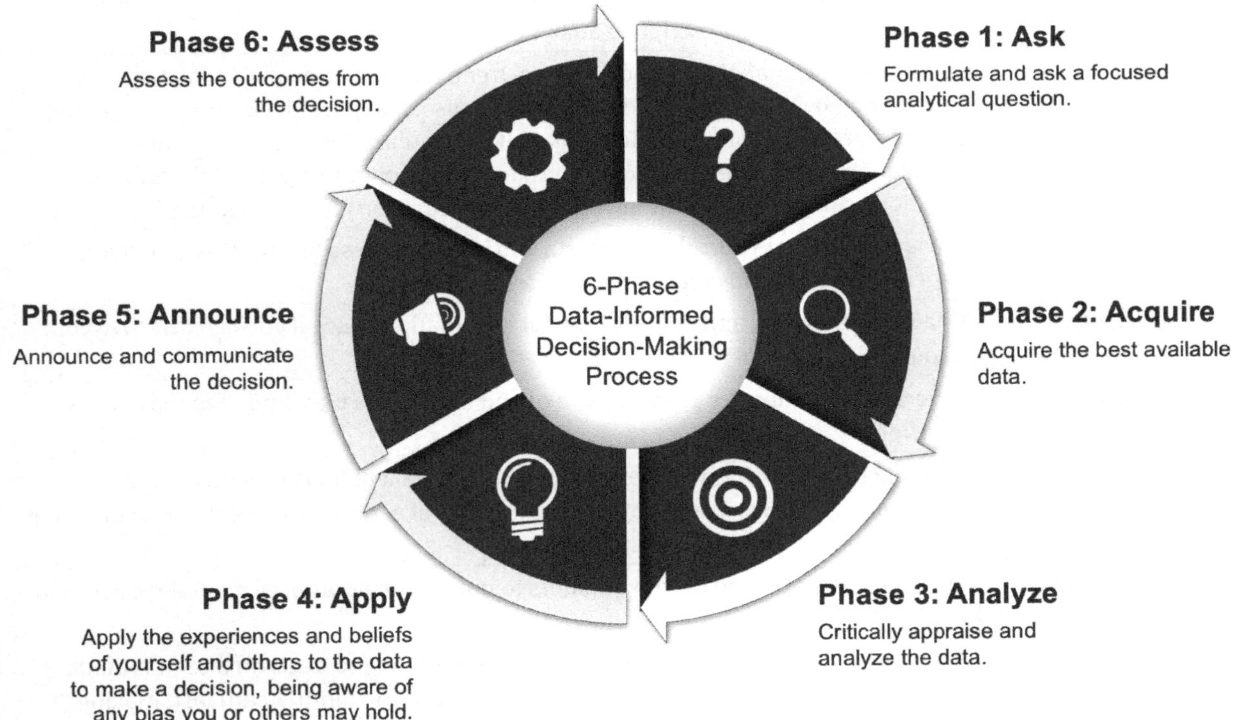

12-Step Data-Informed Decision-Making Methodology

STEP	PHASE	DESCRIPTION
1	Ask	Turn business questions into analytical questions.
2	Ask	Classify the decision needed.
3	Acquire	Find and source all relevant data. Remember to think about the analytical questions systemically and to include any interrelated data that could be relevant. This means not only internal data but external data and information as well.
4	Acquire	Ensure the sourced data is trusted.
5	Analyze	Create a measurement framework to describe your data with key performance indicators (KPIs) and descriptive analytics.
6	Analyze	Use diagnostic analytics to find patterns, trends, and relationships that may exist but not be obvious to start to drill into root cause. If applicable, leverage inferential statistics to take a sample of data and make generalizations about the entire population, predictive analytics to run simulations or to test potential decisions/ solutions, and prescriptive analytics to act on situations as they happen.
7	Apply	Review and orient yourself to the data and information so far, apply your personal experiences to it, and create a hypothesis.
8	Apply	Challenge the data, and actively look for information to see if you can disprove your hypothesis.
9	Apply	Leverage strategies to become aware of and to mitigate bias, and then make a decision.
10	Announce	Announce your decision at the right level to ALL stakeholders (direct, indirect, upstream, and downstream) by leveraging tools like reframing, the Pyramid principle, and the Rule of Three in your storytelling.
11	Announce	Provide adequate time for stakeholders to unlearn any outdated mental models and to learn new ones.
12	Assess	Set up a review mechanism to monitor the impacts of the decision after it is made and acted upon. Leverage that review mechanism, and fail/fix/learn fast, making improvements to data, measurement frameworks, accountability, decisions, and anything else relevant.

Logic Model

INPUTS/RESOURCES	ACTIVITIES	OUTPUTS	OUTCOMES	IMPACTS
What resources should be used?	**What activities should be performed?**	**What assets/info should be created/ used to support the intended outcomes?**	**What changes should be made in the next 3 months (short term) or 12 months (intermediate)?**	**What changes are expected in 1–2 years due to the outcomes?**
People Processes Technology			Short term Intermediate	

Behavior Engineering Model (BEM)

	INFORMATION	RESOURCES	INCENTIVES
ENVIRONMENT			
	KNOWLEDGE/SKILLS	**CAPACITY**	**MOTIVES**
INDIVIDUAL			

Pugh Matrix

CRITERIA	BASELINE	WEIGHTING	OPTION 1		OPTION 2		OPTION 3	
			SCORE	TOTAL	SCORE	TOTAL	SCORE	TOTAL
Criterion 1								
Criterion 2								
Criterion 3								
Criterion 4								
Criterion 5								
TOTAL								

CRITERIA	WEIGHTING	OPTION 1		OPTION 2		OPTION 3	
		SCORE	TOTAL	SCORE	TOTAL	SCORE	TOTAL
Criterion 1							
Criterion 2							
Criterion 3							
Criterion 4							
Criterion 5							
TOTAL							

Force Field Analysis

FORCES	+4	+3	+2	+1	0	-1	-2	-3	-4
Driving force #1									
Driving force #2									
Driving force #3									
Restraining force #1									
Restraining force #2									
Restraining force #3									
TOTAL									

Zig-Zag Process Model for Problem-Solving

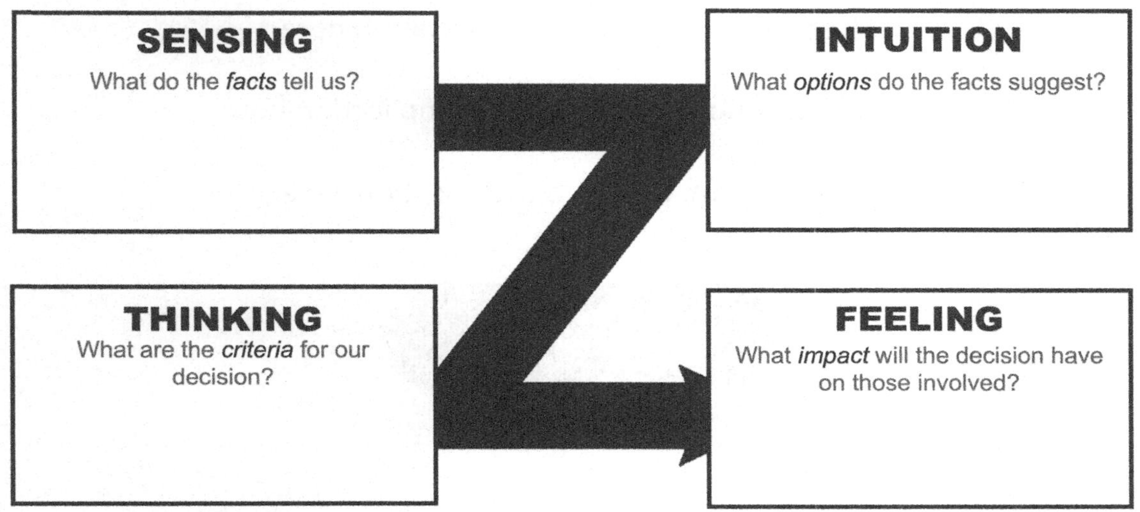

Pyramid Principle and Rule of Three

The situation. Describe the situation here.

The complication. Describe the complication here.

The question. Describe the question here.

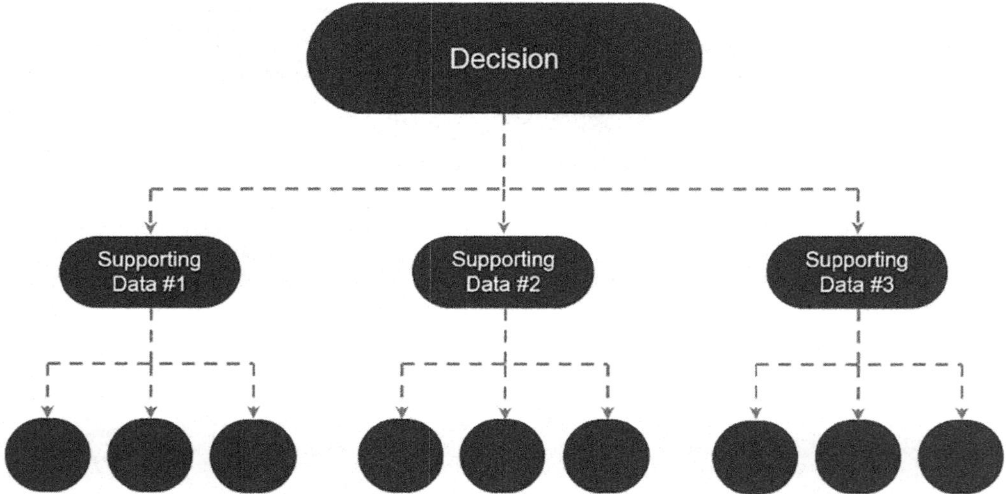

CHAPTER 12

EXAMPLE USE CASES AND CASE STUDIES

This chapter provides a few complete end-to-end examples of how the six-phase data-informed decision-making process and its twelve-step methodology can be applied to various problems. It is important to remember that the methodology is iterative, and certain steps may occur multiple times. Similarly, some decisions may not need to leverage all twelve steps from the methodology. These examples also include some of the tools, frameworks, and models from chapter 10 in action.

Example #1 – A Personal Data-Informed Decision

Many years ago, when one of my sons was just beginning elementary school, he started having a lot of "behaviors" while he was at school. The school staff as well as my wife and I were concerned about the escalating behaviors. After an initial meeting to discuss the situation, the decision was made to give our son a one-to-one aide to help keep him on task and to provide support when he needed it. A few months went by, and we did not see the behaviors decrease. In fact, the behaviors continued to escalate.

1. **Turn business questions into analytical questions. (Ask)**
   Decision-making should always start with the goal in mind. Going into a meeting and asking "How is our son doing?" would not have done much good because it is not an analytical question. Analytical questions need to be clear, specific, scoped, quantifiable, and data oriented. In this example, the goal was trying to decrease behaviors of our son. We turned that goal into multiple analytical questions—for example, "Are the behaviors decreasing since the introduction of a one-to-one aide?"

2. **Classify the decision needed. (Ask)**
   This decision would be a programmed decision because the event was reoccurring and a Type 2 decision because it would be something we could revert back from if needed.

3. **Find and source all relevant data. Remember to think about the analytical questions systemically and to include any interrelated data that could be relevant. This means not only internal data but external data and information as well. (Acquire)**
   At the team meeting, we asked to see the data collected. The school provided us logs where they had performed data collection on behaviors.

4. **Ensure the sourced data is trusted. (Acquire)**
   We then asked the school how the data was collected. They mentioned that the teacher reported on the number of behaviors at the end of each day. At this point, we were not completely sure we could trust the data. The teacher may have missed behaviors or may have forgotten to document them. Even if the teacher had collected the information accurately, was any of it really useful? Did this information, in and of itself, help us understand how to resolve the escalating behaviors?

5. **Create a measurement framework to describe your data with key performance indicators (KPIs) and descriptive analytics. (Analyze)**
   We asked the school to continue capturing the data. However, we wanted to revisit the Acquire phase, so we asked them to collect additional data. The additional data my wife and I asked to be collected included what time of day the behavior happened, what our son was doing before it occurred, what the specific behavior was (using a categorization of four types of behaviors), and what his consequence was as a result of his behavior.

6. **Use diagnostic analytics to find patterns, trends, and relationships that may exist but not be obvious to start to drill into root cause. If applicable, leverage inferential statistics to take a sample of data and make generalizations about the entire population, predictive analytics to run simulations or to test potential decisions/solutions, and prescriptive analytics to act on situations as they happen. (Analyze)**
   Remember that descriptive analytics like a dashboard/measurement framework does not answer questions of why. We knew at this point that our son's behaviors were escalating. But did we know why? Could we make a decision on how to course correct if we did not know why? This is when diagnostic analytics entered in to help us create a hypothesis into what might have been happening.

   Through diagnostic analytics, along with the additional data we asked to be collected, we were able to view the data across multiple dimensions to see that the overwhelming majority of our son's incidents happened at times of the day when the setting was unstructured and he did not have a one-to-one aide (like during lunch and recess).

7. **Review and orient yourself to the data and information so far, apply your personal experiences to it, and create a hypothesis. (Apply)**
At the next school meeting, we discussed what we had found. Since the behaviors were happening during unstructured times without an aide, the logical decision would be to request the aide to stay with our son during those times. This is what was recommended by the school. However, this is when we needed to challenge the data, apply our perspective and experience, and get input from others who might have different perspectives and experiences.

8. **Challenge the data, and actively look for information to see if you can disprove your hypothesis. (Apply)**
My wife and I did challenge the data and apply our perspective and experience. We went back to the data and diagnostic analytics and were able to determine that for just about all of the behaviors, the consequence was for our son to either be sent to the principal's office or back into the classroom with a teacher. My wife and I applied our perspective in knowing that our son craved adult attention for stimulation and would rather be with adults than kids. People without this experience would just apply their own mental model that a punishment of being sent to the principal's office is seen as a negative thing.

   As a result, we came up with a new hypothesis. Our son was having the behaviors because he wanted adult attention. According to the data, the consequences were such that he was getting that adult attention when he acted up. What was happening was actually enabling the behavior.

9. **Leverage strategies to become aware of and to mitigate bias, and then make a decision. (Apply)**
We asked around at the meetings if anyone was aware of reasons our hypothesis may not be valid. There were none, but a decision was made to try to widen the net of our data collection and to acquire more data. In this case, we decided to talk to the principal and get her input on the time our son was in her office. She highlighted that he was always happy and engaged and asked lots of questions. This was enough evidence to help us feel confident to move forward with our

new decision. The decision was then that when these behaviors happened, our son was not to be given time with an adult. He was to instead be sent to his desk by himself.

10. **Announce your decision at the right level to ALL stakeholders (direct, indirect, upstream, and downstream) by leveraging tools like reframing, the Pyramid principle, and the Rule of Three in your storytelling. (Announce)**
We ensured that every single adult at the school—including the bus driver, the cafeteria workers, all teachers, and all staff—were made aware of this decision and were provided with instructions in the form of a decision tree of what to do when certain behaviors came up in the future. (For a reminder visual of a decision tree, see figure 60 in chapter 6.)

11. **Provide adequate time for stakeholders to unlearn any outdated mental models and to learn new ones. (Announce)**
Since the updated consequences were just steps from the decision tree and not skills, there was no need for any mental models to be relearned. However, as a side effect, school faculty were aware going forward that going to the principal's office was not a negative consequence for our son.

12. **Set up a review mechanism to monitor the impacts of the decision after it is made and acted upon. Leverage that review mechanism, and fail/fix/learn fast, making improvements to data, measurement frameworks, accountability, decisions, and anything else relevant. (Assess)**
When we saw the next round of data one month later, we saw that behaviors during that time period in fact trended downward. There was a spike in the beginning, but then gradually it came down.

Keep in mind that, with change, things may get worse before they get better. This is why it is important to fully analyze and understand your data to not only ensure that root causes are investigated but also to see if the data truly shows a new pattern or just some symptomatic waves from the change being made.

Example #2 – Declining Revenue

An e-commerce company reported that its revenue was down 8 percent from the same quarter the past year. Therefore, the company kicked off a project to determine why and to put an action plan into place to stop the decline from continuing.

1. **Turn business questions into analytical questions. (Ask)**
   In this example, the analytical questions were "Why is revenue down 8 percent from the same quarter last year?" and "What can be done to stop the revenue decline from continuing next quarter?"

2. **Classify the decision needed. (Ask)**
   This decision would be a nonprogrammed decision because the event was not reoccurring and a Type 2 decision because it was something the company could revert back from if needed.

3. **Find and source all relevant data. Remember to think about the analytical questions systemically and to include any interrelated data that could be relevant. This means not only internal data but external data and information as well. (Acquire)**
   The leadership team huddled together to brainstorm what might be causing the revenue decline. They did not follow a formal systemic approach but did ask everyone for their hypothesis. The team was asked to look at the gap from multiple perspectives, considering potential external, organizational, job, and individual factors.

   The result was a short list of theories on why the revenue had declined, which included changes in the company's marketing spend for its e-commerce site and a rise in abandonment on the site.

   Armed with these theories, the team began to explore data they had acquired to help review each hypothesis. This data included impressions, clicks, and conversations happening on the website. It also included new-customer acquisition.

4. **Ensure the sourced data is trusted. (Acquire)**
   The organization had a sound data strategy in place already, and so all the data acquired, including the qualitative data, was trusted.

5. **Create a measurement framework to describe your data with key performance indicators (KPIs) and descriptive analytics. (Analyze)**
   The leadership team already had a measurement framework in place, which is what alerted them to the fact that revenue was down 8 percent from the same quarter last year.

6. **Use diagnostic analytics to find patterns, trends, and relationships that may exist but not be obvious to start to drill into root cause. If applicable, leverage inferential statistics to take a sample of data and make generalizations about the entire population, predictive analytics to run simulations or to test potential decisions/solutions, and prescriptive analytics to act on situations as they happen. (Analyze)**
   After performing some diagnostic analytics, the leadership team was able to drill into the data and find a pattern. They realized that the revenue decline mapped up to a similar decreasing trend in new-customer acquisition.

7. **Review and orient yourself to the data and information so far, apply your personal experiences to it, and create a hypothesis. (Apply)**
   The team then applied their beliefs and perception to that hypothesis to try to understand why customer acquisition was declining. They thought systemically about what activities drove customer acquisition and revisited the Acquire phase to find any data related to that. Then, they came up with the following activities to go back and gather data about: search engine optimization, referral programs, optimized landing pages, and updated high-quality content.

8. **Challenge the data, and actively look for information to see if you can disprove your hypothesis. (Apply)**
   One data set that was discussed were results from Google on the company's search engine status. It turned out that nothing internally had changed, but externally, the website's search algorithm had been updated. This update was making the company's site harder to find.

9. **Leverage strategies to become aware of and to mitigate bias, and then make a decision. (Apply)**
   This step was not a distinct step within this decision; it was actually leveraged across steps 3–8 to ensure that any bias was mitigated. The team worked with

a cross-functional set of employees to ensure that they were thinking of all possible elements of the system.

10. **Announce your decision at the right level to ALL stakeholders (direct, indirect, upstream, and downstream) by leveraging tools like reframing, the Pyramid principle, and the Rule of Three in your storytelling. (Announce)**
    The leadership team communicated the decision out to all stakeholders and highlighted their action plan, which was to learn more about the algorithm updates to understand how they can revise their search engine optimization strategy.

11. **Provide adequate time for stakeholders to unlearn any outdated mental models and to learn new ones. (Announce)**
    For the direct stakeholders involved in the company's website and search engine optimization strategy, time was dedicated to unlearn the old search strategy and to learn and adopt the new, required search strategy.

12. **Set up a review mechanism to monitor the impacts of the decision after it is made and acted upon. Leverage that review mechanism, and fail/fix/learn fast, making improvements to data, measurement frameworks, accountability, decisions, and anything else relevant. (Assess)**
    While the search engine team was working on updates to the company's search engine optimization strategy, the leadership team continued to monitor the latest Google results data in case their decision that the decreased revenue was due to the algorithm changes was incorrect. In addition, they revisited their KPIs and measurement framework and added in a few key indicators based on this exercise, such as new-customer acquisition rate.

In this example, you can see the value of following a systematic and systemic methodology. Had the leadership team only looked at the problem internally, they would never have uncovered that at least one of the root causes impacting them was due to a change occurring in their external environment.

Example #3 – Missing Sales Quotas

A software organization reported that it had missed its sales quota for five of the past six quarters. Leaders and decision-makers were asked to investigate why and to decide what to do to improve the situation.

1. **Turn business questions into analytical questions. (Ask)**
   The sales team had missed their quota five of the past six quarters. The leadership team wanted to understand why this had happened and what could be done to help the sales team improve. This focus helped the leadership team create a series of analytical questions as they first wanted to break down the sales-quota attainment by region and then by tenure of employee. These analytical questions were the following: 1) What was our sales attainment against quota in each of our regions for the past six quarters?, and 2) What was our sales attainment against quota for the past six quarters for each of the following categories of sales-employee tenure: first year, 1–3 years, 3–5 years, and more than 5 years?

2. **Classify the decision needed. (Ask)**
   This decision would be a nonprogrammed decision because the decision was not reoccurring and a Type 2 decision because it was something that could be reverted back from if needed.

3. **Find and source all relevant data. Remember to think about the analytical questions systemically and to include any interrelated data that could be relevant. This means not only internal data but external data and information as well. (Acquire)**
   The original data provided showed the forecast for each region and tenure compared to budget. The team was able to see from those numbers that the overall sales forecast was $10 million below budget and that the gap percentage-wise was almost equally split between the regions. They were also able to see that percentage-wise the largest gap to quota attainment was in the employees who had been with the organization for 1–3 years.

4. **Ensure the sourced data is trusted. (Acquire)**
   The sales leaders were shown the data and the analysis, and none of the leaders or the operations team questioned the data. They all trusted it.

5. **Create a measurement framework to describe your data with key performance indicators (KPIs) and descriptive analytics. (Analyze)**

With the analysis up until now, leadership knew there was a gap in hitting sales quotas for five of the past six quarters, and they were now seeing that the largest percentage of the gap was coming from employees who had been with the organization for 1–3 years. Still, they could not confirm just yet that the missed sales quotas had only to do with newer employees. They also did not have enough data to determine what had caused the shortage. In addition, they didn't have any system set up to proactively alert this as an issue. This is partly because the data being measured up to this point were all lagging indicators. Therefore, the recommendation going forward was to add in some leading indicators, like number of opportunities added, opportunities lost, open jobs that have not been filled within the sales team, and compliance with the sales process.

The team then went back to step 3 to acquire all of this new leading-indicator data to help determine root causes.

6. **Use diagnostic analytics to find patterns, trends, and relationships that may exist but not be obvious to start to drill into root cause. If applicable, leverage inferential statistics to take a sample of data and make generalizations about the entire population, predictive analytics to run simulations or to test potential decisions/solutions, and prescriptive analytics to act on situations as they happen. (Analyze)**
With the larger set of data now available, analysts used diagnostic analytics to try to determine patterns, trends, and relationships. After having done so, they uncovered some interesting data:

   A. The organization's sales-department attrition rate (employees who leave the organization) was 15 percent higher than it had been in the past, and the time to get new sales employees up to speed was taking longer than it used to, as measured by the average time it took a new employee to close his or her first deal.

   B. Feedback in the reports that sales employees completed when they lost a deal were coded to various categories to allow analysts to measure the frequencies of reasons. The reports highlighted that a majority of the reasons for not winning the deal were due to product pricing. The second most-used reason was product quality.

   C. There seemed to be variability in territories of sales employees. The ones who were missing their quotas were in territories with all brand-new opportunities and customers.

D. Sales employees were closing the same percentage of deals they had previously closed on. They just had fewer leads and opportunities at this point than they had in previous years.

7. **Review and orient yourself to the data and information so far, apply your personal experiences to it, and create a hypothesis. (Apply)**
The team met to discuss the results of the diagnostic analytics. This appeared to be a complex, multifaceted problem with many causes that all impacted the end result. Everyone in the team was able to add their experiences to validate the data points from the diagnostic analysis. They agreed that the fundamental problem they should try to resolve was the shortage in leads. Their hypothesis was that the sales decline was caused in part by less leads, which caused fewer opportunities.

8. **Challenge the data, and actively look for information to see if you can disprove your hypothesis. (Apply)**
During this same meeting, the team looked at all the data and tried to find some that contradicted their hypothesis. There were some sales reps who made their quotas despite having fewer leads, but in general, the team agreed that it was hard for sales reps to hit their quota with less leads and that this was the main cause. The team also wanted to understand how this related to employees who had been with the organization for 1–3 years. The analysis had shown that this group had the largest percentage of the gap. In talking to the leaders, a new hypothesis formed. New hires were given mentors and coaches who helped them along the process. This guidance helped them close their deals. However, after they reached their one-year anniversary, sales employees received less support. The hypothesis was that new employees received the right support, and employees who had lasted at the organization for over three years knew what they needed to know by then, but the group in years 1–3 were not given as much support.

9. **Leverage strategies to become aware of and to mitigate bias, and then make a decision. (Apply)**
The team met again to decide what actions to take to try to improve this issue

systemically. They used a Pugh matrix to prioritize actions as well as to understand how likely changes made from the decision would be adopted by the broader team.

CRITERIA	WEIGHTING	LEAD-GENERATION TEAM		SALES COACHES TO SUPPORT EMPLOYEES BEYOND NEW HIRES		SALES-MANAGER TRAINING		REALIGNMENT OF TERRITORIES	
		SCORE	TOTAL	SCORE	TOTAL	SCORE	TOTAL	SCORE	TOTAL
Ease of implementation	1	1	1	2	2	3	3	4	4
Cost of implementation	2	1	2	2	4	3	6	4	8
Long-term benefit	4	4	16	3	12	2	8	1	4
Support from business	3	4	12	3	9	1	3	2	6
TOTAL			**31**		**27**		**20**		**22**

The results were that the sales organization was going to invest in a new lead-generation team who would be compensated for the quality of leads they obtained. They were also going to invest in some processes to better support existing employees who had fallen out of the new-hire category. These processes included having sales coaches available to review deals with. While there were other possible actions to take, these were decided upon as the best way to start.

10. **Announce your decision at the right level to ALL stakeholders (direct, indirect, upstream, and downstream) by leveraging tools like reframing, the Pyramid principle, and the Rule of Three in your storytelling. (Announce)**
    This decision was communicated out to all stakeholders. These included not only the direct people in the sales organization but also the marketing team who would be responsible for providing the new lead-generation team with materials to use. It also included the operations team who would need to support this new team from a systems and tools perspective. The communications focused on the opportunity this decision presented and its intended positive results on the organization and were framed on what was in this decision for each of the stakeholder groups.

11. **Provide adequate time for stakeholders to unlearn any outdated mental models and to learn new ones. (Announce)**
    In this case, there were not any old mental models that needed to be unlearned.

12. **Set up a review mechanism to monitor the impacts of the decision after it is made and acted upon. Leverage that review mechanism, and fail/fix/learn fast, making improvements to data, measurement frameworks, accountability, decisions, and anything else relevant. (Assess)**
    The leadership team had used the newly updated measurement framework, which included more leading indicators, to monitor if more leads were created and if that helped the sales team to reach their sales quotas. Leadership did not forget that this was a multifaceted problem, so they continued to look at the other indicators from the diagnostic analysis, including territory alignment and sales-department attrition.

Example #4 – Declines in Soup Sales

A canned-soup company noticed that sales of its soup have been on a downward trend, specific to the supermarket distribution channel. Leaders and decision-makers were asked why.

1. **Turn business questions into analytical questions. (Ask)**
   In this example, the analytical questions were the following:

    - How did the soup sales for the current quarter and year compare to the previous quarter and year?
    - What were the differences in soup sales for the current quarter and year compared to the previous quarter and year across different distribution channels?

2. **Classify the decision needed. (Ask)**
   This decision would be a nonprogrammed decision because the event was not reoccurring and a Type 2 decision because it was something the company could revert back from if needed. (Later, however, you will see that this decision became a Type 1 decision.)

3. **Find and source all relevant data. Remember to think about the analytical questions systemically and to include any interrelated data that could be relevant. This means not only internal data but external data and information as well. (Acquire)**
   The organization gathered a diverse team in the office to brainstorm possible causes for the sales decline. The team was asked to think about possible causes from both an internal and external perspective, including any specific events that had occurred during the time period of the decline that could be factors as well. The following potential causes were identified:

   External

   lower prices from competition

   changes in weather

   Internal

   changes in marketing campaigns

   changes in coupon strategy

   The team then collected the necessary data for all of these potential causes.

4. **Ensure the sourced data is trusted. (Acquire)**
   This data was collected, organized, and cataloged using the organization's data strategy. Any data that was collected from surveys or interviews was coded and handled ethically via the organization's policies on ethical standards for data.

5. **Create a measurement framework to describe your data with key performance indicators (KPIs) and descriptive analytics. (Analyze)**
   The organization already had a measurement framework in place to show current data, but it did not include things like quarter-over-quarter and year-over-year analysis. These were added into the measurement framework.

6. **Use diagnostic analytics to find patterns, trends, and relationships that may exist but not be obvious to start to drill into root cause. If applicable, leverage inferential statistics to take a sample of data and make generalizations about the entire population, predictive analytics to run simulations or to test potential decisions/solutions, and prescriptive analytics to act on situations as they happen. (Analyze)**

The team then performed diagnostic analytics to drill down, find patterns, and discover any relationships and correlations within the data. They performed the following actions as part of the diagnostic analytics process:

- They analyzed the data to see if there were any other channels impacted or just the supermarket channel.
- They analyzed the data to see if there was any seasonality or other trends in the sales.
- They analyzed the data to see if the decline was specific to one soup product or to the entire portfolio of soup products. If it was one specific soup, the team drilled down deeper into that soup—for example, was it a specific type of soup or soup can that maybe was going out of style?
- They analyzed third-party weather data to see if there were any major weather events during the time period that could have potentially caused a decrease in demand (like unseasonably warm weather)?
- They analyzed the data regarding the marketing campaigns for the time period to see if there were any changes in the marketing campaigns that could have impacted the sales.
- They analyzed employee data for the time period to see if there were any trends or patterns around attrition.
- They analyzed information from sales leaders responsible for the supermarket channel to determine if there were any other potential causes for the drop in sales that were not identified.

At the end of the diagnostic analytics, it was determined that the decline was across multiple channels, not just one. However, it was determined that the decline was mostly due to one specific family of soups, not the entire portfolio.

7. **Review and orient yourself to the data and information so far, apply your personal experiences to it, and create a hypothesis. (Apply)**
   The team discussed these findings. From experience, they knew that this soup family in particular was a condensed soup, and it was the only family of condensed soups they had. Therefore, they now had a hypothesis that the decline in sales within this soup family was due to the fact that consumers no longer wanted to buy condensed soup.

8. **Challenge the data, and actively look for information to see if you can disprove your hypothesis. (Apply)**
   Rather than deciding on a possible intervention specific to this soup family, the team wanted to ensure they were really looking at the root cause and not a symptom and were not making a biased decision. Therefore, they decided to do a consumer survey that would give them the information they needed about whether the issue was that people no longer wanted to purchase condensed soup. The survey was done using proper sampling techniques, and results indicated that the soup family definitely had a negative sentiment associated with it.

   The recommendation from the team was to begin the process of replacing the condensed-soup family with a newer ready-to-eat soup model. Since this ultimately became a Type 1 decision, meaning it would be really hard to revert back from, the decision focused on beginning the replacement process by testing it out in one region only.

9. **Leverage strategies to become aware of and to mitigate bias, and then make a decision. (Apply)**
   The team used strategies at multiple stages of the process to be aware of and to mitigate bias. The group that was invited to brainstorm on possible causes was a diverse group to help avoid groupthink and sunk cost bias. During the initial discussions, the organization only allowed each potential cause to be mentioned once to avoid confirmation bias and bandwagon bias. During those discussions, the team visualized the possible causes on the whiteboard. This helped lessen the cognitive load on the team, which helped them avoid biases caused by cognitive overload and having too-much information to process.

10. **Announce your decision at the right level to ALL stakeholders (direct, indirect, upstream, and downstream) by leveraging tools like reframing, the Pyramid principle, and the Rule of Three in your storytelling. (Announce)**
    The organization announced the decision to all stakeholders, including the ones externally impacted, like the suppliers in the supply chain and the distributors who purchased the product. The announcements included data to show why the decision had been made and how it would impact each stakeholder.

11. **Provide adequate time for stakeholders to unlearn any outdated mental models and to learn new ones. (Announce)**
    The soup developers were provided the information from the surveys to understand specifics about the old soup that were negative. This would help them in their innovation process of coming up with a replacement.

12. **Set up a review mechanism to monitor the impacts of the decision after it is made and acted upon. Leverage that review mechanism, and fail/fix/learn fast, making improvements to data, measurement frameworks, accountability, decisions, and anything else relevant. (Assess)**
    Since the team decided to launch in one region only to begin, they were able to test the sales as a pilot in that region to determine what they should do in the future. During their innovation process, they used surveys and focus groups along with market and customer demographics to validate their models and to test out their product before and after launch.

Example #5 - Lower-Than-Planned Profits

In this final example, a software company was experiencing lower profits than planned. Therefore, the company performed an analysis to determine what was causing these lower profits and what decisions they should make to improve the situation. The analysis included using surveys, interviews, and focus groups as well as some tools like the Behavior Engineering Model and the Force Field Analysis.

1. **Turn business questions into analytical questions. (Ask)**
   In this example, the analytical questions were the following:

   - What factors led to the organization missing its profit target for the past three years?
   - What strategies should be implemented to help improve the organization's ability to hit its profit target?

2. **Classify the decision needed. (Ask)**
   This decision would be a nonprogrammed decision because the event was not reoccurring and a Type 2 decision because it was something the company could revert back from if needed.

3. **Find and source all relevant data. Remember to think about the analytical questions systemically and to include any interrelated data that could be relevant. This means not only internal data but external data and information as well. (Acquire)**
   The leaders got together to understand what factors would be systemically related to and impacting the profits of the organization. The following system components diagram was created. The shaded circles indicate the identified gaps, and the black circle indicates the focus of the initial question.

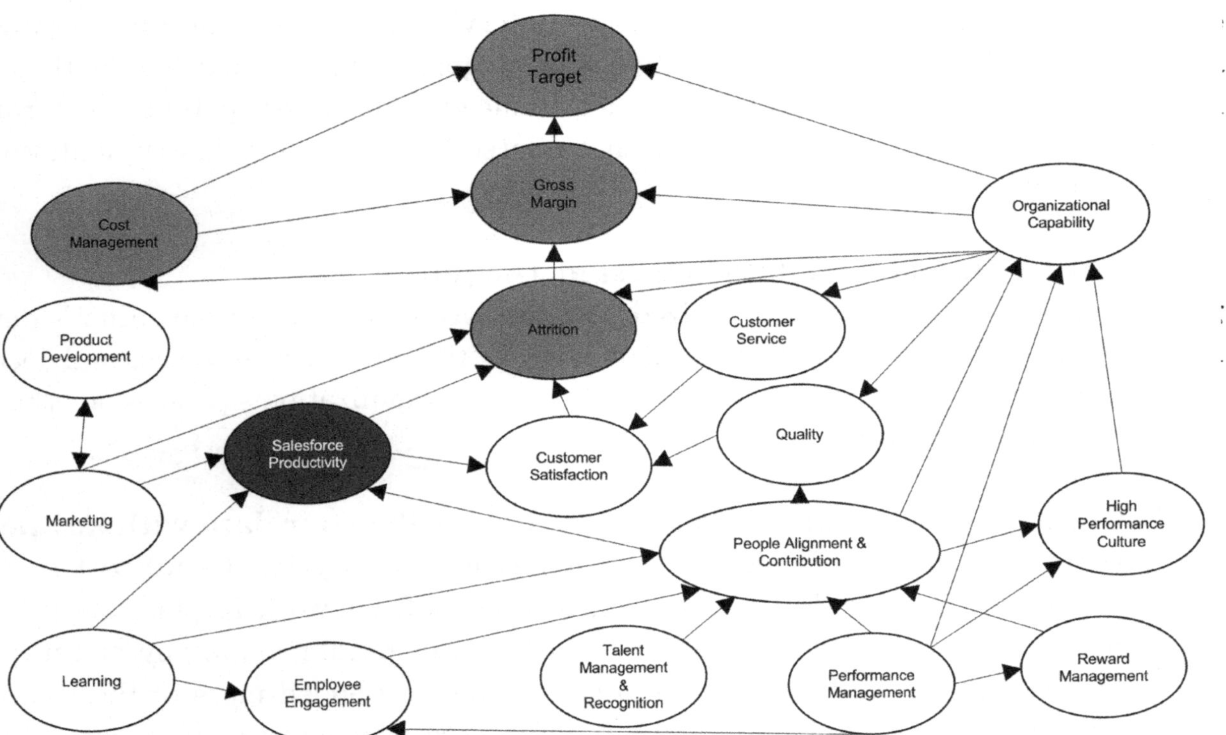

The gap between the profit and the profit target had been quantified by the organization as approximately $34.5 million in the past three years.

After this process, related data, both quantitative and qualitative, was collected in three phases:

Phase 1. Phase 1 was a collection and analysis of extant (existing) organizational data. This included performance data related to quota attainment; forecast accuracy (how accurate a sales employee's forecast was at the start of a given quarter compared to how the employee actually finished the quarter);

attrition (how many employees left the organization); and exit interviews (interviews conducted with employees who were leaving the organization).

Phase 2. Phase 2 featured an external review to determine performance standards within the sales industry as they related to software sales and forecasting. (Remember the importance of **data triangulation**, discussed in the Acquire phase chapter?)

Phase 3. Phase 3 focused on identifying core issues faced by the sales team within the organization. A survey, interviews, and focus groups were designed, and then the information was categorized and coded using the Behavior Engineering Model (BEM) as a framework to explore potential environmental and individual factors that related to information, instrumentation, and motivation.

4. **Ensure the sourced data is trusted. (Acquire)**
   The data was collected, organized, and cataloged using the organization's data strategy. Any data that was collected from the survey, interviews, and focus groups was coded and handled ethically via the organization's policies on ethical standards for data.

5. **Create a measurement framework to describe your data with key performance indicators (KPIs) and descriptive analytics. (Analyze)**
   The organization did not have a measurement framework in place, so it had missed the opportunity initially to see the lower profits coming by measuring leading indicators. However, the organization now added more of the leading indicators to the assessment and ultimately created a new measurement framework later on during the Assess phase (see step 12).

6. **Use diagnostic analytics to find patterns, trends, and relationships that may exist but not be obvious to start to drill into root cause. If applicable, leverage inferential statistics to take a sample of data and make generalizations about the entire population, predictive analytics to run simulations or to test potential decisions/solutions, and prescriptive analytics to act on situations as they happen. (Analyze)**
   The following approaches were used to analyze the collected data:

1. Each question in the survey was mapped to one of the BEM categories. The quantitative questions in the survey used a scale of 1–5 (with one being the worst score). The average for each question was then calculated.
2. The BEM was leveraged to analyze the key themes from the survey, interviews, and focus groups. Below are the high-level results of the BEM:

	INFORMATION	RESOURCES	INCENTIVES
ENVIRONMENT	**Onboarding** Onboarding is impersonal; there is no training for the sales tools; there is no continued support after initial self-paced learning; onboarding is a one-time event and not ongoing; and blended learning is not used. **Performance management** There's a lack of coaching, and management support is inconsistent. **Information** There's a lack of clear information regarding sales methodology and sales cycle, and there are no guides on how to use the sales tools.	**Resources** Resources that the sales reps can tap into are lacking. There's no community of practice, mentors, customer champions, or marketing materials. **Technology** Sales tools are too hard to use and take a lot of time to figure out.	**Territory** Success is seen as hinging on the territory you are assigned. **Quota** The quota is seen as too high.
	KNOWLEDGE/SKILLS	**CAPACITY**	**MOTIVES**
INDIVIDUAL	**Management and employee disconnect** Employees feel they are knowledgeable enough to do the job, but management doesn't feel like the new hires have the skills.	**Previous experience** Being successful is dependent on previous experience rather than on what is learned from the company. **Attrition consequences** The selling environment is negative when the customers have had several different sales reps, and there is no support to handle this.	**Negative environment** The many company changes have led to an unstable and negative work environment.

7. **Review and orient yourself to the data and information so far, apply your personal experiences to it, and create a hypothesis. (Apply)**
The team reviewed the data and information and came to the conclusion that this was a complex problem with multiple factors. The data frequently indicated that sales onboarding was too dense and was carried out over an inadequate amount of time. This prevented learners from synthesizing critical knowledge related to their essential duties and their role. Furthermore, there did not appear to be systems in place to ensure a transfer of knowledge to the workplace after onboarding had concluded nor to provide any kind of performance support to learners in the field. This left incoming sales employees at a disadvantage, as they were unprepared to fulfill their responsibilities to meet sales quotas and to forecast sales accurately.

8. **Challenge the data, and actively look for information to see if you can disprove your hypothesis. (Apply)**
In this example, the team challenged the data multiple times during the process.

9. **Leverage strategies to become aware of and to mitigate bias, and then make a decision. (Apply)**
There were six proposed suggestions for how to improve the problem. For each suggestion, the driving and restraining forces were compared and analyzed using Lewin's Force Field Analysis.
An example Force Field Analysis for one of the proposed suggestions (revamp of the onboarding program) is shown below:

FORCES	+4	+3	+2	+1	0	-1	-2	-3	-4
Improved learning outcomes for the new hires on job expectations									
Data tracker to learn progress									
Allow new users to practice in a safe and coached setting									
New employees are provided feedback rather than just a quiz score									
Considerable increase in onboarding program expenses									
TOTALS	13				4				

With this proposed suggestion, the total magnitude of driving forces was 13. The total magnitude of restraining forces was 4. Since 13 is greater than 4, this suggestion appeared significantly more likely to succeed than fail.

Of the six proposed suggestions, the following four were recommended:

1. Revamp the onboarding program to be more scenario based, and increase the duration to allow learners more of an opportunity to synthesize and apply what they are learning.
2. Implement a leadership performance assessment and training program.
3. Create learning experiences and assets that enable the sales force to realize the full potential of tools and resources.
4. Implement a community of practice using Microsoft Teams or Salesforce Chatter as a platform to share knowledge and successful methods.

The team made the decision to propose suggestions that were more operational than strategic to start with. This was partly due to the earlier classification of the decision as a Type 2 decision so that the organization could revert back from it and reassess if necessary.

The team used multiple strategies during this decision-making process to help mitigate bias. When they were looking at information from the employees, they used a survey, focus groups, and interviews to triangulate the data to avoid bias. When the team discussed strategies for improving the problems, they used Lewin's Force Field Analysis, and each team member completed his or her own. The results were then pooled together. This helped to prevent groupthink and to mitigate any biases individuals may have had if they had just used their own ranking.

10. Announce your decision at the right level to ALL stakeholders (direct, indirect, upstream, and downstream) by leveraging tools like reframing, the Pyramid principle, and the Rule of Three in your storytelling. (Announce)

The decision to implement four programs to help with the problem was communicated to all the impacted stakeholders, with specific citation of the data and rationale.

11. Provide adequate time for stakeholders to unlearn any outdated mental models and to learn new ones. (Announce)
There were not any old mental models that needed to be unlearned in this case.

12. Set up a review mechanism to monitor the impacts of the decision after it is made and acted upon. Leverage that review mechanism, and fail/fix/learn fast, making improvements to data, measurement frameworks, accountability, decisions, and anything else relevant. (Assess)
The team set up a process to review the impacts of the decisions. Below is the system components diagram shown earlier. The proposed interventions are the circles with the lightest shading, the performance gap is the circle with the darkest shading, and the downstream metrics are the circles with the middle shading. A new measurement framework was put into place with these metrics to monitor any changes.

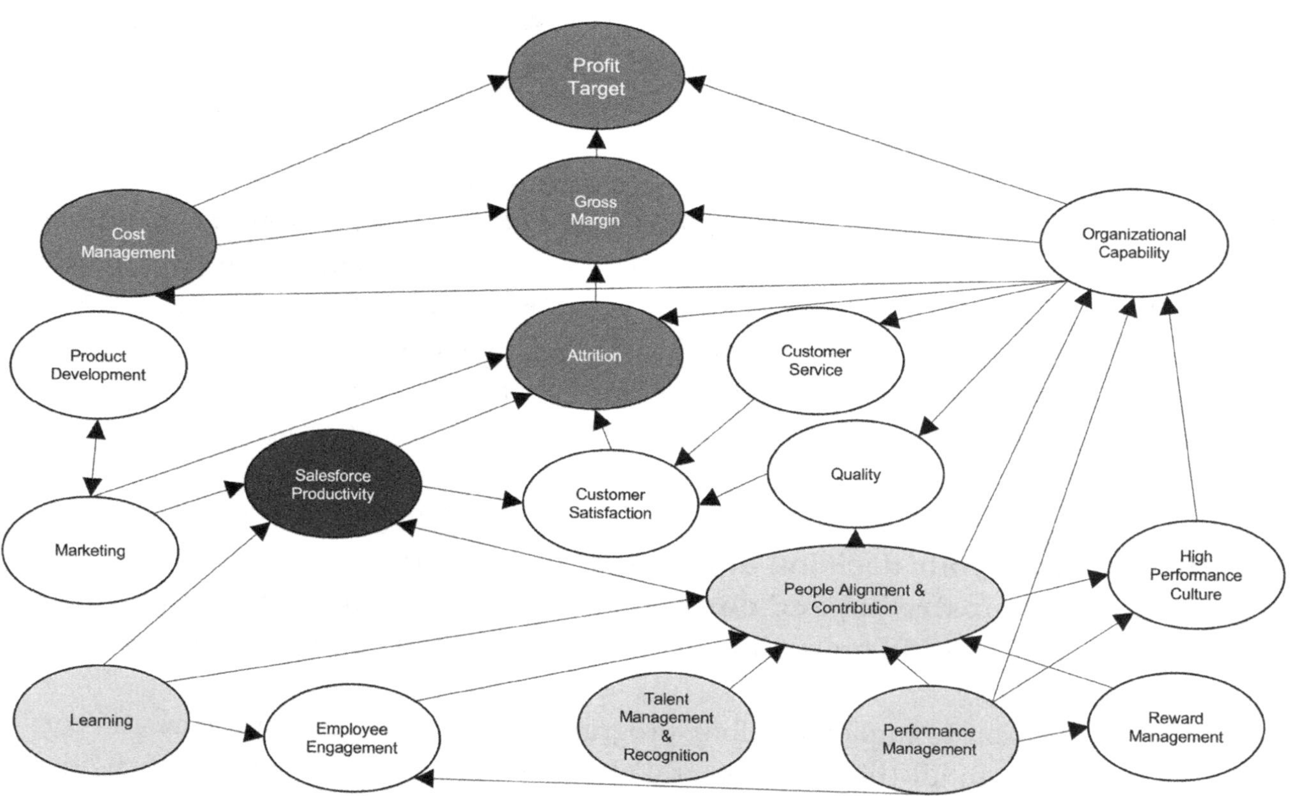

GLOSSARY OF TERMS

Absolute zero. Absolute zero is a point at which there is no measurement.

Aggregate data. Aggregate data is data that has been summarized using an aggregation (a cluster of things that have been brought together) such as sum, mean, or median, to name a few.

Algorithm. An algorithm is a set of instructions that get executed when triggered. An algorithm can be thought of as a recipe of step-by-step tasks to be completed.

Analytical questions. Analytical questions are questions that can be answered with data and analytics. Analytical questions must be clear, specific, scoped, data oriented, and answerable.

Analytics. Analytics can be defined as the process of transforming raw data into insights.

Artificial intelligence. Artificial intelligence is any program that can sense, reason, act, and adapt. The ultimate goal of artificial intelligence is for a piece of software to help in the decision-making process by thinking like a human can.

Assumptions. Assumptions are implicit or explicit thoughts that are accepted as true without any proof.

Big data. Big data is a term that describes large volumes of data that are analyzed in order to make decisions. Big data is said to have higher velocity, which means the data is more quickly received, analyzed, and then acted upon. The data is also said to have lots of variety, which means it comes in many forms, including structured data, such as from spreadsheets and databases, and unstructured data, such as from social media posts, images, and video files.

Binary. A binary variable is a variable that can only have two values—for example, a variable that has the values true or false.

Categorical data. Categorical data, also called qualitative data, is nonnumerical data for which the values can be one of several categories. For example, gender and marital status are categorical variables.

Central tendency. Central tendency is a value that describes the center of a given variable.

Cognitive bias. Cognitive bias can be defined as an unconscious, systematic, and reproducible failure in information processing that gets in the way of logical thinking. Also referred to as unconscious bias.

Cognitive diversity. Cognitive diversity is the inclusion of people who have different styles of problem-solving and can offer unique perspectives because they think differently.

Context. Context is defined as the circumstances that form the setting for an event or idea so that event or idea can be fully understood and assessed.

Continuous data. Continuous data is quantitative data for which the values are not restricted to specific values. For example, continuous data can be sales-revenue numbers, time, weight, and height.

Data collection. Data collection is the process of gathering and potentially measuring data from a variety of sources.

Data governance. Data governance is the overall practice of managing your data with guidance to make sure that the data aligns with the company's goals.

Data-informed decision-making. Data-informed decision-making is the ability to transform information into actionable and verified knowledge to ultimately make business decisions.

Data literacy. Data literacy is the ability to read, work with, analyze, and argue with data.

Data management. Data management is the implementation of the processes, policies, technology, and training to ensure that those within an organization can achieve its data-governance goals.

Data quality. Data quality refers to the overall level of quality, or utility, of data.

Data strategy. A data strategy is a strategy for collecting, storing, governing, and using data within an organization.

Data triangulation. Data triangulation is the process of gathering and validating information from two or more sources.

Dependent and independent variables. A dependent variable is a variable that depends on the values of the independent variable. The dependent variable represents the output or outcome. Typically, it is the dependent variable that is being studied in inferential statistics to see if the independent variable causes an effect on it. For example, say we want to see if there is a relationship between marketing spend and sales revenue. In this test, the independent variable is the marketing spend, and we want to see what impact it has on the dependent variable, which is the sales revenue.

Descriptive analytics. Descriptive analytics is a type of analytics designed to give you an overview of your data, both quantitative and qualitative.

Diagnostic analytics. Diagnostic analytics is a type of analytics used to find connections and unknown relationships in your data.

Discrete data. Discrete data is quantitative data that can be counted and that only takes specific values, typically whole numbers.

Dispersion/measures of spread. Dispersion, also called measures of spread, helps to determine how spread out the data is.

Double-loop learning. Double-loop learning is a reflective process in which a decision-making team challenges the assumptions, norms, and objectives for a decision.

Groupthink. Groupthink is the tendency to favor choices of mass populations and to strive for consensus at the cost of rational assessments of alternate decisions.

Hard skills. Hard skills are teachable abilities or skill sets that relate to specific technical knowledge and are easily measurable.

Heuristics. Heuristics are rules of thumb and mental shortcuts that can be applied to guide decision-making based on a limited subset of the available information.

Inferential statistics. Inferential statistics is used to help draw conclusions about a larger population.

Interval data. Interval data is quantitative data that has no absolute zero. With interval data, you can add and subtract, but you cannot multiply and divide.

Key performance indicators (KPIs). Key performance indicators (KPIs) are metrics that tie to a strategic objective of the organization.

Leading and lagging indicators. Leading and lagging indicators are types of KPIs. Leading indicators are metrics that can be used to predict future success toward a goal. Lagging indicators are outcome metrics and provide information into past performance specific to a goal.

Machine learning. Machine learning is a subset of artificial intelligence. It is any algorithm whose performance improves over time as it is exposed to more and more data. The goal of machine learning is for the algorithm to continue to learn and improve its decision-making without any alteration.

Mean. The mean, also referred to as the arithmetic mean, is the average of all the numbers in a given set of numbers.

Measurement framework. A measurement framework is a visual representation of the data that is being used to answer your analytical question.

Median. The median is defined as the middle of a sorted list of numbers in a set. The median is often used when the data contains a few outliers that could greatly influence the mean and distort what might be considered typical.

Mental model. A mental model is an individual's explanation of how the world works —a framework through which the individual views the world. Mental models shape what we think and how we understand. They are related to heuristics, but whereas heuristics are used during System 1 decisions, or unconscious or intuition-based decisions, mental models can be used during System 2 decisions, or conscious decisions that require deductive reasoning and problem-solving. Mental models explain someone's thought process and why different people perceive the world differently.

Metaevaluation. A metaevaluation is an evaluation of a decision after the decision has been made. The evaluation focuses on what went well, why it went well, what can be improved, and how you think it can be improved.

Mode. The mode is defined as the most common number in a set of numbers.

Nominal data. Nominal data is qualitative data that has no sense of sequential order—for example, gender, makes of a car, or types of fruit.

Nonprogrammed decisions. Nonprogrammed decisions are one-off decisions that are not part of a routine.

Normal distribution. Data can be distributed in many ways. When the distribution of data is around the central value (mean, median, or mode), with 50 percent of the data below the central value and 50 percent above the central value, it is said to be normally distributed. Normal distributions allow statisticians to make inferences about the data with a high degree of probability. Normal distribution is an important part of inferential statistics as various statistical tests depend on whether the data is normally distributed or not.

Ordinal data. Ordinal data is qualitative data that has a sense of order and can be ordered in a sequence—for example, rankings from one to five or from good to better to best.

Organizational culture. An organizational culture comprises the values, beliefs, assumptions, and behaviors that are shared by all members of an organization and that contribute to the environment of an organization.

Outlier. An outlier is a number that lies outside of most of the other numbers in a set.

Population. A population is the entire pool from which a sample is drawn. Samples are used in statistics because of how difficult it can be to study an entire population.

Predictive analytics. Predictive analytics is a type of analytics that uses data to make predictions about future events.

Prescriptive analytics. Prescriptive analytics is a type of analytics that builds on the predicted outcomes from predictive analytics and then makes recommendations on one or more courses of action to take.

Programmed decisions. Programmed decisions are reoccurring decisions.

Qualitative data. Qualitative data, also called categorical data, is descriptive information about characteristics that are difficult to define or measure or that cannot be expressed numerically. Qualitative data can be put into categories like gender and sales regions.

Quantitative data. Quantitative data, also called numerical data, is numerical information that can be measured or counted.

Ratio data. Ratio data is quantitative data with an absolute zero. With ratio data, you can not only add and subtract but also multiply and divide.

Raw data. Raw data is data that is collected from a source and not cleaned, transformed, or edited in any way.

Sample. A sample is a subset of the population we care about. For example, it may not be possible to survey every single customer from a retail store, so the retail store would survey a sample. The population would be all customers from that retail store.

Significance level. A statistically significant result is one that cannot be explained by chance or random error.

Soft skills. Soft skills are personal habits or traits that shape how an individual works and how the individual works with others.

Standard deviation. Standard deviation measures how widely data values are dispersed from the mean.

Statistics. Statistics is a branch of mathematics that deals with collecting, processing, analyzing, and interpreting quantitative data (numerical information that can be measured or counted).

Statistically significant. A statistically significant result is one that cannot be explained by chance or random error.

Strategic decision. A strategic decision is a type of decision that has a major impact on a business.

System 1 decision. A System 1 decision is a type of decision that is fast, automatic, effortless, and unconscious.

System 2 decision. A System 2 decision is a type of decision that is deliberate and conscious and requires effort and controlled mental processing along with rational thinking.

Systems thinking. Systems thinking is an approach to analysis that focuses on the way that all parts of a system relate to one another.

Type 1 decision. A Type 1 decision is a type of decision that is not reversible, like quitting a job or changing a product direction.

Type 2 decision. A Type 2 decision is a type of decision that you can always revert back from if the decision ends up not being ideal. Examples include executing a specific marketing campaign or changing a vendor in your supply chain.

Unlearning. Unlearning is the ability to choose an alternative and more-current mental model over a mental model that is outdated.

Variable. A variable is a characteristic, number, or quantity that can be measured. In a general sense, it can be seen as a column of data.

ENDNOTES

1. "Tim O'Reilly," AZquotes, Wind and Fly LTD, 2020, accessed April 12, 2020, https://www.azquotes.com/quote/218170.

2. Commvault, "7 Reasons Your Data Is Now More Important Than Ever," Commvault, February 7, 2018, https://www.commvault.com/blogs/7-reasons-your-data-is-now-more-important-than-ever.

3. Alison Mairena, "Personalizing Drug Development Using Big Data," UA-News, August 19, 2019, https://news.arizona.edu/story/personalizing-drug-development-using-big-data.

4. "42% of Global Coal Power Plants Run at a Loss, Finds World-First Study," Carbon Tracker, November 30, 2018, https://carbontracker.org/42-of-global-coal-power-plants-run-at-a-loss-finds-world-first-study/.

5. Mike Gualtieri and Noel Yuhanna, *The Forrester Wave™: Big Data Hadoop Solutions, Q1 2014* (Forrester Research, Inc., February 27, 2014), http://hortonworks.com/wp-content/uploads/2014/02/The_Forrester_Wave__Big_Data_Solutions_Q1_2014.pdf.

6. "Overcoming the 'Cobra Effect' in Your Business," Continuous Business Planning, accessed June 21, 2020, https://www.continuousbusinessplanning.com/blog/02082019123204-overcoming-the--cobra-effect--in-your-business/.

7. Brian Tayan, "The Wells Fargo Cross-Selling Scandal," Harvard Law School Forum on Corporate Governance, December 19, 2016, https://corpgov.law.harvard.edu/2016/12/19/the-wells-fargo-cross-selling-scandal/.

8. Jeffrey P. Bezos, EX-99.1 [2016 Letter to Shareholders], U.S. Securities and Exchange Commission, accessed April 13, 2020, https://www.sec.gov/Archives/edgar/data/1018724/000119312517120198/d373368dex991.htm.

9. Amy Shira Teitel, "Challenger Explosion: How Groupthink and Other Causes Led

to the Tragedy," History, January 25, 2018, last modified December 13, 2019, https://www.history.com/news/how-the-challenger-disaster-changed-nasa.

10. Elizabeth A. Banset and Gerald M. Parsons, "Communications Failure in Hyatt Regency Disaster," *Journal of Professional Issues in Engineering* 115, no. 3 (1989): 273–288, https://ascelibrary.org/doi/10.1061/%28ASCE%291052-3928%281989%29115%3A3%28273%29.

11. Julie (Alumni), "Target Using Predictive Analytics to Increase Value Capture," Digital Initiative [Harvard Business School], November 22, 2015, https://digital.hbs.edu/platform-digit/submission/target-using-predictive-analytics-to-increase-value-capture/.

12. "B.J. Neblett > Quotes > Quotable Quotes," Goodreads, accessed April 13, 2020, https://www.goodreads.com/quotes/1222185-we-are-the-sum-total-of-our-experiences-those-experiences.

13. PwC, *23rd Annual Global CEO Survey: Navigating the Rising Tide of Uncertainty* (PwC, 2020), https://www.pwc.com/gx/en/ceo-agenda/ceosurvey/2020.html.

14. Armand Ruiz, "The 80/20 Data Science Dilemma," InfoWorld, September 26, 2017, accessed April 26, 2020, https://www.infoworld.com/article/3228245/the-80-20-data-science-dilemma.html.

15. W. Edwards Deming, *Out of the Crisis* (Cambridge, Massachusetts: The MIT Press, 2018).

16. Cordell Hensley, "The Illusion of Knowledge?" Cordell Hensley (website), April 29, 2014, https://www.cordellhensley.com/leadership/the-illusion-of-knowledge.

17. *Albert Einstein Quotes and Facts*, EasyBib, https://www.easybib.com/guides/quotes-facts-stats/albert-einstein/.

18. Sigmund Freud, *The Interpretation of Dreams* (Buccaneer Books, 1985).

19. Nick Morgan, "How to Master Yourself, Your Unconscious, and the People Around

You – – 3," *Forbes*, March 7, 2013, https://www.forbes.com/sites/nickmorgan/2013/03/07/how-to-master-yourself-your-unconscious-and-the-people-around-you-3/#39de45c36762.

20. Daniel Kahneman, *Thinking, Fast and Slow* (New York: Farrar, Straus and Giroux, 2011).

21. Nick Morgan, "How to Master Yourself, Your Unconscious, and the People Around You – – 3," *Forbes*, March 7, 2013, https://www.forbes.com/sites/nickmorgan/2013/03/07/how-to-master-yourself-your-unconscious-and-the-people-around-you-3/#39de45c36762.

22. Amos Tversky and Daniel Kahneman, "Judgment Under Uncertainty: Heuristics and Biases," *Science* 185, no. 4157 (September 27, 1974): 1124–1131, https://www2.psych.ubc.ca/~schaller/Psyc590Readings/TverskyKahneman1974.pdf.

23. Ibid.

24. Ibid.

25. Pete Pachal, "How Kodak Squandered Every Single Digital Opportunity It Had," *Mashable*, January 20, 2012, https://mashable.com/2012/01/20/kodak-digital-missteps/.

26. Alexandra Panzer (lesson plan) and SmarterEveryDay (video), "The Backwards Brain Bicycle: Un-doing Understanding," TEDEd, accessed April 13, 2020, https://ed.ted.com/featured/bf2mRAfC.

27. Image: ©public domain, retrieved from https://mathworld.wolfram.com/YoungGirl-OldWomanIllusion.html.

28. Wayne Weiten, *Psychology: Themes and Variations* (Boston, MA: Cengage Learning, 2015).

29. Jerome S. Bruner and Leo Postman, "On the Perception of Incongruity: A Paradigm," *Journal of Personality* 18, no. 2 (1949): 206–223, https://onlinelibrary.wiley.com/doi/abs/10.1111/j.1467-6494.1949.tb01241.x.

30. Roger N. Shepard, *Mind Sights: Original Visual Illusions, Ambiguities, and Other Anomalies, with a Commentary on the Play of Mind in Perception and Art* (New York: W.H. Freeman and Company, 1990).

31. Dan Lovallo and Olivier Sibony, "The Case for Behavioral Strategy," *McKinsey Quarterly* (2010): 30–40, https://www.mckinsey.com/business-functions/strategy-and-corporate-finance/our-insights/the-case-for-behavioral-strategy.

32. Peter C. Wason, "On the Failure to Eliminate Hypotheses in a Conceptual Task," *Quarterly Journal of Experimental Psychology* 12, no. 3 (1960): 129–140, https://www.tandfonline.com/doi/abs/10.1080/17470216008416717.

33. Edgar H. Schein, *Organizational Culture and Leadership: A Dynamic View* (San Francisco: Jossey-Bass, 1991).

34. Ibid.

35. "Large List of Quotes by W. Edwards Deming," *The W. Edwards Deming Institute Blog*, accessed April 13, 2020, https://blog.deming.org/w-edwards-deming-quotes/large-list-of-quotes-by-w-edwards-deming/.

36. Ibid.

37. Dan Lovallo and Olivier Sibony, "The Case for Behavioral Strategy," *McKinsey Quarterly* (2010): 30–40, https://www.mckinsey.com/business-functions/strategy-and-corporate-finance/our-insights/the-case-for-behavioral-strategy.

38. Jeffrey P. Bezos, EX-99.1 [Letter to Shareholders], U.S. Securities and Exchange Commission, accessed April 13, 2020, https://www.sec.gov/Archives/edgar/data/1018724/000119312516530910/d168744dex991.htm.

39. Ibid.

40. "Gautama Buddha > Quotes > Quotable Quotes," Goodreads, accessed April 13, 2020, https://www.goodreads.com/quotes/59840-all-things-appear-and-disappear-because-of-the-concurrence-of.

41. "Newton's Laws of Motion," *Oxford Reference*, accessed April 13, 2020, https://www.oxfordreference.com/view/10.1093/oi/authority.20110803100232420.

42. Russell L. Ackoff, *Creating the Corporate Future: Plan or Be Planned For* (New York: John Wiley & Sons, 1981).

43. Ray Dalio, *Principles* (New York: Simon & Schuster, 2017).

44. Jeffrey Keisler, "A Framework for Organizational Decision Analysis" (doctoral thesis, Harvard University, 1992).

45. Leandro DalleMule and Thomas H. Davenport, "What's Your Data Strategy?," *Harvard Business Review*, May 2017, https://hbr.org/2017/05/whats-your-data-strategy.

46. Peter F. Drucker, *The Practice of Management* (Harper Business, 2006).

47. Michael Lewis, *Moneyball: The Art of Winning an Unfair Game* (New York: W.W. Norton & Company, 2004).

48. Gareth Morgan, *Images of Organization* (Thousand Oaks, CA: SAGE Publications, 2006).

49. Paul Burrin, "Case Study: How Google Uses People Analytics," Sage People, December 1, 2019, https://www.sagepeople.com/about-us/news-hub/case-study-how-google-uses-people-analytics/.

50. "About the IAT," Project Implicit, accessed April 13, 2020, https://implicit.harvard.edu/implicit/iatdetails.html.

51. Scott E. Page, *The Difference: How the Power of Diversity Creates Better Groups, Firms, Schools, and Societies* (Princeton, NJ: Princeton University Press, 2008).

52. Ibid.

53. Irving L. Janis, *Victims of Groupthink: A Psychological Study of Foreign-Policy Decisions and Fiascoes* (Boston, MA: Houghton Mifflin, 1972).

54. Peter M. Senge, *The Fifth Discipline: The Art & Practice of the Learning Organization* (New York, NY: Doubleday, 1994).

55. Gail T. Fairhurst and Robert A. Sarr, *The Art of Framing: Managing the Language of Leadership* (San Francisco: Jossey-Bass, 1996).

56. Lee G. Bolman and Terrence E. Deal, *How Great Leaders Think: The Art of Reframing* (San Francisco: Jossey-Bass, 2014).

57. Daniel Goleman, Richard Boyatzis, and Annie McKee, *Primal Leadership: Realizing the Power of Emotional Intelligence* (Boston, MA: Harvard Business School Press, 2002).

58. Chris Argyris and Donald A. Schön, *Organizational Learning: A Theory of Action Perspective* (Reading, MA: Addison-Wesley, 1978).

59. Leo Saini, "How Netflix Destroyed Blockbuster in Just 6 Years," Medium, November 16, 2019, https://medium.com/better-marketing/how-netflix-destroyed-blockbuster-in-just-6-years-4c5c3006fe3e.

60. E. Mazareanu, "Enplaned Passengers on Domestic Flights – Airlines in U.S. 2011–2019," Statista.com, April 1, 2020, https://www.statista.com/statistics/445641/united-states-domestic-enplaned-passengers-of-leading-airlines/.

61. Jeffrey P. Bezos, EX-99.1 [2016 Letter to Shareholders], U.S. Securities and Exchange Commission, accessed April 13, 2020, https://www.sec.gov/Archives/edgar/data/1018724/000119312517120198/d373368dex991.htm.

62. Brent Dykes, "Data Storytelling: The Essential Data Science Skill Everyone Needs," *Forbes*, March 31, 2016, https://www.forbes.com/sites/brentdykes/2016/03/31/data-storytelling-the-essential-data-science-skill-everyone-needs/?sh=609bbc5052ad.

63. Amy Shira Teitel, "Challenger Explosion: How Groupthink and Other Causes Led to the Tragedy," History, January 25, 2018, last modified December 13, 2019, https://www.history.com/news/how-the-challenger-disaster-changed-nasa.

64. Yael Zofi, *A Manager's Guide to Virtual Teams* (New York: AMACOM, 2012).

65. Edward T. Hall, *The Silent Language* (New York: Anchor Books, 1990).

66. Edward T. Hall, *Beyond Culture* (New York: Doubleday, 1989).

67. Stephen Few, "Data Visualization for Human Perception," in *The Encyclopedia of Human-Computer Interaction*, 2nd ed., ed. Mads Soegaard and Rikke Friis Dam (Aarhus, Denmark: Interaction Design Foundation, 2013).

68. Michael S. Sweeney, *Brain: The Complete Mind: How It Develops, How It Works, and How to Keep It Sharp* (National Geographic, 2009).

69. George A. Miller, "The Magical Number Seven Plus or Minus Two: Some Limits on Our Capacity for Processing Information," *Psychological Review* 63, no. 2 (1956): 81–97, https://psycnet.apa.org/doiLanding?doi=10.1037%2F0033-295X.101.2.343.

70. Colin Ware, *Information Visualization: Perception for Design* (Waltham, MA: Morgan Kaufmann, 2012).

71. "How to Use the Gestalt Principles for Visual Storytelling #PoDV," March 28, 2014, FusionCharts, https://www.fusioncharts.com/blog/how-to-use-the-gestalt-principles-for-visual-storytelling-podv/.

72. George A. Miller, "The Magical Number Seven Plus or Minus Two: Some Limits on Our Capacity for Processing Information," *Psychological Review* 63, no. 2 (1956): 81–97, https://psycnet.apa.org/doiLanding?doi=10.1037%2F0033-295X.101.2.343.

73. Jorge A. Barraza and Paul J. Zak, "Empathy toward Strangers Triggers Oxytocin Release and Subsequent Generosity," *Annals of the New York Academy of Sciences* 1167, no. 1 (2009): 182–189, https://nyaspubs.onlinelibrary.wiley.com/doi/abs/10.1111/j.1749-6632.2009.04504.x.

74. Barbara Minto, *The Pyramid Principle: Logic in Writing and Thinking* (London: Financial Times Prentice Hall, 2010).

75. Alexandra Panzer (lesson plan) and SmarterEveryDay (video), "The Backwards Brain Bicycle: Un-doing Understanding," TEDEd, accessed April 13, 2020, https://ed.ted.com/featured/bf2mRAfC.

76. Leon Megginson, "Lessons from Europe for American Business," *Southwestern Social Science Quarterly* 44, no. 1 (June 1963): 3–13, https://www.jstor.org/stable/42866937?seq=1.

77. "Thomas A. Edison Quotes," BrainyQuote, https://www.brainyquote.com/quotes/thomas_a_edison_132683.

78. Jeffrey P. Bezos, EX-99.1 [2016 Letter to Shareholders], U.S. Securities and Exchange Commission, accessed April 13, 2020, https://www.sec.gov/Archives/edgar/data/1018724/000119312517120198/d373368dex991.htm.

79. John R. Boyd, *The Strategic Game of ? and ?* (unpublished briefing, 1987), retrieved from https://www.colonelboyd.com/boydswork.

80. Klaus Schwab, "Are You Ready for the Technological Revolution?" World Economic Forum, February 19, 2015, https://www.weforum.org/agenda/2015/02/are-you-ready-for-the-technological-revolution.

81. Chet Richards, *Certain to Win: The Strategy of John Boyd, Applied to Business* (Philadelphia, PA: Xlibris, 2004).

82. Jeffrey P. Bezos, EX-99.1 [2016 Letter to Shareholders], U.S. Securities and Exchange Commission, accessed April 13, 2020, https://www.sec.gov/Archives/edgar/data/1018724/000119312517120198/d373368dex991.htm.

83. Roger Chevalier, "Updating the Behavior Engineering Model," *Performance Improvement* 42, no. 5 (2003): 8.

84. Ibid.

85. Ibid.

86. Victor H. Vroom and Arthur G. Jago, *The New Leadership: Managing Participation in Organizations* (Englewood Cliffs, NJ: Prentice Hall, 1988).

87. Ibid. (Visual created by author using information from Victor H. Vroom and Arthur G. Jago, *The New Leadership*.)

88. Eric Griggs, "The Z-Model for Deciding & Planning," Medium, April 21, 2018, https://medium.com/@ericgriggs/the-z-model-for-deciding-planning-f764d3587e32.

89. Gordon D. Lawrence, *People Types and Tiger Stripes: Using Psychological Type to Help Students Discover Their Unique Potential*, 4th ed. (Gainesville, FL: Center for Applications of Psychological Type, 2009).

90. Edward Cornish, *Futuring: The Exploration of the Future* (Bethesda, MD: World Future Society, 2005).

91. Marvin Weisbord and Sandra Janoff, *Future Search* (San Francisco: Berrett-Koehler, 1999).

92. Eliyahu M. Goldratt, *What Is This Thing Called Theory of Constraints and How Should It Be Implemented?* (Croton-on-Hudson, NY: North River, 1990).

93. Robert E. Quinn and John Rohrbaugh, "A Competing Values Approach to Organizational Effectiveness," *Public Productivity Review* 5, no. 2 (1981): 122, https://doi.org/10.2307/3380029.

94. "Organizational Culture Assessment Instrument Online," OCAI Online, accessed April 13, 2020, https://www.ocai-online.com/.

BIBLIOGRAPHY

"About the IAT." Project Implicit. Accessed April 13, 2020. https://implicit.harvard.edu/implicit/iatdetails.html.

Ackoff, Russell L. *Creating the Corporate Future: Plan or Be Planned For*. New York: John Wiley & Sons, 1981.

Albert Einstein Quotes and Facts. EasyBib. https://www.easybib.com/guides/quotes-facts-stats/albert-einstein/.

Argyris, Chris, and Donald A. Schön. *Organizational Learning: A Theory of Action Perspective*. Reading, MA: Addison-Wesley, 1978.

Banset, Elizabeth A., and Gerald M. Parsons. "Communications Failure in Hyatt Regency Disaster." *Journal of Professional Issues in Engineering* 115, no. 3 (1989): 273–288. https://ascelibrary.org/doi/10.1061/%28ASCE%291052-3928%281989%29115%3A3%28273%29.

Barraza, Jorge A., and Paul J. Zak. "Empathy toward Strangers Triggers Oxytocin Release and Subsequent Generosity." *Annals of the New York Academy of Sciences* 1167, no. 1 (2009): 182–189. https://nyaspubs.onlinelibrary.wiley.com/doi/abs/10.1111/j.1749-6632.2009.04504.x.

Bezos, Jeffrey P. EX-99.1 [Letter to Shareholders]. U.S. Securities and Exchange Commission. Accessed April 13, 2020. https://www.sec.gov/Archives/edgar/data/1018724/000119312516530910/d168744dex991.htm.

Bezos, Jeffrey P. EX-99.1 [2016 Letter to Shareholders]. U.S. Securities and Exchange Commission. Accessed April 13, 2020. https://www.sec.gov/Archives/edgar/data/1018724/000119312517120198/d373368dex991.htm.

"B.J. Neblett > Quotes > Quotable Quotes." Goodreads. Accessed April 13, 2020. https:

//www.goodreads.com/quotes/1222185-we-are-the-sum-total-of-our-experiences-those-experiences.

Bolman, Lee G., and Terrence E. Deal. *How Great Leaders Think: The Art of Reframing*. San Francisco: Jossey-Bass, 2014.

Boyd, John R. *The Strategic Game of ? and ?*. Unpublished briefing, 1987. Retrieved from http://dnipogo.org/john-r-boyd/.

Bruner, Jerome S., and Leo Postman. "On the Perception of Incongruity: A Paradigm." *Journal of Personality* 18, no. 2 (1949): 206–223. https://onlinelibrary.wiley.com/doi/abs/10.1111/j.1467-6494.1949.tb01241.x.

Burrin, Paul. "Case Study: How Google Uses People Analytics." Sage People. December 1, 2019. https://www.sagepeople.com/about-us/news-hub/case-study-how-google-uses-people-analytics/.

Chevalier, Roger. "Updating the Behavior Engineering Model." *Performance Improvement* 42, no. 5 (2003): 8.

Commvault. "7 Reasons Your Data Is Now More Important Than Ever." Commvault. February 7, 2018. https://www.commvault.com/blogs/7-reasons-your-data-is-now-more-important-than-ever.

Cornish, Edward. *Futuring: The Exploration of the Future*. Bethesda, MD: World Future Society, 2005.

Dalio, Ray. *Principles*. New York: Simon & Schuster, 2017.

DalleMule, Leandro, and Thomas H. Davenport. "What's Your Data Strategy?" *Harvard Business Review*. May 2017. https://hbr.org/2017/05/whats-your-data-strategy.

Deming, W. Edwards. *Out of the Crisis*. Cambridge, Massachusetts: The MIT Press, 2018.

Drucker, Peter F. *The Practice of Management*. Harper Business, 2006.

Dykes, Brent. "Data Storytelling: The Essential Data Science Skill Everyone Needs."

Forbes. March 31, 2016. https://www.forbes.com/sites/brentdykes/2016/03/31/data-storytelling-the-essential-data-science-skill-everyone-needs/?sh=6947fd1652ad.

Fairhurst, Gail T., and Robert A. Sarr. *The Art of Framing: Managing the Language of Leadership*. San Francisco: Jossey-Bass, 1996.

Few, Stephen. "Data Visualization for Human Perception." In *The Encyclopedia of Human-Computer Interaction*. 2nd ed. Edited by Mads Soegaard and Rikke Friis Dam. Aarhus, Denmark: Interaction Design Foundation, 2013.

"42% of Global Coal Power Plants Run at a Loss, Finds World-First Study." Carbon Tracker. November 30, 2018. https://carbontracker.org/42-of-global-coal-power-plants-run-at-a-loss-finds-world-first-study/.

Freud, Sigmund. *The Interpretation of Dreams*. Buccaneer Books, 1985.

"Gautama Buddha > Quotes > Quotable Quotes." Goodreads. Accessed April 13, 2020. https://www.goodreads.com/quotes/59840-all-things-appear-and-disappear-because-of-the-concurrence-of.

Goldratt, Eliyahu M. *What Is This Thing Called Theory of Constraints and How Should It Be Implemented?* Croton-on-Hudson, NY: North River, 1990.

Goleman, Daniel, Richard Boyatzis, and Annie McKee. *Primal Leadership: Realizing the Power of Emotional Intelligence*. Boston, MA: Harvard Business School Press, 2002.

Griggs, Eric. "The Z-Model for Deciding & Planning." Medium. April 21, 2018. https://medium.com/@ericgriggs/the-z-model-for-deciding-planning-f764d3587e32.

Gualtieri, Mike, and Noel Yuhanna. *The Forrester Wave™: Big Data Hadoop Solutions, Q1 2014*. Forrester Research, Inc., February 27, 2014. http://hortonworks.com/wp-content/uploads/2014/02/The_Forrester_Wave__Big_Data_Solutions_Q1_2014.pdf.

Hall, Edward T. *Beyond Culture*. New York: Doubleday, 1989.

Hall, Edward T. *The Silent Language*. New York: Anchor Books, 1990.

Hensley, Cordell. "The Illusion of Knowledge?" Cordell Hensley (website). April 29, 2014. https://www.cordellhensley.com/leadership/the-illusion-of-knowledge.

"How to Use the Gestalt Principles for Visual Storytelling #PoDV." March 28, 2014. FusionCharts. https://www.fusioncharts.com/blog/how-to-use-the-gestalt-principles-for-visual-storytelling-podv/.

Janis, Irving L. *Victims of Groupthink: A Psychological Study of Foreign-Policy Decisions and Fiascoes*. Boston, MA: Houghton Mifflin, 1972.

Julie (Alumni). "Target Using Predictive Analytics to Increase Value Capture." Digital Initiative [Harvard Business School]. November 22, 2015. https://digital.hbs.edu/platform-digit/submission/target-using-predictive-analytics-to-increase-value-capture/.

Kahneman, Daniel. *Thinking, Fast and Slow*. New York: Farrar, Straus and Giroux, 2011.

Keisler, Jeffrey. *A Framework for Organizational Decision Analysis*. Doctoral thesis, Harvard University, 1992.

"Large List of Quotes by W. Edwards Deming." *The W. Edwards Deming Institute Blog*. Accessed April 13, 2020. https://blog.deming.org/w-edwards-deming-quotes/large-list-of-quotes-by-w-edwards-deming/.

Lawrence, Gordon D. *People Types and Tiger Stripes: Using Psychological Type to Help Students Discover Their Unique Potential*. 4th ed. Gainesville, FL: Center for Applications of Psychological Type, 2009.

Lewis, Michael. *Moneyball: The Art of Winning an Unfair Game*. New York: W.W. Norton & Company, 2004.

Lovallo, Dan, and Olivier Sibony. "The Case for Behavioral Strategy." *McKinsey Quarterly* (2010): 30–40. https://www.mckinsey.com/business-functions/strategy-and-corporate-finance/our-insights/the-case-for-behavioral-strategy.

Mairena, Alison. "Personalizing Drug Development Using Big Data." UANews. August

19, 2019. https://news.arizona.edu/story/personalizing-drug-development-using-big-data.

Mazareanu, E. "Enplaned Passengers on Domestic Flights – Airlines in U.S. 2011–2019." Statista.com. April 1, 2020. https://www.statista.com/statistics/445641/united-states-domestic-enplaned-passengers-of-leading-airlines/.

Megginson, Leon. "Lessons from Europe for American Business." *Southwestern Social Science Quarterly* 44, no. 1 (June 1963): 3–13. https://www.jstor.org/stable/42866937?seq=1.

Miller, George A. "The Magical Number Seven Plus or Minus Two: Some Limits on Our Capacity for Processing Information." *Psychological Review* 63, no. 2 (1956): 81–97. https://psycnet.apa.org/doiLanding?doi=10.1037%2F0033-295X.101.2.343.

Minto, Barbara. *The Pyramid Principle: Logic in Writing and Thinking*. London: Financial Times Prentice Hall, 2010.

Morgan, Gareth. *Images of Organization*. Thousand Oaks, CA: SAGE Publications, 2006.

Morgan, Nick. "How to Master Yourself, Your Unconscious, and the People Around You--3." *Forbes*. March 7, 2013. https://www.forbes.com/sites/nickmorgan/2013/03/07/how-to-master-yourself-your-unconscious-and-the-people-around-you-3/?sh=34f013b86762.

"Newton's Laws of Motion." *Oxford Reference*. Accessed April 13, 2020. https://www.oxfordreference.com/view/10.1093/oi/authority.20110803100232420.

"Organizational Culture Assessment Instrument Online." OCAI Online. Accessed April 13, 2020. https://www.ocai-online.com/.

"Overcoming the 'Cobra Effect' in Your Business." Continuous Business Planning. Accessed June 21, 2020. https://www.continuousbusinessplanning.com/blog/02082019123204-overcoming-the--cobra-effect--in-your-business/.

Pachal, Pete. "How Kodak Squandered Every Single Digital Opportunity It Had." *Mashable*. January 20, 2012. https://mashable.com/2012/01/20/kodak-digital-missteps/.

Page, Scott E. *The Difference: How the Power of Diversity Creates Better Groups, Firms, Schools, and Societies*. Princeton, NJ: Princeton University Press, 2008.

Panzer, Alexandra (lesson plan), and SmarterEveryDay (video). "The Backwards Brain Bicycle: Un-doing Understanding." TEDEd. Accessed April 13, 2020. https://ed.ted.com/featured/bf2mRAfC.

PwC. *23rd Annual Global CEO Survey: Navigating the Rising Tide of Uncertainty*. PwC, 2020. https://www.pwc.com/gx/en/ceo-agenda/ceosurvey/2017/us.

Quinn, Robert E., and John Rohrbaugh. "A Competing Values Approach to Organizational Effectiveness." *Public Productivity Review* 5, no. 2 (1981): 122. https://doi.org/10.2307/3380029.

Richards, Chet. *Certain to Win: The Strategy of John Boyd, Applied to Business*. Philadelphia, PA: Xlibris, 2004.

Ruiz, Armand. "The 80/20 Data Science Dilemma." InfoWorld. September 26, 2017. Accessed April 26, 2020. https://www.infoworld.com/article/3228245/the-80-20-data-science-dilemma.html.

Saini, Leo. "How Netflix Destroyed Blockbuster in Just 6 Years." Medium. November 16, 2019. https://medium.com/better-marketing/how-netflix-destroyed-blockbuster-in-just-6-years-4c5c3006fe3e.

Schein, Edgar H. *Organizational Culture and Leadership: A Dynamic View*. San Francisco: Jossey-Bass, 1991.

Schwab, Klaus. "Are You Ready for the Technological Revolution?" World Economic Forum. February 19, 2015. https://www.weforum.org/agenda/2015/02/are-you-ready-for-the-technological-revolution.

Senge, Peter M. *The Fifth Discipline: The Art & Practice of the Learning Organization*. New York, NY: Doubleday, 1994.

Shepard, Roger N. *Mind Sights: Original Visual Illusions, Ambiguities, and Other*

Anomalies, with a Commentary on the Play of Mind in Perception and Art. New York: W.H. Freeman and Company, 1990.

Shira Teitel, Amy. "Challenger Explosion: How Groupthink and Other Causes Led to the Tragedy." History. January 25, 2018. Last modified December 13, 2019. https://www.history.com/news/how-the-challenger-disaster-changed-nasa.

Sweeney, Michael S. *Brain: The Complete Mind: How It Develops, How It Works, and How to Keep It Sharp*. National Geographic, 2009.

Tayan, Brian. "The Wells Fargo Cross-Selling Scandal." Harvard Law School Forum on Corporate Governance. December 19, 2016. https://corpgov.law.harvard.edu/2016/12/19/the-wells-fargo-cross-selling-scandal/.

"Thomas A. Edison Quotes." BrainyQuote. https://www.brainyquote.com/quotes/thomas_a_edison_132683.

"Tim O'Reilly." AZquotes. Wind and Fly LTD. 2020. Accessed April 12, 2020. https://www.azquotes.com/quote/218170.

Tversky, Amos, and Daniel Kahneman. "Judgment Under Uncertainty: Heuristics and Biases." *Science* 185, no. 4157 (September 27, 1974): 1124–1131. https://www2.psych.ubc.ca/~schaller/Psyc590Readings/TverskyKahneman1974.pdf.

Vroom, Victor H., and Arthur G. Jago. *The New Leadership: Managing Participation in Organizations*. Englewood Cliffs, NJ: Prentice Hall, 1988.

Ware, Colin. *Information Visualization: Perception for Design*. Waltham, MA: Morgan Kaufmann, 2012.

Wason, Peter C. "On the Failure to Eliminate Hypotheses in a Conceptual Task." *Quarterly Journal of Experimental Psychology* 12, no. 3 (1960): 129–140. https://www.tandfonline.com/doi/abs/10.1080/17470216008416717.

Weisbord, Marvin, and Sandra Janoff. *Future Search*. San Francisco: Berrett-Koehler, 1999.

Weiten, Wayne. *Psychology: Themes and Variations*. Boston, MA: Cengage Learning, 2015.

Zofi, Yael. *A Manager's Guide to Virtual Teams*. New York: AMACOM, 2012.

ABOUT THE AUTHOR

Kevin Hanegan is chief learning officer at Qlik, a data analytics company and a *Fast Company* top-10 innovator in Social Good. Kevin's passion is the intersection of business, technology, learning, and psychology. He promotes diversity and inclusion within company processes and brings a human approach to topics that may at first seem dry or intimidating. Kevin holds a master of science in organizational performance and workplace learning and a bachelor of science in mathematics and computer science. He has authored a number of computer software and language books, regularly blogs for Qlik, and has taught online university courses for respected institutions since 2006. He lives with his wife and four children in Massachusetts.

For additional resources related to this book or to further your learning, visit www.turningdataintowisdom.com.

Made in the USA
Columbia, SC
16 May 2021